BEYOND
FEMINISM,

Cornelius F. Murphy, Jr.

BEYOND
FEMINISM,

Toward a Dialogue on Difference

The Catholic University of America Press
Washington, D.C.

The paper used in this publication meets the minimum
requirements of American National Standards for Information
Science—Permanence of Paper for Printed Library materials,
ANSI Z39.48-1984.
∞

LIBRARY OF CONGRESS CATALOGING-IN-PUBLICATION DATA
Murphy, Cornelius F.
    Beyond feminism : toward a dialogue on difference / by
Cornelius F. Murphy.
                p.   cm.
    Includes bibliographical references and index.
    1. Feminist theory—United States.   2. Femininity
(Psychology)   3. Masculinity (Psychology)   4. Oppression
(Psychology)   I. Title.
HQ1140.M87   1994
305.3—dc20
93-47404
ISBN 0-8132-0806-8 (cl : alk. paper).
ISBN 0-8132-0807-6 (pa : alk. paper)

For my three sisters: Nancy, Joan, and Mary

The hour is coming, in fact has come, when the vocation of women is being achieved in its fullness, the hour in which woman acquires in the world an influence, an effect, and a power never hitherto achieved.

Closing message, Second Vatican Council

The orientation of the sexes on one another . . . can be summed up under three heads. They are to consider one another, to hear the question which each puts to the other, and to make responsible answer to one another.

Karl Barth

A new age of Christendom, if it is to come, will be an age of reconciliation of that which was disjoined.

Jacques Maritain

I have never seen in any country—and I have seen most of the countries of the world—such unsatisfactory personal relations between men and women as there are in America.

Pearl Buck

CONTENTS

PREFACE

Through the assertion of their grievances against men, feminists have broken the bonds of a patriarchal culture. At home and in the workplace, women have begun to vindicate their need to be recognized as persons in their own right, entitled to respect and fulfillment, in every aspect of life. This movement toward emancipation has now reached a point where collaboration, rather than antagonism, must characterize the relations between the sexes. There is a growing recognition within the women's movement that further progress toward a new humanism requires the development of an equality that affirms the differences, as well as the similarities, between men and women. These essays constitute a reflection upon those differences.

While they have struggled to overcome conventional stereotypes and gender bias, feminists have also insisted upon the recognition of legitimate sexual differences. Distinctions are of practical importance with respect to the responsibilities connected with the bearing and raising of children. But an emphasis upon the uniqueness of being a woman has a deeper purpose. There is a desire to understand a distinctive feminine sexuality which influences every important aspect of a woman's existence. Among men, there is now a comparable inquiry into the integration of gender and personality. Books such as Robert Bly's *Iron John* and Sam Keen's *Fire in the Belly* explore the distinctive attributes of men and describe the influence of those qualities upon male attitudes toward the meaning and purposes of their lives. These developments, taken together, demonstrate that neither men nor women will allow their self-understanding to be determined by the virtues or values of the opposite sex. Nor will they be satisfied with an androgynous conception of what it means to be fully human.

If harmony, rather than discord, is to prevail in relations between men and women, we must open up a new dialogue; a
conversation between the sexes based upon the premise that
it is something valuable, in itself, to be either a masculine or a
feminine human being. The shared articulation and affirmation of separate identities will have a beneficial influence upon
every aspect of human encounter. Such a project of reconciliation must be based upon an awareness that men and women
are neither superior nor inferior in relation to each other. As
persons who are either masculine or feminine, they are simply,
but profoundly, different. Both have aspirations for happiness
and fulfillment; both suffer disappointment and frustration.
As a man or a woman, every individual strives for personal
autonomy, yet none can avoid vital interdependencies. Much
of the antagonism that has arisen between the sexes in recent
years is traceable to the failure of all to acknowledge these elementary truths.

Sexual oppression exists whenever the personal destiny of
any individual is subject to the power or purposes of someone
of the opposite sex. This study begins with an exploration of
how such an experience of subservience has become an integral part of lives of both men and women.

Throughout Western history women have been subjected to
the indignities of a patriarchal system that has pervaded every
aspect of their lives. Beginning in the ancient world, the rule
of the fathers confirmed the supremacy of men within the
home as well as their dominance throughout the whole of the
social and political world. Often considered to be a primary
source of evil, women were denied opportunities for personal
growth that were made available to males. Women were also
prevented from having any direct influence upon the broader
life of the community. The first chapter reviews the principal
themes of that history as well as the theoretical justifications
for the subordination of women. It then moves to the beginning of the arduous struggle for emancipation.

By the end of the eighteenth century, women were beginning to protest actively against the governance of men. Inspired by the ideals of the Enlightenment as well as those of the American and French revolutions, gifted women, such as Abigail Adams and Mary Wollstonecraft, protested against sexual injustice and demanded that men make an authentic commitment to the principles of liberty and equality. Their efforts were encouraged by works such as John Stuart Mill's essay *On the Subjugation of Women,* in which he condemned the control that the mass of men of his time were exercising over their wives.

In the present century, some distinguished women such as Eleanor Roosevelt sustained the hopes for equality, but a general effort toward the full emancipation of women did not begin in earnest until after the Second World War. Works such as Simone de Beauvoir's *The Second Sex* and Betty Friedan's *The Feminine Mystique* were particularly influential. These writings, as well as many others, dramatically exposed the sufferings of women who, by either law or custom, were confined to the home. It was gradually realized that the sexuality of women was being used to deny them their legitimate aspirations as human persons.

Given the gravity of the oppression that has been imposed upon women, it is extremely difficult to come to an awareness of any reciprocal experience. Modern feminism has achieved an understanding of the extent of the harms that men have inflicted upon women, and feminists have brought these deprivations to the attention of their oppressors. What is not sufficiently appreciated is the subtle range of mutual abuse and subservience that can arise within the dynamics of intimate encounter. Radical feminists insist that the impalpable power of men is rooted in the hierarchical sexual structure of the family, yet it is precisely within this most fundamental experience that women, as well as men, can effectively oppose the deepest aspirations of the person closest at hand.

In the second half of the opening chapter I examine the breadth of sexual oppression and its influence upon masculine, as well as feminine, self-esteem. I rely primarily upon the

testimony of literature. Novels and stories that inquire into
heterosexual experience from a male point of view have been
justly criticized for the attitudes of contempt and exploitation
they manifest toward women. Yet such reflections may also
contain insights of great importance to the mutual quest for
sexual equality. All significant literature is concerned with the
loss, or acquisition, of personal identity, and by drawing upon
a wide sampling of dramatic fiction I hope to show how men
can undergo serious confusion, frustration, and deep unhappiness within the circle of domestic existence.

As this chapter draws to a close, I consider some of the psychological and anthropological implications of sexual difference. The distinctiveness of the experience of being either a
male or a female person must be examined as fully as possible,
so that both may be enabled to realize all of their capacities.
The objective is to develop, in a dialogue of mutual respect,
whatever potentialities may be attributed to masculine or to
feminine existence. Such a dialogue is not only important to
the equality of public opportunity but also to the future of love
between the sexes.

In ending these initial reflections, I raise questions that will
be the subject matter of the chapters that follow.

One of the most powerful forms of sexual oppression is the
control of understanding. Knowledge is power; it is also a
means by which men have maintained their control over
women. Women who are seeking to express their insights and
develop their talents within professional and intellectual communities often find that they are expected to conform to standards of thought and action upheld by men. In the second
chapter, which I have entitled "Reason and Gender," I explore
some of the varied dimensions of such cognitive tyranny.

The attachment of men to the values of abstract rationality
is a substantial obstacle to the aspirations of women for full
participation in the development of human culture. Since the
time of Descartes, the exercise of mental powers has been conceived as a conversation of the mind with itself, and this mas-

culinization of thought has perpetuated the ancient prejudice that women lack the ability to fully exercise the powers of reason. A similar discrimination can be found in the disposition to believe that the acquisition of moral knowledge demands a distancing from what are perceived to be the snares of feeling and emotion. As the movement for the emancipation of women gains a consciousness of this oppression, feminists have begun to denounce male claims of intellectual and ethical objectivity. Women have also become disenchanted with the idea that, under conditions of equality, it will become evident that their own cognitive and moral abilities are essentially the same as those of men.

In matters of the mind and heart we reach the deepest aspirations of the human person. At those levels, the personality is so deeply engaged that sexual differences are less obtrusive than they are in other areas of life. However, whenever the human spirit seeks expression, there are nuances of feeling and perception at work that cannot be fully understood if all considerations of gender are suspended. Throughout this chapter, I reflect upon some of the most significant differences of tone and emphasis that can be discerned in the cultural contributions of men and women as they bring their special values and insights into the domain of public discourse. Before exploring those differences, I explain how the modern spirit of rationalism, when combined with an ideology of individualism, has led to an objectification of existence that has distorted the purposes of human culture and done immense harm to all human relations. I contrast these excesses with the primary themes of the classical Christian tradition. Within that tradition, there is an understanding of wisdom that has an important bearing upon the matter of reason and gender. This way of knowing looks upon the moral and intellectual life as involving qualities of intuition, receptivity, and connectedness to being that are much closer to feminine than to masculine sensibility.

I also try to comprehend the roots of women's thought. Among many contemporary feminists there is a revival of interest in mothering. Giving birth to and raising a child is being seen not only as an experience of inherent value but also as an opportunity for women to gain an understanding of certain unique ways of thinking and acting. To be a mother requires the exercise of deliberative imagination and the use of reason under the pressures of particular need. Such experiential understanding disproves the prejudice that the mind should be reserved exclusively for theoretical endeavors. While acknowledging the value of this approach, I also argue that the confinement of women's thinking to a world of practices—whether within or beyond the home—would be inconsistent with their full participation in all the possibilities of human existence.

The remainder of this second chapter explores some of the more subtle and fundamental differences between the masculine and the feminine dispositions. A woman is less inclined than a man to transform what she is doing into objective categories. She is also more likely to see the significance of what is present. Men tend to defy rather than accept reality; for a woman, nearness activates moral responsibility. Such differences are, at best, generalizations rather than exact truths; but much of the potential harmony or discord between men and women will depend upon whether one recognizes, or ignores, such differences. While respecting these divergences, I also try to confront the tensions that exist between a feminine concern with what is immediate and the masculine impulse toward the outer ranges of abstract reflection.

In the third chapter I address both the distinctions that have traditionally been drawn between public life and the efforts of modern women to overcome them. For Aristotle and his followers, the *polis* is a place for men to display the excellences of their character and to have a life experience higher than that which is possible within the world of domesticity. Feminism is a protest against such discrimination and a demand for participation in all the modes of social life that exist beyond the home. It is also a rejection of the governance of men.

From a deeper perspective, the movement rejects the violent style of male political action, which women see as endangering the continuity of existence. As they bring domestic values more directly to bear upon the public sphere, women hope to develop alternatives to the destructive behavior of men. The negative images of masculinity are echoed in the self-conceptions of many contemporary males. At the beginning of this chapter, I explain how men in modern western societies have become generally satisfied with a belligerent notion of their character. As this conception of manliness becomes widely accepted, men are increasingly oblivious to those higher versions of political existence originally articulated by the ancient Greeks. A loss of enlarged images of what it means to be a man has contributed to the deplorable political situation so well documented by feminists. As the chapter develops, I draw upon both mythology and experience to suggest some more positive standards of masculine behavior.

The entry of large numbers of talented women into the legal profession vindicates the principles of equal opportunity for which earlier feminist reformers so valiantly struggled. Women legal scholars have had considerable influence upon legal doctrines and practices that either explicitly or by implication discriminate against women. These reforms are part of a broader effort to remove the last vestiges of patriarchy from our culture. In the middle section of this third chapter, I review these developments and also examine some of the features of feminist legal reasoning. This inquiry provides an opportunity to reconsider in greater depth some of the issues concerning knowledge and values that I introduced in the chapter "Reason and Gender." I use the abortion controversy as an example of the disparity between a particularistic approach to matters of public importance and one that looks upon abstraction as a means of protecting important values. Extending this reflection upon knowledge and experience, I hope to show not only how the generalizations of the legal process increase jural intelligibility but also that this liberation from detail is an important weapon in the battle against abuses of power.

In insisting upon a sharp distinction between public and private life the Aristotelians have ignored the intrinsic importance of the family. But the separation between the two spheres has been maintained for reasons that are not necessarily of a discriminatory nature. It is possible to maintain an idea of living well beyond the home without demeaning reproductive values or desiring to exclude women from public life. However, the opportunities for fulfillment within the public sphere for both men and women are threatened by the expansion of the economic dimension of social life. In the final section of this chapter I examine some of the implications of this inflation of necessity.

When the vulnerabilities of existence come to dominate the public agenda, other important values of peace, permanence, and stability tend to be neglected. The experience of simply being together out of a need to survive impairs the ability of both men and women to make significant contributions to the broader well-being of their societies. By raising these issues I hope to redirect the dialogue over the relation between the personal and the public domains and set new directions for the values of caring and connectedness which have been so eloquently expressed by feminists.

At the conclusion of the first chapter I raised questions concerning the future of sexual attraction in a world where men and women have become liberated from the conventional burdens of gender. Women will no longer live their lives through a man; but neither men nor women will be able to live for themselves alone. The desire to make masculinity or femininity an integral part of the experience of being a person will not eliminate the mutual attraction of the sexes. I return to these themes in the final chapter, which I have entitled "Love and Marriage."

Since the time of Plato, love has been deemed a subject suitable for reflection. Although in the modern world we tend to understand its experiential and autobiographical aspects, one must not set up an inherent opposition between thought and feeling in an area of such vital importance to human happiness. I seek to avoid that danger through an extended exploration of the nature of the erotic dimension of existence.

Eros is bound up with sexuality, but at its most fundamental level it reflects the inclination of the human person toward a life of happiness and fulfillment. As an elementary impulse, eros is self-serving, but it also seeks the good to be attained through a union with another. In the first section of this final chapter, I argue for a reconsideration of the value of eros to the viability and flourishing of heterosexual love. I explain the necessity of freeing eros from its bondage to instinct and of directing its energies toward the possibilities of human happiness. To comprehend these possibilities it is necessary to grasp the subtle links between self-love and love for another.

To be a participant in the dynamics of mutual love, one cannot exaggerate individual self-sufficiency. As finite creatures, neither men nor women can fully exist unless they are being affirmed by the love of another. The richest possibilities of such affirmation are to be found in some form of heterosexual encounter. The crisis of modern sexuality lies with our inability to determine the appropriate form and duration of such encounters.

For sexuality to be compatible with human dignity, it cannot function in isolation from deeper desires for personal stability and happiness. In mature sexual love, the lovers desire to love each other not just as they love themselves, but with the love of themselves, and it is this aspiration that draws them toward marriage. The final pages of the initial section of this chapter are devoted to a reflection upon the role of the will in the realization of a permanent, espoused love. I argue that the failures of married love so painfully obvious in our culture suggest a lack of understanding of the relation between personal choice and the objective requirements of heterosexual happiness.

The second section of this final chapter is devoted to an inquiry into the effect of procreation upon marital unity. The birth of a child marks the beginning of a family and, while this is a joyful event, it can also adversely affect the relationship between the spouses. As married persons become parents, they assume the responsibilities of being a mother and a father. But they remain a husband and a wife. To retain the balance between these ways of loving, the prospect of a child must be seen in relation to the love the spouses bear for one another. Procreation is, or should be, a consequence of that love rather than an occurrence that supersedes it.

I also argue for a revitalization of the family. It is important that the family find new ways of flourishing and, to that end, begin to resist the intrusions of an external culture that so relentlessly tries to subject the family to its materialistic ends. Adequate resistance requires a restoration of the dignity of parental life in its paternal as well as its maternal aspects. Such restoration will also require greater attention to the distinctions between age and youth. I also point out the need to discover the relation between the natural habitat of the home and the development of a sense of individual human dignity.

In a final section, I analyze some of the tensions between the desire for personal fulfillment and the obligations of marital life. I consider the proposition that a principle of equality should govern the division of labor between a husband and wife and compare it with the bonds relative to the nature of espousal. I also suggest that the measure of fulfillment to be achieved through mutual association contains satisfactions of a higher order than those that can be realized through the pursuit of individual autonomy.

The completion of this book was made possible by a sabbatical semester leave from my usual tasks at Duquesne University School of Law. A travel grant from the American Philosophical Society made it possible for me to study developments in gender studies in Spain. I wish to thank both, and also to express my gratitude to the staff, faculty, and students of the Catholic University of Navarra, who helped to make my Spanish visit so memorable.

Drafts of various chapters were read and critiqued for me by various colleagues at Duquesne and by friends at other universities. At the risk of unintended omission, I want specifically to thank at Duquesne, Anne Clifford and William Thompson of the department of theology, Robert Madden in philosophy, and Foster Provost of the English department. Wallace Watson of that department, good friend as well as colleague, went through the whole manuscript with surgical care. Nicholas Rescher of the University of Pittsburgh, Virginia Black of Pace University, and Ralph Lindgren of Lehigh all read some earlier versions of particular chapters. Thanks, also, to friend and writer Nick Demas for important suggestions of style. I am also grateful to Susan Needham for her rigorous, but constructive, editorial suggestions. While grateful to all, I, of course, accept full responsibility for the final product.

Susan Holtzman and, especially, Lorraine Bender assumed the arduous task of typing. I thank them both.

1. SEXUAL OPPRESSION AND PERSONAL FREEDOM

I. *The Power of Patriarchy*

Patriarchy, the rule of the fathers, is the basic cause of women's oppression. Its roots lie deep in Western history. Under the Hebrew patriarchs, female deities were overthrown and the reverence attributed to them was replaced by the worship of a male Father-god, Yahweh. In the book of Genesis, woman, being created from man, was subordinated to him. As a temptress she was considered to be a source of evil. Both men and women were blessed by God, but the covenant was centered upon the male and his pursuit of immortality through compliance with God's will.[1]

Having been subject to the will of a woman, man had been disobedient to God. Fidelity to one had led to infidelity to the other. Thus, at the beginning of our common history, the seeds of a fundamental opposition were being sown. Female sexuality became a symbol of human weakness, and Holy Writ, given by God to men, could be interpreted only by male priests who partook of the gender chosen to mediate between God and humanity.

In Hebrew culture a woman was honored in her role as mother, but she was ruled by men. As the social and economic roles of women became restricted, their honor, their very lives, were increasingly subject to the power of the male heads of

1. Gerda Lerner, *The Creation of Patriarchy* (New York: Oxford University Press, 1986); W. A. Vissert Hooft, *The Fatherhood of God in an Age of Emancipation* (Geneva: World Council of Churches, 1982). Marilyn French, *Beyond Power: On Women, Men and Morals* (New York: Summit Books, 1985); Mary Daly, *Beyond God the Father: Toward a Philosophy of Woman's Liberation* (Boston: Beacon Press, 1973). See also Adrienne Rich, *Of Woman Born* (New York: W. W. Norton, 1976), and Rosemary Radford Ruether, *Religion and Sexism: Images of Women in the Jewish and Christian Tradition* (New York: Simon and Schuster, 1974).

households. The progressive development of the Hebrew patriarchy marginalized women. They were seen as being essentially different from men, and the difference could be expressed only within the boundaries set by the dominant males.
The principal purpose of life became more linear than cyclical.
Monotheism produced universal symbols and abstract ideals
that elevated Judaic life, but these new explanations of the
world and human destiny were to be interpreted exclusively
by men in the course of their own fulfillment of a divine
plan.[2]

Within the Mediterranean world there had been cults of female goddesses that revealed the importance of women in society and religion. In ancient Greece there were multiple male
gods as well as feminine deities, but in case of conflict the male
prevailed. Primary goddesses, such as Athene, protected masculine heroes and patriarchal values while others like Hestia
reigned over the household.[3] The heroes of Homeric poems
expected women to serve them in subordinate roles while dis-
playing virtues of obedience, modesty, and fidelity. Women
were also perceived as sources of danger. Hesiod recorded the
arrival of the first woman, Pandora, as a being sent by an angry
Zeus to be the cause of men's misery.

By the late fifth and early fourth century B.C. women were
generally excluded, as far as possible, from public life. In ur-
ban Athens, they were neither visible nor valued.[4] They were

2. Lerner, *The Creation of Patriarchy.* See also Sandra M. Schneiders, *Beyond Patching: Faith and Feminism in the Catholic Church* (New York: Paulist Press, 1991). Recent feminist scholarship has done much to correct the patriarchal bias of biblical studies and to accentuate the role of heroic women in Judaic history. See, e.g., Sharon Pace Jeansonne, *The Women of Genesis* (Minneapolis: Fortress Press, 1990); Alice L. Laffey, *An Introduction to the Old Testament* (Phil-adelphia: Fortress Press, 1988). See also Naomi R. Goldberg, *Changing the Gods* (Boston: Beacon Press, 1979). For a general evaluation of these developments see Cullen Murphy, "Women and the Bible," *Atlantic Monthly* (August 1993).

3. Gillian Clark, *Women in the Ancient World* (Oxford: Oxford University Press, 1988); Eva Cantarella, *Pandora's Daughters,* trans. Maureen Bifant (Bal-timore & London: Johns Hopkins University Press, 1981); Charles Seltman, *Women in the Ancient World* (New York: St. Martin's Press, n.d.) See also Riane Eisler, *The Chalice and the Blade* (San Francisco, Harper and Row, 1987).

4. Sarah Pomeroy, *Goddesses, Whores, Wives and Slaves* (New York: Schocken

not allowed to serve as magistrates or jurors or in other civic offices. The legal status of a woman was determined by her relationship to a man.

Within philosophical circles there was some recognition of the abilities and virtues of women. Socrates thought that women, if not equal to men, were not necessarily inferior. In *Oeconomicus*, Xenophon noted some equality between the sexes with respect to intelligence and moral ability; but he affirmed a division of labor that would direct feminine energies to the maintenance of the conjugal home.[5] In the writings of Plato the distinctions between the sexes were minimized: men begot, and women bore children. Reaching beyond that variation, Plato believed that in the common life of the Guardians, men and women should receive the same education and share equally in all public duties.[6] But the philosophy of Aristotle would lead to a deepening of the subordination of women and a further frustration of their desires for fulfillment.

Aristotle's world view was hierarchical and divided. He drew distinctions within, and between, the varieties of exis-

---

Books, 1975); Eva Cantarella, *Pandora's Daughters*. Seltman argues that Athenian vases and marble figures show that the cult of goddesses was more important than the worship of male gods (*Women in the Ancient World*, chap. 8). This view gains some support from Robert Graves's poetic reinterpretation of ancient history. Arguing that the Hebrews and Greeks perverted the values of matriarchal societies, Graves reaffirmed the value of the "White Goddess": "All saints revile her and all sober men Ruled by the God Apollo's golden mean" (*Collected Poems* [Garden City: Doubleday, 1961], 247). See John B. Vickery, *Robert Graves and the White Goddess* (Lincoln: University of Nebraska Press, 1972).

5. Gillian Clark, *Women in the Ancient World*.

6. "No one ever argued, outside Plato's *Republic*, that you should choose the best person for the job regardless of sex, and no one proposed the social changes, beginning with education, that were needed for women to develop their abilities. But it was something to have it said that sex is not relevant to natural ability and moral capacity" (Clark, *Women in the Ancient World*, 5). Eva Cantarella contends that Plato does not deserve to be called a feminist champion because his later works reasserted the subordination of women (chap. 5).

The Stoics gave some recognition to the equality of women by promoting a "kinship of the wise," which included them. This was, however, limited to consent to carnal union. J. M. Rist, *Stoic Philosophy* (Cambridge: Cambridge University Press, 1969), chap. 4.

tence. The *polis*, the central human reality—a domain of ex-
cellence—was sharply distinguished from the darker world of
domesticity. Whereas the household was subject to the demands of survival, virtue flourished beyond the hearth. Men,
and men alone, would find moral fulfillment through their participation in the political life of the community. The exclusion
of women from the higher realm of politics and culture was
coupled with more pervasive discriminations. Their subordination was firmly linked to their procreative function, a function described as passive in nature. This bodily labor would
fulfill the plans and designs of the male, who was being raised
to a position of supremacy.[7]

In the Hellenistic age there were some changes in the status
of women. Their legal capacities were extended, but in other
than in exceptional circumstances they were excluded from
political power and public office. While a deeper understanding of conjugal relations led to a decline in misogyny, there
were also increased efforts to reinforce the confinement of
women to the domestic arena.[8]

7. Gerda Lerner, *The Creation of Patriarchy*, chap. 10; Wendy Brown, *Manhood and Politics, A Feminist Reading in Political Theory* (Totowa, N.J.: Rowman
and Littlefield, 1980); Jean Bethke Elshtain, *Public Man, Private Woman* (Princeton: Princeton University Press, 1981), chap. 1; Susan Moller Okin, *Women in
Western Political Thought* (Princeton: Princeton University Press, 1979). Hannah
Arendt was a principal exponent of Aristotelian thought. See *The Human Condition* (Chicago: University of Chicago Press, 1974). She is criticized for adopting that outlook in Brown, *Manhood and Politics*.

8. In *The Politics*, I, II, 6–9, 12, Aristotle lays down the principles of authority and subordination and applies them to the relations between husbands
and wives. Similar observations are made in *The Nicomachean Ethics* Bk. X.5.
The quality of friendship between the parties is discussed in Bk. XI.4 and
XII.7. These relations are developed more fully in *The Oeconomica*, in which
the woman is referred to as a "free associate" who makes primary claim upon
the household. Part V deals with the rules that should govern a man's treat-
ment of his wife "and the first forbids him to do her wrong." I am grateful to
Professor Enrique Alarcon of the Department of Philosophy, University of Navarra, for the references to *The Oeconomica*.

Marital circumstances in another part of the ancient world are examined in
Sarah B. Pomeroy, *Women in Ancient Egypt* (New York: Schocken Books, 1984).
The cultural situation in ancient China also led to male dominance. See gen-
erally, Francis L. K. Hsu, *American and Chinese, Passages to Differences*, 3d ed.
(Honolulu: University of Hawaii Press, 1985).

Similar movements of advance and regression also marked the situation of women in the Roman world. Although Etruscan women enjoyed considerable liberty of movement, they remained subservient to their husbands. And from its beginnings Roman law reflected the values of a patriarchal society. Only male citizens who were heads of households possessed full legal and political rights. Women, even if unmarried, had no political rights, and their legal capacities were subject to the humiliation of guardianship. By marriage a woman became subject to a new master. Roman family organization became firmly subject to the *pater potestas*. While some women sought to live out alternative images of femininity, the prevailing model was that of the *Matrona*, a wife and mother who found fulfillment in family life.[9]

The role of women in Roman society was more complex than in classical Greece. Roman women of the upper classes participated in the lives of men and, in the last years of the Republic, their legal rights were increased. Yet they were still excluded from the *virilia officia*, the offices of government, and the strict application of principles of sexual morality reinforced their restricted status.[10] With such basic discriminations, the opposition between the masculine and feminine modes of existence which had begun in the Judaic world began to congeal into a basic aversion.

The advent of Christianity reinforced the subordination of

9. J.P.V.D. Balsdon, *Roman Women* (New York: Barnes and Noble, 1983).

10. The *Institutes of Gaius*, written in the second century A.D., reflect changes in the legal status of women. A woman was released from her father's *potestas* by coming, by marriage, under the power (manus) of her husband. She could compel her husband to release her by notice of divorce. Francis de Zulueta, *The Institutes of Gaius*, Part 1, Book 1, 137a (Oxford: Clarendon Press, 1940). The *Institutes* also reflect a developing understanding of the intelligence of women. Guardianship over any individual was justified because of immaturity, yet "hardly any valid argument seems to exist in favor of women of full age being in *tutela*. That which is commonly accepted, namely that they are very liable to be deceived owing to their instability of judgment and that therefore in fairness they should be governed by the *auctoritas* of tutors seems more specious than true. For women of full age conduct their own affairs, the interposition of their tutor's *auctoritas* in certain cases being merely a matter of form" (*Institutes*, Book 1, 190).

women within the home, in public life, and in the sphere of religious ritual. The church fathers refined and extended the biblical symbolism that had attributed demonic power to female sexuality. For Augustine the distinctions that arose from physical differences were directed, by analogy, to the inward subjection of the passions to the power of deliberative action. In medieval theology the dominance of the male was given a higher justification. While it was conceded that both men and women had rational souls, the man was seen to be, in himself, the image of God, while a woman approached the divine through her husband.[11]

The dialectic between Christianity and the ancient world had other consequences that were more favorable to women. St. Paul insisted upon their obedience to their husbands, but he also called upon husbands to govern their wives with a sincere and sacrificial love.[12] And, by insisting upon the equality

11. "God created one sole individual, not that he was meant to remain alone deprived of human companionship, but in order that the unity of society and the bond of harmony might mean more to man, since men were to be united not only by the likeness of nature but also by the affection of kinship. God did not even wish to create the woman who was to be mated with man in the same way that He created man, but, rather, out of him, in order that the whole human race might be derived entirely from one single individual" (St. Augustine, *The City of God*, ed. Vernon J. Bourke [New York: Image Books, 1958], Book 12, chap. 22). On the demonology of the early church fathers, see Mary Daly, *Beyond God the Father*, chap. 2. It is worth noting that Tertullian, who was most vehement in his attacks upon women—seeing them as the Devil's Gateway—eventually took up attitudes toward sexuality that were deemed heretical by the church. For a generally balanced view of the attitude of the church fathers toward women, see John M. Rist, *Human Values* (Leiden: Brill, 1982), chap. 3.

12. Ephesians 5:25–30; see also Galatians 3:18–20. In his commentary on this passage, John Paul II holds that the obligation of the husband to love his wife is a recognition of the dignity of the woman as a person. "This affirmation makes it possible for the female personality to develop fully and be enriched" (*Mulieris Dignitatem*, Apostolic Letter on the Dignity and Vocation of Women [1988], 83). The subjection referred to by St. Paul is seen by the Holy Father as having a twofold character. The obedience of the wife is balanced by the submission of the husband's will to Christ's command of self-sacrificing love. In the same work, John Paul II interprets the biblical injunction "He shall rule over you" (Gen. 3:16) as an indication of one of the consequences of that orig-

of all within the body of Christ, Paul laid some of the foundations for the subsequent rehabilitation of the feminine. In comparison to the hierarchies of the ancient world—which set master over slave, Greeks over barbarians, as well as men over women—the Christian apostles made the audacious claim that all were called to the contemplation of the Divine Mercy.

There were other influences at work in Western civilization that were gradually elevating the status of women. In medieval Europe, practices of courtship and courtesy began to emerge that would eventually become the chivalric code of gallantry toward women. The figure of Beatrice in Dante's *Divine Comedy* brought to new heights a sense of woman as a source of inspiration and salvation—an ennobling that had been only feebly suggested by the ancients. And the growing cult of the Virgin Mary bestowed immeasurable spiritual esteem upon all women in Christian society.[13] Yet this elevation of the feminine did not remove the basic obstructions to women's fulfillment.

In medieval society, widows who inherited land participated in feudal assemblies and ruled over extensive territories, but women were otherwise excluded from office. The limitations imposed upon them were justified under church law because of their presumed secondary role in human procreation and their responsibility for original sin. Their testimony was excluded from trials and they suffered discriminations in the impositions of legal punishments.[14] Christianity, like Judaism, barred women from religious office, but the celibate life of a

---

inal sin for which both Adam and Eve were responsible. Such domination, which may be rightfully resisted, is incompatible with the natural order of spousal love. The pope immediately adds that such rightful opposition "must not under any conditions lead to the 'masculinization' of women. In the name of liberation from male 'domination' women must not appropriate to themselves male characteristics contrary to their own feminine 'originality' (37–41).

13. Eileen Power, *Medieval Women* (Cambridge: Cambridge University Press, 1984). Shulamith Shahar, *The Fourth Estate: A History of Women in the Middle Ages*, trans. Chaya Galai (London and New York: Methuen, 1983).

14. Shulamith Shahar, *The Fourth Estate*, chap. 2. For a study of the position of women in late medieval Italy, see Thomas Kuehn, *Law, Family, and Women* (Chicago: University of Chicago Press, 1991).

nun was presented as an alternative avenue of spiritual growth. In such a theocentric world, a St. Theresa of Avila might find some outlets for her immense talents, but outside the religious sphere the basic divisions between public and private life were rigorously maintained.[15]

Women were exalted—but in their roles as wives and mothers. In spite of these repressions, however, there were liberating influences at work in Western culture. Christine de Pisan, a fifteenth-century writer, drew upon ancient and Christian sources to dispel masculine myths and improve the conditions of women.[16] Other freeing impulses, inspired by the advance of liberal and democratic ideals, would eventually emerge, but they would begin to appear only after the ideology of patriarchy had been given a definitive form in the philosophy and culture of Europe.

In the reflective world of medieval theology the separateness of masculine and feminine identity had been articulated at the furthest boundaries of abstract thought. The vital operations toward which life is principally directed were seen as being guided by the intellect, and it was man, exercising his reason, who symbolized this primacy. The greatest thinker of the age, St. Thomas Aquinas, saw this intellectual capacity as the quality that defined the distinctiveness of human nature. Women, as well as men, were endowed with reason; but feminine existence was not explained on the same basis as that of men. The meaning of woman was derived from the original state of creation. Her existence was natural, symbolizing generation. But she was by nature subject to man.[17]

15. George Eliot makes some interesting observations on this point in her introduction to *Middlemarch*. St. Catherine of Siena, who was not a nun, had an enormous influence upon the papacy of her time.

16. See Christine De Pizan, *The Book of the City of Ladies*, trans. Earl Jeffrey Richards (New York: Persea Books, 1982).

17. Her subjection was by nature rather than because of sin, "For the human group would have lacked the benefit of order had some of its members not been governed by others who were wiser. Such is the subjection in which woman is by nature subordinate to man because the power of rational dis-

The essential subordination of women was also developed on the plane of political theory. In the period of the Renaissance, women such as Isabel of Spain and Elizabeth I of England showed that women are capable of exercising supreme political authority. Yet as the practice of politics was increasingly perceived as a combative struggle of conquest and power, it was thought of as a field of endeavor more suitable for the actions of men than for the influence of women.

In the theoretical defenses of monarchical absolutism, patriarchal images abounded. Connections were drawn from the principle of *pater familias* to the highest levels of political authority.[18] And, as male energy was increasingly expended upon trade and commerce, it became necessary to formulate new rationalizations for the confinement of women to the domestic sphere. Paternalistic dominance, and the relations of superiority and inferiority which inhered in patriarchy, had to be explained in terms of some plausible allocations of individual rights and responsibilities.[19]

---

cernment is by nature stronger in man" (St. Thomas Aquinas, *Summa Theologiae*, 1A. 92, 1 reply 12 [Blackfriars, 1964], 37–39). See also reply 11. Man and woman are both created in God's image, i.e., they both have a rational nature; but according to Thomas there is an essential hierarchy: "Thus after saying in *Genesis, after God's image he created him*, i.e. man, it adds *male and female he created them*; and it put *them* in the plural, as Augustine says, in case it should be supposed that the sexes were combined in one individual.

But as regards a secondary point, God's image is found in man in a way in which it is not found in woman; for man is the beginning and end of woman, just as God is the beginning and end of all creation" (*Summa Theologiae* IA, 93, 5).

See further, Genevieve Lloyd, *The Man of Reason* (1964), 28–36; Lloyd, "Augustine and Aquinas," in *Feminist Theology, A Reader*, ed. Ann Loades (Louisville: John Knox Press, 1990). See also Sandra M. Schneiders, *Women and the Word* (New York: Paulist Press, 1986).

In the Middle Ages, the speculative hierarchy was subverted by pastoral practices which elevated the spiritual sensibilities of women and reduced the religious role of the husband (Silvana Vecchio, "The Good Wife," in II *A History of Women*, ed. Christiane Klapisch-Zuber, chap. 4).

18. Gordon J. Schochet, *Patriarchalism in Political Thought* (New York: Basic Books, 1975). Susan Moller Okin, *Women in Western Political Thought* (Princeton: Princeton University Press, 1975). These developments are more fully analyzed in Chapter 3 of the present work.

19. Zillah R. Eisenstein, *The Radical Future of Liberal Feminism* (New York: Longman, 1981).

In the Puritan revolt of the seventeenth century, Milton tried to justify domestic male supremacy by attributing the authority of the husband to the consequences of the Fall.[20] And while John Locke's critique of monarchical rule undercut the patriarchal foundations of government, it did not reach its roots in family life. Locke acknowledged an equality of parental authority between spouses, but he reaffirmed paternal supremacy. A woman was still subject to her husband. Thus, rule within the home was separated from political legitimacy in the broader world.[21]

Locke's thinking reflected the rise of bourgeois man. The power of the king was transferred to independent individuals, who would choose for themselves the appropriate form of political organization. In the market there would be no dependent relations as there had been in the feudal and aristocratic ages. Equality of opportunity was to replace an antiquated social hierarchy. An individual was to be responsible for *his* own welfare.

This progressive development did not include women, but it established a liberal ideology that would eventually inspire feminists seeking equal freedom for the sexes.[22] These liberating possibilities would, however, face further frustrations. During the Enlightenment, new justifications for masculine predominance would be advanced as men of power and influence sought to fix the boundaries between public and private life.

Rousseau believed that the differentiations that had marked the evolution of civil society reveal a mutual dependence that is inevitable whenever individuals are members of a particular community. He thought that interdependence was rooted in the fundamental structures of personal existence. Sexual attraction indicated a need not only to be complemented by another, but also the desire of both to dominate. Although males

---

20. See Mary O'Brien, *Reproducing the World: Essays in Feminist Theory* (Boulder: Westview Press, 1989), chap. 9.
21. Zillah R. Eisenstein, *The Radical Future of Liberal Feminism*, chap. 3.
22. Ibid., 43–44.

have superior physical power, their sexual initiatives are subject to the approval and the manipulation of women. If a
woman has such power in the realm of sexuality—a power
that threatens man's independence—she must be subjugated
to him in other spheres if there is to be, overall, a rational balance of power. Rousseau believed that conjugal interdependence
weakens the male and this vulnerability can be redressed by
an understanding of woman's dependence upon him. This
subservience was to be expressed not only in the family but
also through the actions of the male in the public world.[23]

Rousseau's explication of the power relations between the
sexes was a modern extension of the traditional distinctions between men and women. As in the past, women were thought
of as physical and sensual, men as creative and intellectual.
Men had infinite potential; the happiness of women would depend upon their willingness to accept their reproductive role.
A woman's education in refinement and sensibility was a
training designed to help her fulfill that essential function.
Men, by contrast, were to overcome conventional authority
and to be educated to realize their unlimited possibilities.[24]

Philosophical justifications of sexual inequality were further
developed by Kant. He concentrated upon the nature of marriage, which he saw as the only means of validating sexuality.
Sexual relations are by nature animal relations. They are made
human by the marriage contract, through which each acquires
a right to the enjoyment of the other on the condition that the
other be treated as a person. Kant was convinced that such
reciprocity could not be found outside of marriage. If a woman
was to be a man's mistress, the relationship would be unequal.

23. Susan Moller Okin, *Women in Western Political Thought* (Princeton:
Princeton University Press, 1979), chap. 5; Zillah Eisenstein, *The Radical Future
of Liberal Feminism*, chap. 4. See also Emily Gill, "Models of Family and Polity,"
in *Perspectives on the Family*, ed. Moffat, Gric and Bayles (1990).

24. Broader aspects of Rousseau's thought are traced in Allan Bloom, *Love
and Friendship*, Part 1 (New York: Simon and Schuster, 1993); Jean Starobinski,
Jean-Jacques Rousseau, trans. A. Goldhammer (Chicago: University of Chicago
Press, 1988); and Ernst Cassirer, *The Question of Jean-Jacques Rousseau* (New
York: Columbia University Press, 1963).

She would then be treated as a thing without receiving a lasting commitment in return.[25] Kant was not only concerned with determining the conditions upon which sexual relations could be morally justified. He also wanted to determine the legitimate distributions of power and authority within those relations.

Like Rousseau, Kant thought that in all sexual relations there was as much exploitation of the man as there was of the woman. While in marriage the women was in many respects dominated, the condition could, in part, be explained as a requirement of order.[26] Such subordination was also justified because it was, in subtle ways, reciprocal:

> If a union is to be harmonious and indissoluble, it is not enough for two people to associate as they please; one party must be *subject* to the other, and, reciprocally, one must be the *superior* of the other in some way, in order to be able to rule and govern him. For if two people who cannot dispense with each other make *equal* claims, self-love produces nothing but wrangling. As *culture* advances, each party must be superior in his own particular way: the man must be superior to the woman by his physical strength and courage; the woman to the man, however, by her natural talent for gaining mastery over his desire for her.[27]

These distinctions had a wider social and moral significance. The bearing of children by women preserved the continuation of the species, but it also led to the cultivation and refinement of society. This elevation of life was traceable to the power of women within the family. The modesty of their speech and

25. Immanuel Kant, *Lectures on Ethics* (New York: Harper and Row, 1963). See also Kant's *Political Philosophy* (New York: St. Martin's Press, 1983), chap. 5; Irving Singer, *The Nature of Love*, vol. 2 (Chicago: University of Chicago Press, 1984), chap. 12.

26. Immanuel Kant, *Anthropology from a Pragmatic Point of View*, trans. Mary J. Gregor (The Hague: Martinus Nijhoff, 1974). Compare Kant, *Observations on the Feeling of the Beautiful and the Sublime* (1764).

27. *Anthropology from a Pragmatic Point of View*, 167. Compare the criticism of Kant's conception in Carole Pateman, *The Sexual Contract* (Stanford: Stanford University Press, 1988), chap. 6. Ms. Pateman's work does not avert to the reciprocities of power. For a general survey of Kant's views see Steven G. Smith, *Gender Thinking* (Philadelphia: Temple University Press, 1992), chap. 5.

expression provided a cultivation of sensibility that was indispensable to the moral development of all. While a woman lacked the intellectual power and initiative of the male, she was, in tenderness and feeling, his superior.

Harmonious family life was widely seen as being indispensable to the stability and prosperity of the rising bourgeois class. But if the family was to be of supreme importance to civil society, it had to be based upon foundations that were superior to the randomness of trade or the capricious nature of individual will. Hegel insisted that marriage, in its essentials, was not a contractual relation. Although marriage begins in contract, it is "a contract to transcend the standpoint of contract, the standpoint from which persons are regarded in their individuality as self-subsistent units."[28]

For Hegel, the family is, in itself, an ethical entity. If it is to endure, the relationships among its members have to be grounded upon something more substantial than romantic love. Hegel argued that the spiritual bond of marriage refines what is merely physical and subjective out of the consciousness of the parties. This deeper connection raises both to the thought of what is substantive in the relationship between them.[29]

In spite of this Hegelian enhancement of family life, the principles of patriarchy were left intact. The father retained unlimited power over his spouse and children—especially through his control of money, which was the real substance of family existence. These practical realities reinforced a domestic submission to his will. And the separation of the spheres of public and private life provided grounds for the view that a wife should find her ethical destiny in the family, while her husband was to find fulfillment in civil society and the state. As we move further into the modern world, however, the inequalities

28. Hegel, *The Philosophy of Right*, sect. 163. Trans. T. M. Knox. (London: Oxford University Press, 1952).

29. "The ethical aspect of marriage consists in the parties' consciousness of this unity as their substantive aim, and so in their love, trust, and common sharing of their entire existence as individuals" (*Philosophy of Right*, sect. 163).

of the patriarchal regime would be gradually exposed and challenged.

II. *The Struggle for the Emancipation of Women*

In the thought of Hegel, the separateness of individual male and female existence could be overcome in marriage if the partners would give themselves to the expansive unity that they had created out of their love. In such a conception, any assertion of independent right was antithetical to the relationship. A subsistent, personal autonomy would be incompatible with the intrinsic familistic community. This theory of marriage justified a power of husbands over their wives that was increasingly perceived as tyrannical. An emerging protest began to challenge the patriarchal foundations of married life.

Mary Wollstonecraft sought to apply liberal values to the aspirations of women in order to relieve them from sexual bondage. Appealing to the idea of a universal human nature, she argued that women, as well as men, should pursue the virtues that can elevate them both.[30] Abigail Adams urged her spouse not to permit husbands to have unlimited power in the American republic. Lawless men would use such power with cruel impunity.[31] The same criticism was more fully expressed by John Stuart Mill. Mill saw the subjugation of women within the family as a relation that was essentially unjust:

The relation between husband and wife is very like that between Lord and vassal, except that the wife is held to more unlimited obedience than the vassal was. . . . The self-worship of the monarch, or of the feudal superior, is matched by the self-worship of the male. Human beings do not grow up from childhood in the possession of unearned distinctions, without pluming themselves upon them. Above all,

30. Mary Wollstonecraft, *A Vindication of the Rights of Women*, ed. Charles W. Hagelman, Jr. (New York: W. W. Norton, 1967). See also Zillah R. Eisenstein, *The Radical Future of Liberal Feminism*, chap. 5.

31. Letter of Abigail Adams to John Adams, March 31, 1776, in *The Feminist Papers*, ed. Alice S. Rossi (New York: Bantam Books, 1973), 10–11. In literature, other protests were being expressed. One of the most extraordinary came from South Africa, with the publication of Olive Schreiner, *The Story of an African Farm*. (New York: A. L. Burt, 1883).

when the feeling of being raised above the whole of the other sex is combined with personal authority over one individual among them, the situation . . . is . . . a regularly constituted Academy or Gymnasium for training them in arrogance and overbearingness.[32]

Mill not only attacked the domestic dominance of men. He also protested against the exclusion of women from civic and public life. Enslavement was not just political, it was also economic. Financial independence was as indispensable to freedom as any other form of liberation. When recognized as equal citizens, women should be allowed to compete for all lawful occupations. Mill also saw that women were entitled to the education necessary to such pursuits. Once women became free to develop their inherent capacities, these opportunities for self-fulfillment would not only benefit themselves but would also enrich the whole of human society.

In the latter half of the nineteenth century, women protested, with mixed results, against the social, legal, and political disabilities that had been imposed upon them through patriarchal governance. Reformers such as Elizabeth Cady Stanton fought for equality of opportunity and for the right of women to determine their own destiny. These efforts brought only limited success.[33] Within the common law tradition, women

32. John Stuart Mill, "The Subjugation of Women," in vol. 21 of *Collected Works*, ed. John M. Robson (Toronto: University of Toronto Press, 1984).

33. At the time of the French Revolution, Olympe de Gouges had fought for a sexual equality of rights and responsibilities. During the nineteenth century, the rise of socialist theory provided a basis for a new attack upon the bourgeois family. Engels underminded the belief in the immutability of sexual relations by revealing their character as social phenomena. This also helped to overcome the sentimentality which had, until then, protected the family from reform. Andrea Nye, *Feminist Theory and the Philosophies of Man* (New York and London: Routledge, 1988).

In the United States, the seminal event was the Seneca Falls Convention of 1848. See generally, Ellen Carol DuBois, *Feminism and Suffrage: The Emergence of an Independent Woman's Movement in America, 1848–1869* (Ithaca: Cornell University Press, 1978). On the legal situation see Deborah L. Rhode, *Justice and Gender* (Cambridge: Harvard University Press, 1989). See also Zillah Eisentein, "Elizabeth Cady Stanton: Radical Feminist Analysis and Liberal-Feminist Strategy," in *Feminism and Equality*, ed. Anne Phillips (New York: New York University Press, 1987), 77; Betty Friedan, *The Feminine Mystique* (New York:

were more separate than equal. Some statutory reforms improved the legal status and powers of women, but women were excluded from the legal profession.[34] Yet, in spite of these disappointments, emancipatory forces had been set in motion that, in our time, would substantially alter the patriarchal structures that distort our domestic and social life.

A society is organized along patriarchal lines whenever women are excluded by law or custom from political participation and lack the full legal capacities necessary for the exercise of all civil and personal rights. In such a society only males are educated and children are not free to choose their own marriage partners.[35] In most modern Western societies the explicit, formal obstacles to the emancipation of women have been removed. Much of course remains to be done to protect women from the violence of men and to correct discriminatory practices which still impede their economic, social, and professional advancement. Yet it would be a mistake to reduce the problematic of patriarchy and sexual oppression to the necessities of political and legal reform.

Contemporary feminism is a struggle to correct laws and practices that prevent women from achieving full equality with men in all aspects of domestic and public life. But the deeper struggle is against attitudes that sustain such discriminatory practices. What has been achieved by way of emancipation and formal equality of status is all too often a concession to pressure rather than an honest recognition of right. Moreover, the power of men to define themselves is the most pervasive power in the world. This power can be corrected only when it is matched by a comparable capacity of women to fully express

---

W. W. Norton, 1963), chap. 4. I discuss these questions more fully in Chapter 3 of the present work.

34. Bradwell v. State, 83 U.S. 130 (1872).

35. Jean Bethke Elshtain, *Public Man, Private Woman,* 214–15. When formal barriers are removed, patriarchy remains a system by which men, through "ritual, tradition, law and language, customs, etiquette, education, and the division of labor, determine what part women shall or shall not play" (Adrienne Rich, *Of Woman Born: Motherhood as Experience and Institution* [New York: Norton, 1976], 57).

their own experience and gain a positive and equal influence upon the course of human events.[36] From the point of view of radical feminism, the impalpable power of men derives from a sexual hierarchy whose influence precedes the elaboration of social and political relations. This understructure can be overcome only by reaching its roots in the family. Patriarchy is not based upon maleness as such, but rather upon the social position held by the male as head of a household:

The radical feminist analysis traces all the dominance relations in the social order to the system of universal hierarchical dualism that finds its first and basic instance as well as its paradigm in the dominance/ subordination relationship between male household head and wife mother that is the principle of the patriarchal family unit. In short, patriarchy is . . . the root of all hierarchical relationships . . . while it is not exclusively a male over female structure it is essentially and pervasively sexual, drawing its psychic energy as well as its basic example from the dominance relation of male to female in the familial unit. . . .

Radical feminist analysis . . . perceives the interconnectedness of all forms of oppression and draws the necessary conclusion that sexist oppression cannot be overcome unless all forms of domination and oppression are overcome, and this requires the transformation of society literally from the root up."[37]

The family structure must be reconstructed, because it is within the domestic sphere that the vulnerability of women and the imbalances of power, esteem, and opportunity in relations between the sexes is most intensely experienced. To understand this need to eradicate the fundamental roots of patriarchy, the agenda of domestic reform must be seen in relation to the general struggle for the realization of human liberty.

In the great liberal and democratic movements of modern

36. Mary O'Brien, *Reproducing the World*. See also J. C. Smith, *The Neurotic Foundation of Social Order* (New York: New York University Press, 1991).

37. Sandra M. Schneiders, *Beyond Patching: Faith and Feminism in the Catholic Church* (New York: Paulist Press, 1991), 24. See also Hester Eisenstein, *Contemporary Feminist Thought* (Boston: G. K. Hall, 1983), chap. 1, and Susan Moller Okin, *Justice and the Family* (New York: Basic Books, 1989). For a general study of changes in law and custom, see Mary Ann Glendon, *The Transformation of Family Law* (Chicago: University of Chicago Press, 1989).

life, personal freedom and emancipation from oppression have become the paramount ideals of a new humanism. Men have striven to achieve freedom and equality for themselves in the public world. Women were not expressly included in these progressive developments, but they could not be completely excluded from the benefits. The spirit of freedom will not suffer sexual confinement; its influence appears in the dynamics of private as well as public life. The spread of liberating values to the conditions of women was an imperative demand of logic and ethics. It was also inherent in the dynamics of married life.

The perception of inequity begins at home. In modern life, whatever respect is conferred upon a woman as mother and homemaker does not compensate for the personal frustration implicit in the domestic experience. A housewife marks time. Perpetuating the present, she rarely senses the accomplishment of a positive good. She has no direct influence upon the world. If she merely fulfills a role, her destiny is not in her own hands. The divide between her circumstances and her awareness of her inherent value as a person can become virtually unbearable. A woman may desire political and legal emancipation, but, above all, she hopes to experience a greater degree of personal happiness.

The "feminine mystique," which promised the fulfillment of femininity through the loss of an independent existence, no longer persuades. A modern woman will not accept the exchange through which she yielded the public sphere to the male while she reigned at home:

It is urgent to understand how the very condition of being a housewife can create a sense of emptiness, non-existence, nothingness, in women. There are aspects of the housewife role that make it almost impossible for a woman of adult intelligence to retain a sense of human identity, the firm core of self or "I" without which a human being, man or woman, is not truly alive. For women of ability, in America today, I am convinced there is something about the housewife state itself that is dangerous. In a sense that is not as far-fetched as it sounds, the women who "adjust" as housewives, who grow up wanting to be "just a housewife," are in as much danger as the millions who walked to their own death in the concentration camps—

and the millions more who refused to believe that the concentration camps existed.[38]

A woman rebels against a destiny created for her by men, and she insists upon fashioning a future of her own. And, like men, she will exercise a will to power if this is the only means by which she can find meaning in her life.[39]

While she may address public discrimination through political activism, the modern feminist seeks relief from domestic oppression in the dynamics of interpersonal encounters. In her struggle with the male closest at hand, a woman will take her revenge:

One does not play a part when free: the free woman will often act as such against man. Even the Sleeping Beauty may awaken with displeasure; she may not regard her awakener as a Prince Charming at

38. Betty Friedan, *The Feminine Mystique* (New York: W. W. Norton, 1963), 305. Compare Pearl Buck, "America's Medieval Women," (Harper's, 1938) in *An American Retrospective*, ed. Ann Marie Cunningham (1985). Buck, writing in the 1930s, covered much of the same ground that would later bring public acclaim to Betty Friedan. To Ms. Buck, the frustrations of the traditional woman confined to domestic life led her too often to become "a petty dictator in the home, a nag to her husband and children, and a gossip among her woman friends." "When," Buck argued, "will American men learn that they cannot expect happiness with a wife who is not her whole self?" Pearl S. Buck, "America's Medieval Women" (Harper's, 1938) in *An American Retrospective* ed. Ann Marie Cunningham (1985), 110.

The drudgery of middle class domestic life is observed by Lenin in his essay "Women and Society." See *The Woman Question, Selections from the Writings of Karl Marx, Frederick Engels V.I. Lenin and Joseph Stalin* (New York: International Publishers, 1951), 55–57. The theme is repeated in Simone de Beauvoir, *The Second Sex*, ed. and trans. H. M. Parshley (New York: Alfred A. Knopf, 1952), chap. 16. See also Alice Beal Parsons, *Woman's Dilemma* (New York: Thomas Y. Crowell, 1926), and H. L. Mencken, *In Defense of Woman* (New York: Knopf, 1917).

39. " 'But some women,' said Waldo, . . . 'some women have power.' . . . 'Power!' she said suddenly, . . . 'yes, we have power; and since we are not to expend it in tunneling mountains, nor healing diseases, nor making laws, nor money, nor on any extraneous object, we expend it on *you*. You are our goods, our merchandize, our material for operating on; we buy you, we sell you, we make fools of you. . . . And they say, truly, there was never an ache or pain or broken heart but a woman was at the bottom of it. We are not to study law, nor science, nor art, so we study you' " (Olive Schreiner, *The Story of an African Farm* [1883], pt. 2, chap. 4, 185–86).

all, she may not smile. . . . The hero's wife listens indifferently to the tale of his exploits; the Muse of whom the poet dreams may yawn when she listens to his stanzas. . . . The Roman women of the decadence, many American women of today, impose their caprices or their rule upon men. Where is Cinderella?

Man wants to give, and here is woman taking for herself. It is becoming a matter of self-defense, no longer a game. From the moment when woman is free, she has no other destiny than what she freely creates for herself. The relation of the two sexes is then a relation of struggle. . . . The same dialectic makes the erotic object into a wielder of black magic, the servant into a traitress, Cinderella into an ogress, and changes all women into enemies: it is the payment man makes for having in bad faith set himself up as the sole essential.[40]

These tactics are used against the male not just to manifest the woman's will to power. They are also meant to deny him his higher ambitions; to "humiliate the male sex rather than to do away with it."[41] As a free person, the woman resents the man's position and his unfair access to opportunities for self-fulfillment that he has reserved for himself in the world outside the home. As she becomes disenchanted with male prestige, she will exercise to the full the authority over men that tradition has allotted to her. Freedom is her primary need, and its frustration will be compensated by her capacity to retaliate.

Resentment is the obverse of dependence. The actions of a woman against her man are derived more from frustration with powerlessness than as a rebellion against his authority. Through their subordination under patriarchy, women experienced both physical and psychological oppression. The unjust laws, customs, and practices that traditionally sustained masculine domination marked women with a stigma of inferiority. The repression of their legitimate aspirations led them to a feeling of inadequacy in the overall scheme of existence. Since this lack of self-esteem was most intensely experienced by women through their confinement to domestic roles, the

40. *The Second Sex*, pt. 3, chap. 9, 178–79. There is a good analysis of the relation between socialist thought and the work of de Beauvoir in Andrea Nye, *Feminist Theory and the Philosophies of Man*, chap. 4.

41. *The Second Sex*, pt. 5, chap. 16, 467.

struggle for emancipation arises first in the private contexts of a common life.

Within the home, power is personal and it is not limited to physical violence. Hidden modes of control—more psychological than physical—which can damage the self-esteem of either partner, can be operative. The one undergoing the ordeal is subject to a situation that impairs his or her desire for a more meaningful existence. Under such conditions, intimacy can reverse the order of sexual hierarchy. Within these heterosexual dynamics, relations between the parties can undergo changes that may leave men as well as women with an experience of oppression.[42]

III. *The Masculine Experience of Sexual Oppression*

Patriarchy was the rule of the fathers. From its beginnings, when Abraham and the Hebrew tribes made a covenant with the male God, the supremacy of husbands in the home, as well as their dominance in social and religious activities, has been the primary theme of the patriarchal culture. As we have seen, this ideology has been perpetuated throughout the history of the West. As late as the nineteenth century, the absolute power of the husband over his wife, as well as his children, as sanctioned by law and custom, was considered the critical element in the overall social structure. In this century, in the West, that

42. For a discussion of the embedded nature of oppression see Marion Young, *Justice and the Politics of Difference* (Princeton: Princeton University Press, 1990). For feminists, the most intense experiences of oppression come from the sexual, interpersonal power which is used by men to dominate women. There are graphic illustrations of this physical exploitation in Kate Millet, *Sexual Politics* (New York: Avon Books, 1969). See also Catharine A. MacKinnon, *Toward a Feminist Theory of the State* (Cambridge: Harvard University Press, 1989), chap. 7. The point of the present reflections is that such power is, in subtle ways, reciprocal.

While this point must be persuasively argued, it should be pointed out that a conviction that radical feminism exaggerates the force of masculine power is not exclusively a male prejudice. For example, Andrea Nye observes that power, as an explanatory principle, is too crude an instrument to explain the complexity of heterosexual interaction (*Feminist Theory and the Philosophies of Man*, 95–103).

assumption has been fundamentally swept away. Fathers no longer possess a decisive authority within their families, and, except in abusive situations, they no longer control the life and destiny of their wives. Nor does the culture at large confer a dominance upon the man at home. Whatever may be his power in business or government, as husband and father he has become an "Archie Bunker" figure—more the object of ridicule or suspicion than of respect.[43]

Men have always had ambivalent feelings about the benefits of marriage and family life. The uncertainties first manifest in the Hebrew and Christian Scriptures have continued through-out the literature of Western civilization. Adonis vacillates be-tween intimacy and isolation.[44] Juvenal's sixth satire is de-signed to prove that men cannot find happiness in marriage. Medieval classics such as the *Romance of the Rose*, or Chaucer's *Wife of Bath's Tale*, while more optimistic, see women as do-mestic masters. They wished to have the most of love, and sov-ereignty over their husbands.

With the advance of civilization the benefits of matrimony become more problematic. Milton felt a profound tension be-tween the attractions of domestic life and his aspirations for spiritual perfection.[45] On a more mundane level, Francis Bacon observed how "he that hath wife and children hath given hos-tages to fortune."[46] The responsibilities of home and family inevitably impinged upon a man's broader social and political

43. See, generally, Robert Bly, *Iron John* (1990).
44. Similar themes appear in the plays of Shakespeare. See Copelia Kahn, *Man's Estate: Masculine Identity in Shakespeare*, (Berkeley: University of Califor-nia Press, 1981), and Allan Bloom, *Love and Friendship*, part 2. *The Romance of the Rose*, written in the thirteenth century, describes the woes of marriage, although it insists upon the equality of husband and wife. "True love cannot for long endure when . . . reciprocal annoyances exist and men treat their own wives like property" (Guillaume de Lorris and Jean de Meun, *Romance of the Rose*, ed. and trans. Harry W. Robbins (New York: E. P. Dutton, 1962), chap. 41. Chaucer was influenced by the *Romance*, and the *Wife of Bath's Tale* deals with similar objections to the power of women. Christine de Pisan, a medieval woman scholar and writer, defended women against the antifeminism of the *Romance*. See Shulamith Shahar, *The Fourth Estate*, 165–68.
45. Mary O'Brien, *Reproducing the World*, chap. 9.
46. Francis Bacon, *Of Marriage and the Single Life* (1625).

ambitions. Men who married had compromised their voca-
tions. Even John Stuart Mill, who berated men for exercising
an unjust power over their wives, noted how a wife who was
not endowed with the same natural talents as her husband
would eventually frustrate his higher ambitions.[47]

On the plane of dramatic literature, a more fundamental opposition between masculine fulfillment and the demands of
domesticity appeared. George Bernard Shaw used his plays to
launch a provocative assault upon the whole range of conventional Victorian morality. He mocked prevailing views of sexual polarity by reversing the pursuit of women by men. In
courtship it was the man who ostensibly took the initiative;
Shaw tried to show that in reality the male was being drawn
into the orbit of the female's desire. A similar reversal was
made in marital relations. While marriage was considered as
requiring her subordination it was, in reality, designed to serve
her purposes. From a woman's point of view, a man was simply a means to the begetting and raising of children. In *Man
and Superman* Don Juan expresses this view:

Sexually, Man is Woman's contrivance for fulfilling Nature's behest
in the most economical way. She knows by instinct that far back in
the evolutionary process she invented him, differentiated him, created
him in order to produce something better than the single-sexed process can produce. Whilst he fulfills the purpose for which she made
him, he is welcome to his dreams, his follies, his ideals, his heroisms,
provided that the keystone of them all is the worship of women, of
motherhood, of the family.[48]

47. *The Subjection of Women*, 331, in XXI Collected Works. That same frustration was apparently the experience of T. S. Eliot in his first marriage. See
Lyndall Gordon, *Eliot's New Life* (Oxford: Oxford University Press, 1988). Ms.
Gordon reports Eliot's ordeal as involving "the whole oppression, the un-
reality of the role she . . . imposed upon me" (150).

48. George Bernard Shaw, *Man and Superman*, in *Nine Plays* (New York:
Dodd, Mead, 1946), 624. Compare Schopenhauer's aphorism "Marriage is a
trap which nature sets for us." Elaborating, this pessimistic philosopher argued that "poets and philosophers who are married men incur by that very
fact the suspicion that they are looking to their own welfare and not to the
interests of science and art." Arthur Schopenhauer, *The Art of Controversy and
Other Posthumous Papers*, trans. T. Bailey Sanders (New York: MacMillan, 1896),

Shaw provided comic relief. But other dramatists would give a much bleaker report of both married life and the general state of relations between the sexes.

Shaw was humorous; Ibsen was deadly serious. Plays like *The Doll's House* documented the suffering of wives under the patriarchal ethos, but *Hedda Gabler* brought into the open the darker side of the modern woman. The wife's frustration of her husband's ambitions was not, as with Mill, the pitiable resentment of a limited woman whose only desire was to protect herself and her children. Now a different force is operative, one that reveals a more destructive attitude which a woman might adopt toward her husband and his work. Provoked by a belief that she is not an object of his erotic desire, Hedda must weaken her husband. By turning his manuscript to ashes she annihilates his ambitions toward higher ideals. Hedda is a type: a phallic woman. Envious of her husband, she views her femininity as a deprivation. For such a woman, marriage is not a union of love but a struggle for domination. The power in question is far removed from the oppressive myths of patriarchy. Now two souls encounter each other in a cycle of assertion and defense as they become entangled in a neurotic struggle for supremacy.[49]

The writings of D. H. Lawrence constitute a search for a deeper understanding of the developing combat. Lawrence led a tortured existence. There is little doubt that adverse childhood experiences within his own family gave him a distorted view of the prospects of erotic love and contributed to his misogynous outlook.[50] Nevertheless, he had some important in-

93. For a penetrating appraisal of Schopenhauer's misogyny see Karl Stern, *The Flight from Woman*, chap. 6.

49. See the account in Karl Stern, *The Flight From Woman*, chap. 8. Compare Karen Horney, *Feminine Psychology*, ed. Harry Kelman (New York: W. W. Norton, 1967), chap. 8.

50. On his misogyny and perversions, see Kate Millet, *Sexual Politics*, III, five. General criticism can be found in T. S. Eliot, "The Victim and the Sacrificial Knife," in *D. H. Lawrence and the Critical Heritage*, ed. R. P. Draper (New York: Barnes and Noble, 1970); David Cavitch, *D. H. Lawrence and the New World* (New York: Oxford University Press, 1969); Eliseo Vivas, *D. H. Lawrence, The*

sights into the nature of dysfunctional marriage and the growing antagonism between men and women. His central observation was that under modern conditions men have conceded
the initiative in life to women. As a consequence, the delicate
balance of power which had previously sustained the structure
of family life had now shifted in favor of the woman:

> [L]et us remember the actual state of affairs today, when the poles are
> reversed between the sexes. The woman is now the responsible party,
> the law-giver, the culture-bearer. She is the conscious guide and di-
> rector of the man. She bears his soul between her two hands. And
> her sex is just a function or an instrument of power. This being so,
> the man is really the servant. . . .
> Which is all very well while the fun lasts.[51]

This concession of authority to woman was matched by an increasing male passivity. Lawrence faulted the men of his time
for not adopting a more positive and venturesome attitude toward themselves and their future. He also believed that intense sexual union between a husband and his wife might
renew the man's activities in the social world. But these possibilities were always threatened by what he saw as the de-
vouring power of women.

For Lawrence, modern woman was insatiable in her need
for love and personal fulfillment. He believed that she has become destructive to the degree that she rejects the possibility
of a creative union with a man. While Lawrence placed inordinate hopes in the restorative powers of sex, he was also

---

Failure and The Triumph of Art (Evanston: Northwestern University Press, 1969);
John Middleton Murry, *Son of Woman: The Story of D. H. Lawrence* (New York:
Johnathan Cape & Harrison Smith, 1931).

51. D. H. Lawrence, *Fantasia of the Unconscious* (New York: Viking Press,
1960), 172. See also D. H. Lawrence, *Studies in Classical American Literature*
(New York: Thomas Seltzer, 1923). Compare H. L. Mencken, *In Defense of
Woman*, secs. 22–23. Mencken points out that all the older rights of men relative
to marriage have been turned into obligations; as a result of treating women
with great reverence, men have "created for her a vast and growing mass of
immunities, culminating . . . in the astounding doctrine that, under the contract of marriage, all the duties lie upon the man and all the privileges apper-
tain to the woman" (123).

deeply aware of the dangers which sensual indulgence posed to higher aspirations. He was convinced that a man's greatest desire is to have some purposive activity in the public world. If a man should make sexuality and the reproductive cycle the center of his existence, he would not only forfeit the opportunity for such activity; he would inevitably fall into despair.

The psychological opposition that men experience in marriage has been recorded by other writers whose credentials are less controversial than those of Lawrence. The Nobel laureate François Mauriac saw as the fundamental problem the primacy that a married woman inevitably gives to her maternal character. In his study of bourgeois family life, *The Nest of Vipers*, Mauriac draws the portrait of Louis, a dying lawyer, who experiences the disintegration of the original bond between himself and his beloved. Following their marriage, they gradually become alienated from each other. He pursues his profession; children and property become her center of interest and the boundaries of her affections. The role of wife is eclipsed by that of mother. And while the husband retains some financial power, he completely loses his self-esteem.[52]

In the plays and novels by modern men, more is lost than gained through heterosexual love. In encounters with women the important symbols are those of fear and rejection. Pursuit is motivated more by lust or fascination than by any sense of wholesome attraction.[53] The physical consummation, if it occurs at all, is often conceived as a retaliation for some injury to the male ego rather than as an act of personal union. Throughout, there is no confidence in fulfillment within the dynamics of heterosexual love. A complete relationship, which would unite sexuality with love, seems to have been lost. Ancient myths of woman's destructive power are renewed as

52. See K. R. Iyenfar, *François Mauriac* (London: Asia Publishing House, 1963), chap. 15, and Francis F. Maloney, *François Mauriac* (Denver: Alan Swallow, 1958).

53. See the discussion of the novels of Lawrence, Henry Miller, and Norman Mailer in Kate Millet, *Sexual Politics*, iii.

women are increasingly seen to be manipulative, domineering, and intent upon emasculating men.[54]

There is, of course, a good bit of "macho" nonsense in some of this literature, as well as the blatant exploitation of women. But, at a deeper level, the sensibility concerns something more profound than a diminution of sexual power. All significant literature is concerned with the acquisition, or loss, of personal identity. In these works, the recurring theme is that of an undoing of personal identity and of a humiliation that is attributed to the inability, or unwillingness, of a woman to affirm the man's potential. The male protagonist hopes to marry the woman of his heart; he is more likely, as in Bellow's novel, to "die of heartbreak." Oppressed by the domestic role imposed upon him, the male becomes increasingly incapable of maintaining a meaningful existence of his own.[55]

As a matter of psychoanalysis, these effusions of need may be traced to primitive deprivations, which women, as well as men, suffer at the hands of their mothers. The fear of the will of a woman is based, at least in part, upon that primordial experience. We are originally dependent upon a maternal authority which can either encourage, or deny, our desires for independence.[56] And it is certainly the case that serious maternal deprivation in infancy can, as in the case of Tolstoy, lead the male to a subsequent hatred of women. It must also be admitted that in the literary expressions of a man's hope for a

54. This is a recurrent theme in the works of Hemingway. See Theodore Bardacke, "Hemingway's Women," in *The Man and His Work*, ed. John K. M. McCaffern (New York: Cooper Square Publishers, 1969), 340. Leslie Fielder has observed that in American male fiction there are no positive encounters between men and women (*Life and Death in the American Novel* [New York: Criterion Books, 1960], xix). Compare Barbara Ehrenreich, *The Hearts of Men* (New York: Anchor Press, 1983).

55. T. S. Eliot felt that the tension between himself and his first wife was such that "she . . . made him incapable of any existence of his own" (*Eliot's New Life*, 150). In Mauriac's *Nest of Vipers*, the male protagonist is reduced to the role of provider.

56. Nancy Chodorow, *The Reproduction of Mothering* (Berkeley: University of California Press, 1978); Dorothy Dinnerstein, *The Mermaid and the Minotaur* (New York: Harper and Row, 1977).

woman's love, it is difficult to distinguish adult from infantile longings.[57]

A man's craving for a woman may also suggest a search for a kind of inspiration which only someone of a different sex can provide. Robert Graves's adulation of the White Goddess is an extreme expression of a more general masculine tendency.[58] Feminist writers tend to dismiss these assertions of need as nothing more than refined expressions of an arrested development. Yet there is something simplistic in the assertion that what men fear most is that women will no longer mother them.

While ridiculing the need that men have for women, Virginia Woolf recognized how great men are dependent, in a significant way, upon women. Beyond flattery and pleasure, they receive "some stimulus, some renewal of creative power which is in the gift only of the opposite sex to bestow."[59] If that much is conceded, it is important that such personal affirmation not be restricted to the privilege of an elite. Love is a need. All human beings need a love from others that is appropriate to their sex, age, and circumstances.

Such a love must be mutual and mature. The lives of both adult men and women are equally impoverished if the love of a mother for a child is taken as the exclusive measure of human affection. Grown men and women both need self-esteem. A proper appreciation and acceptance of oneself is the most fundamental of all human needs, and if the need is not satisfied,

57. E.g.: "[T]he real fierceness of desire, the real heat of a passion long continued and withering up the soul of a man, is a craving for identity with the woman that he loves. . . . For, whatever may be said of the relation of the sexes, there is no man who loves a woman that does not desire to come to her for the renewal of his courage . . . and that will be the mainspring of his desire for her. We are all so afraid, we are all so alone, we all so need from the outside the assurance of our own worthiness to exist" (Ford Maddox Ford, *The Good Soldier* [New York: Vintage Books, 1989], 127).

58. John B. Vickery, *Robert Graves and the White Goddess* (Lincoln: University of Nebraska Press 1972).

59. Virginia Woolf, *A Room of One's Own* (New York: Harcourt Brace, 1929), 150. Of her relationship with Chopin, George Sand observed that "he complains that I have killed something in him by deprivation" (Letter of May 1847, quoted in Karl Stern, *The Flight from Woman*, 156).

the whole personality is endangered.[60] The absence of self-esteem among contemporary men has been amply demonstrated, and the isolation and desperation that they experience is increasing at an alarming rate. There is also a growing recognition among men that they are primarily responsible for the recovery and maintenance of their masculinity.[61]

Self-confidence cannot be entirely self-generated. Nor can it be derived exclusively from the enhancement of a separate gender identity. The truism that love of self depends upon the love received from others has always included the possibilities inherent in a mutually beneficial love between the sexes. Men, as well as women, need to be loved and esteemed in an adult relationship. However, under the circumstances of modern life, the relationships between men and women have become forms of reciprocal mistrust. Consequently, the capacities which each possesses to empower the other have been greatly neglected.

The biological distinctiveness of women makes them extremely vulnerable to the sexual power of men. Women have become subject to violence and abandonment, with disastrous consequences for both themselves and their offspring. But in the wars between the sexes there have been masculine as well as feminine casualties. Upon the dissolution of a marriage, the man is usually better off financially, but, as his hopes in the future decline, his physical and psychological condition quickly deteriorates. When love is lost, men suffer a more complete rejection. Being separated from the continuities of family life, they rarely enjoy the affective bonds they once had with their children.[62]

60. "To be split off from relationships and to define ourselves solely by our separateness is as pathological as defining ourselves within our relationships, deriving our identity from the nexus of our belonging" (Judith M. Barwick, *In Transition* [New York: Holt, Rinehart and Winston, 1979], 128).

61. Significant works on the need for men to develop a positive sense of their masculine identity include Sam Keen, *Fire in the Belly* (New York: Bantam, 1991); Patrick Arnold, *Wildmen, Warriors and Kings* (New York: Crossroads, 1991); Robert Bly, *Iron John* (1990); George Gilder, *Men and Marriage* (1987); Karl Bednarik, *The Male in Crisis*, trans. Helen Sebba (Westport: Greenwood Press, 1970).

62. Gilder, *Men and Marriage.*

While women suffer from the sexual aggressiveness of men, their overall status in sexual matters is more advantageous. A woman's identity is more secure than that of a man. Feminist literature emphasizes the way that prevailing social standards distort women's self-esteem. But however much the feminine may be influenced by imposed roles, women have a natural being that can only be supplemented, rather than established, by conventional standards. The sexual identity of the male is, however, *essentially* uncertain. It is not a given condition which automatically matures. Sexual activity is one measure of male identity, and, if it is not stabilized by morals and culture, its aimless repetition will have harmful and disruptive effects.

Beyond sexual expression, there are further complications. Manhood is inherently precarious. Its achievement depends upon the fulfillment of the expectations set by others. Considered anthropologically:

[T]rue manhood is a precious and elusive status beyond mere maleness, a hortatory image that men and boys aspire to and that their culture demands of them as a measure of belonging. Although this stressed or embattled quality varies in intensity . . . [it] frequently shows an inner insecurity that needs dramatic proof. Its vindication is doubtful, resting on rigid codes of decisive action in many spheres of life: as husband, father, lover, provider, warrior. A restricted status, there are always men who fail the test.[63]

Masculinity is predominantly a social construct. The realization of manhood involves much greater tensions than those required to conform to, or resist, a sexual stereotype. Men are called upon, as well as conditioned. The meaning of their manhood is contained in standards, myths, and stories, which, in their highest forms, summon the deepest potentials of the male spirit and forecast a man's destiny.

Feminists tend to characterize men as being predatory, violent, and aggressive. But although masculine development

63. David D. Gilmore, *Manhood in the Making* (New Haven: Yale University Press 1990), 17. See also Walter J. Ong, *Fighting for Life* (Ithaca: Cornell University Press, 1981).

may lead to the domination of women, this is not its necessary effect. In a civilized society, men are expected to protect the helpless and the vulnerable and to safeguard the essential interests of the community, particularly those concerned with reproduction and the continuity of life. In all these endeavors, with the risks that they involve, men know that they are expendable.

The combative competitions of men can bring them great power and prestige on the stages of the public world. But men are not as important to the fundamental evolution of life as are women. Women are more powerful shapers of private life and the domestic environment. A mother develops stronger bonds with the children she has borne than does their father. And women are more deeply embedded in the continuities of human existence. Male dynasties come and go, but the fundamental society sustained by women endures.

iv. *From Sexual Asymmetry to Mutual Affirmation*

Masculinity does not, of itself, hold the same fears for women that womanliness holds for men. Women know more about men than men know about themselves. In speech, dress, and behavior, a woman can more easily assimilate male characteristics than the male can adopt feminine traits.[64] More importantly, women intuitively sense the vulnerability of the men in their lives, and they are painfully aware of the male proclivity toward destructive behavior. Women are often the victims of such violence, but they are also spectators. They can watch as men turn their rage inward upon themselves. Women understand how men are prone to self-destruction, and it is often in a woman's power either to arrest or to accelerate that process.[65]

---

64. Ong, *Fighting for Life.*
65. Karl Menninger, *Love against Hate* (New York: Harcourt, Brace, 1942), chap. 4. See also Rollo May, *Love and Will.*
A modern writer describes the disappointment that men experience in marriage: "For thousands of years somehow man believed that when he left his

The violence that men display toward women and that men bring upon themselves is not caused solely by the strain placed upon men in a patriarchal culture. While the frustrations they experience in the workplace will adversely affect the quality of their private life, deeper discords are derived from childhood experiences which are a rehearsal for the later relationships of love and marriage. The problematic of parental love to which we have briefly referred has adverse consequences for children of both sexes. But it has a particular significance for the general predicament of manhood.

At the beginning of life every child has a strong attraction to the parent of the opposite sex and begins a struggle with the parent of the same sex. Under normal circumstances the child will, over time, begin to model himself, or herself, after the parent having the same gender. These identifications are susceptible to considerable variation. On balance, such contingencies do not adversely affect female development. Where the father is the stronger parent, the female child may experience her femininity as a deprivation; if the mother is the stronger, the daughter will have an ambivalence over her own sexual identity. But the likelihood is that she will eventually acquiesce in her own gender. Some hostility toward her mother may persist, but will not prevent the emergence of an independent feminine personality.[66]

---

home he left near the fire a faithful wife. This belief is disappearing . . . so modern man feels that he has really nothing to live for" (*Conversation with Issac Bashevis Singer,* Isaac Bashevis Singer and Richard Burgin [Garden City: Doubleday, 1985], 159).

66. Nancy Chodorow, *The Reproduction of Mothering* (Berkeley: University of California Press, 1978). Karl Stern, *The Flight from Woman.* Freud's explanation of the "Oedipus complex" is criticized in Erich Fromm, *The Sane Society* (1955), chap. 3. See also the observations on "The Dread of Woman," in Karen Horney, *Feminine Psychology* (New York: W. W. Norton, 1967). Horney notes that the menace to the boy's self-respect posed by the anatomical differences between himself and his mother is more severe than the experience of a female child as she becomes aware of the differences between her body and that of her father. The anxiety caused to the male child will affect his general disposition toward women, but a similar effect is not observed in the female's attitude toward men. Horney notes further: "Now one of the exigencies of the

The feminine reconciliation of gender and identity has an important bearing upon adult relationships between men and women. A woman's needs are relational, and the bond of a female child with her mother provides a foundation for the further development of the connectedness that will characterize her adult life. The male child, by contrast, must resist his relationship to his mother if he is to attain an independent personality. Masculinity is determined as much negatively as positively. In the realization of maleness there is an emphasis upon differentiation which leads the male to reject the feminine world and to search for his identity in some broader, non-relational, universe.[67] Yet, no matter how much progress is made in that external direction, the male never fully escapes from his elementary bondage to woman.

The oedipal conflicts of modern man suggest that the mother is the more powerful parent.[68] As a male struggles to deny her psychological authority he may seek to take vengeance upon other women whom he encounters in his adult

---

biological differences between the sexes is this: that the man is actually obliged to go on proving his manhood to the woman. There is no analogous necessity for her. Even if she is frigid, she can engage in sexual intercourse and conceive and bear a child. She performs her part by merely *being*, without any *doing*— a fact that has always filled men with admiration and resentment. The man on the hand has to *do* something in order to fulfill himself" (ibid., 145). For further aspects of these issues see Jacques Lacan, *Feminine Sexuality*, trans. Jacqueline Rose (New York: W. W. Norton, 1982). See also Andrea Nye, *Feminist Theory*, chap. 5. The assertion by feminists that being a woman is something made rather than given is not supported by the biological, psychological, or anthropological evidence. This does not mean that being a woman is the same as being a mother. It is a matter of experience that a woman's occupation—in the home or in public life—does not depend upon her femininity. A female can be a mother but not womanly; conversely, she can be a public figure, such as Justice O'Connor, and remain essentially feminine. See further K. Stern, *The Flight from Woman*, chap. 8.

67. Nancy Chodorow, *The Reproduction of Mothering*. See also Karl Bednarik, *The Male in Crisis*. Greater involvement of men in parenting may moderate the need of the male child to find his identity through separation, but it will not eliminate the process.

68. Dorothy Dinnerstein, *The Mermaid and the Minotaur*, (New York: Harper and Row, 1977); Karl Menninger, *Love against Hate*. See also Robert Bly, *Iron John*, chap. 1.

life. There is also the possibility that he will search for a re-
union with the mother through his attraction to another
woman. But, more importantly, his fundamental dependence
upon the feminine will always frustrate his desire for complete
autonomy.

At the very beginnings of existence, the interdependencies
between men and women are not symmetrical. In the Judaic-
Christian tradition, the domination of women by men has been
traced to the overthrow of the female deities and the covenant
made by the patriarchs with their male-God, Yahweh.[69] But,
at the same time, a significant inversion was also initiated. In
the book of Genesis maleness is given precedence; but it is a
supremacy burdened with a need: "It is not good for man to
be alone."[70] At this elemental level, the woman does not suffer
a comparable deficiency. For good, or ill, her companion is already there.[71]

This Hebraic experience was paralleled by similar changes
throughout the ancient world. While goddess worship was
being publicly eliminated, its reenactment was beginning within the male psyche. Intensely recorded by poets, this primal
dependency, and the male vulnerability to it, have become

69. See the discussion in Part 1, above, and accompanying notes. For a
challenge to the patriarchal personification of the religious symbols of Judaism
and Christianity, see Naomi R. Goldberg, *Changing the Gods* (Boston: Beacon
Press, 1979).

70. Genesis 2:15–25.

71. Walter Ong, *Fighting for Life*. Compare the interpretation of Karl Barth:
"The divine decision that it is not good for man to be alone has been taken
irrevocably; and it applies to woman as well as to man. For both, therefore,
there is only an incidental, external, provisional and transient isolation and
autonomy. They elude themselves if they try to escape their orientation on one
another, i.e., the fact that they are ordered, related and directed to one another. Their being is always and in all circumstances a being with the other"
(K. Barth, *Church Dogmatics*, trans. A. T. MacKay et al. [Edinburgh: T. & T.
Clark, 1961], III/4 168).

In reflecting upon the creation of woman from the rib of Adam (Gen. 2:18–
25), Pope John Paul II affirms that the woman is another "I" in a common
humanity and that both were created to establish a "unity of the two" that is
meant to overcome the original solitude of the man (*Mulieris Dignitatem*,
chap. 3).

a fundamental aspect of masculine experience. In some instances the dependency may be excessive, but it is not, essentially, a sign of abnormality. It is ontological, something "rooted in our being."[72]

The basic asymmetry between the sexes has profound consequences. In the ongoing relations between men and women it can lead to disproportions of power and influence, which must be acknowledged if we are fully to understand the phenomenon of sexual oppression.

The historical subjection of women to the physical, financial, and cultural power of men is well understood. While much remains to be done, the ideology of patriarchy is now in full retreat. But all indices of sexual power and vulnerability should be taken into account if the relations between the sexes are to be based upon equal concern and respect. Men are more emotionally dependent upon women than either men, or women, have been willing to acknowledge. And this dependency of the male has moral, as well as psychological, significance. Called upon to prove that he is not a woman, a man struggles to secure his identity in a demanding public world. He is often drawn toward heterosexual relations as a way of relieving the burdens of that wider contest with impersonal forces. But to look upon this attraction toward the female solely in sensual terms is to miss its deeper meaning.

Man is in awe of woman as much for her spiritual as for her erotic power. Men are acutely aware of the distinct advantages of feminine being. Men sense that a woman's ability to penetrate the depths of reality far exceeds their own limited capacities. And they see her as possessed of a fullness that not only makes up for their deficiencies but also constitutes a potential endowment that can lead them into unknown dimensions of their otherwise impoverished existence. A man entrusts to a woman the responsibility of guarding and weighing values, and he sees in her the incarnation of his ideals. It is for these deeper reasons that he solicits her love. He not only

72. Sam Keen, *Fire in the Belly*, 15.

seeks to possess her but also hopes that she will confirm his projects. Other men may be comrades, but they are, eventually, his competitors. In his solitude, a man looks to a woman to confer an absolute value upon his life.[73]

These emotional ties have been substantially altered by the women's movement. With the passing of patriarchy, women no longer accept their subordination to men or their exclusion by men from the wider world of human possibilities. Nor will they play the role of a desirable object that solicits male adulation. As they make the most of their rising opportunities for self-affirmation, women will no longer reflect back to men a self-enlarging image of themselves.[74]

Distancing is becoming reciprocal. Men, too, are now searching for authentic identities. In that pursuit, they are resisting the power that women possess either to reward or punish them. Men are beginning to develop new images of what it means to be masculine. With the ascendancy of women's values, men have been encouraged to develop the feminine side of their personalities. But while becoming more gentle they are not, on the whole, happier. They now realize that they must understand themselves on the basis of their own experience rather than as they are seen in the eyes of women. Men hope to distinguish what belongs to masculine character from what constitutes male domination. Standing forth in new forms of

73. Simone de Beauvoir, *The Second Sex*, Part III. See also Gertrud von le Fort, *The Eternal Woman*, trans. Placid Jordon, O.S.B. (Milwaukee: Bruce, 1962).

74. "Women have served all these centuries as looking-glasses possessing the magic and delicious power of reflecting the figure of man at twice its natural size. Without that power probably the earth would still be swamp and jungle. The glories of all our wars would be unknown . . . whatever may be their use in civilized societies, mirrors are essential to all violent and heroic action. That is why Napoleon and Mussolini both insist so emphatically upon the inferiority of women, for if they were not inferior, they would cease to enlarge. That serves to explain in part the necessity that women so often are to men. And it serves to explain how restless they are under her criticism. . . . For if she begins to tell the truth, the figure in the looking glass shrinks; his fitness for life is diminished" (Virginia Woolf, *A Room of One's Own*, 60–61). See also Madonna Kolbenschlag, *Kiss Sleeping Beauty Goodbye* (New York: Doubleday, 1979).

virility, they are trying to discover the positive qualities of a heroic but nonviolent life.[75]

All these developments pose an essential question: In a world of gender distinction, what are to be the fundamental relationships between men and women? Gender liberation may reveal a common human nature, but the movement toward separate sexual identity is too far advanced to suggest some culmination in an androgynous world.[76] Men and women are both trying to overcome sexual stereotypes, and they are doing so in order to affirm what is unique to the personal experience of being masculine or feminine. They are both unwilling to collapse their differences into a facile similarity. It remains to be seen whether the increase of gender distinctiveness will jeopardize the sexual polarity that always has been the mainspring of human growth and vitality.

While drawing upon women's gifts to civilized life, society must also renew the positive abilities of men. For men and women to collaborate, there must be a constructive use of sexual differences. These differences make their appearance, in various ways, throughout all aspects of a common life. They take on a unique significance, however, in the realm of sexual intimacy and espoused love. We have already observed how both men and women can experience some form of oppression within the circle of family life. The success of a new humanism will depend, in large measure, on how well the dynamics of sexual polarity are renewed within the fundamental society that arises out of married love.[77]

75. See authorities, n. 61, above.

76. "I do not believe we are simply involved in a straightforward and inevitable progression to an ultimately androgynous society. . . . In periods of intensified social change, men and women, the masculine and the feminine, come closer together" (Juliet Mitchell, "Reflections on Twenty Years of Feminism," in *What Is Feminism?* ed. Juliet Mitchell and Ann Oakley [New York: Pantheon, 1986], 47–48). See also Jean Bethke Elshtain, "Against Androgyny," in *Feminism and Equality*, ed. Anne Phillips (New York: New York University Press, 1987).

77. Pedro-Juan Viladrich, *The Agony of Legal Marriage*, trans. Alban d'Entremont (Pamplona: University of Navarra 1990).

For John Stuart Mill, the highest achievement of men and women would be to live together as equals. Yet, while he insisted that intimacy was not immune from justice, his conception of marital relations was not essentially moralistic. He assumed that where the parties were similarly endowed, and equally desirous of personal fulfillment, they would be drawn together in a sympathetic companionship in which "each can enjoy the luxury of looking up to the other, and can have alternatively the pleasure of leading and being led in the path of development."[78] Mill also thought that in the future, a married woman who enjoys her husband's respect would identify herself more intimately with his own happiness. Under these circumstances, the *affection of equality*—which for Mill was the equivalent of love—would be fully operative.

Many feminists take umbrage with Mill's conception of married love, as they see any such deep association of a wife with her husband's calling as being inconsistent with the right of the woman to have a meaningful existence of her own. Mill might even be charged with inconsistency, since, if a woman should pursue her happiness "by uniting herself to a man whom she loves,"[79] that orientation, logically pursued, might lead to a revival of the very subjugation Mill condemned. These criticisms raise important questions about the hazards connected with an affirming affection, and I shall return to them, in the final chapter, when I explore more fully the nature of love. For the present, it will suffice to point out that the objections to Mill's conception of a unitive married love do not sufficiently account for the degree of fulfillment that a woman may possess from the experience of being married.

Mill attacked the legal tyranny that allows men to control

78. John Stuart Mill, "The Subjugation of Women," 336. Jane Austen's understanding of married love as a union of friendship between a man and a woman is considered. Allan Bloom, *Love and Friendship*, chap. 3.

79. "On Marriage," p. 44, in *Essays on Equality, Law, and Education*, vol. 21, Collected Works. Compare the criticisms of Mill and Harriet Taylor in Zillah R. Eisenstein, *The Radical Future of Liberal Feminism*, chap. 9.

their wives, and he objected to the customs that encourage a woman to manipulate a man so that she might gain some security in marriage. What he found to be more distressing, however, was the absence of mutual sympathy, or the enjoyment of the possibilities of companionship *between* spouses. It was hoped that in the future, as their self-esteem increased, women, as well as men, would be open to these richer experiences. Where companionable affection flourished, the circumstances of each partner would be enhanced by their entry into marriage.[80]

In pursuing the observations initiated by Mill, it is important to realize that if we wish to understand the prospects of reciprocal love, we cannot ignore the significance of procreation. When children are born of a marital union, the woman realizes a unique form of fulfillment. Married persons may achieve and enjoy a pervasive equality, yet the fertility of sexual love shifts the balance of attention in favor of the feminine. Through her capacity to give birth a woman holds "an exceptional position in the order of being."[81] In its strident early expressions modern feminism tended to demean procreative experience. That attitude has been significantly altered. Major women writers now assert the humanistic importance of freely chosen childbirth, and they see it as having a value both to the woman who has become a mother and to the general quality of life.[82]

80. See the brief essay "On Marriage," by Harriet Taylor, in vol. 21, *Collected Works*, 375. Taylor was Mill's companion and after her husband's death she and Mill married. The importance of interpersonal companionship is increasingly reflected in the literature on marriage. See, e.g., Evelyn Eaton Whitehead and James D. Whitehead, *Marrying Well* (New York: Image Books, 1983).

81. Woman is "a mystery defined by modesty which has an exceptional position in the order of being" (Emmanuel Levinas, *Time and the Other*, trans. R. A. Cohen [Pittsburgh: Duquesne University Press, 1987], 84). According to Levinas, erotic love does not have possession as its objective. Rather, it involves a relationship to an unknown future; a relationship which arises out of the response of the male to the radical otherness (alterity) of the feminine.

In *Mulieris Dignitatem*, John Paul II speaks of motherhood as involving a "special communion with the mystery of life" (chap. 6, p. 65).

82. E.g., Virginia Held, "Birth and Death," in *Feminist Political Theory*, ed.

The restoration of the value of procreation has important consequences for married love. Its just, and immediate, significance is to highlight neglected male responsibilities. But there are other implications. Mill's suggestion that a wife might closely identify herself with her husband's projects suggests the need to consider whether a woman who is being fulfilled by motherhood might be drawn, by way of mutual affirmation, to support her spouse in his own creative endeavors.

As men pursue an elusive manhood, women are determined to establish a meaningful existence for themselves. A woman rightly refuses to live her life through a man. But she cannot live for herself alone. Nor are the capacities of a woman for giving of herself to another limited to the affection she can bestow on her child. If she is approached by a man with a love that acknowledges her entire personal value, she may willingly respond to his deeper needs. At the point where love reaches toward respect, affirmation must be mutual. Each needs to receive from the other that degree of confirmation that makes possible the bestowal of reciprocal affection. [83]

Much of modern feminism has been an effort by women incrementally to develop a common consciousness of suffering and to bring this experience to the attention of whose whom they have considered to be their oppressors. In the process,

---

Cass R. Sunstein (Chicago: University of Chicago Press, 1990), 87; Carol McMillan, *Woman, Reason, and Nature* (Princeton: Princeton University Press, 1982); Jean Bethke Elshtain, *Public Man, Private Woman*, xxxiii. See also Betty Friedan, *The Second Stage* (New York: Summit Books, rev. ed. 1986), and Germaine Greer, *Sex and Destiny* (New York: Harper and Row, 1984). The significance of these developments for the intellectual life will be explored in the following chapter.

83. Karl Stern, *The Flight from Woman*, chap. 8. See also Irving Singer, *The Nature of Love*, vol. 3, chap. 10. Singer contends that in married love there is a basic dialectic between need and bestowal. All love involves a transcendence of self-interest, yet the need to have our deepest interests satisfied is an integral part of all intimate heterosexual relationships. Mutual need is also recognized in Judith M. Barwick, *In Transition* (New York: Holt, Rinehart and Winston, 1979). I shall explore these themes in Chapter 4 of the present work.

patriarchy has diminished, but the image of manhood has not been enlarged. In some respects it has been demeaned. The traditional masculine fear and hatred of women is too often matched by an equally virulent misandry.[84] This hostility toward men is not always just a weapon in a battle for liberation; it can also express the power of women to oppose men's deepest aspirations.[85]

At the dawn of feminism, reformers were confident that, once the oppression of women was ended, the relations between the sexes would improve. When a woman became a man's equal, she would understand him more completely. It was expected that they would both experience an increase in well-being. These hopes have not been fulfilled. Male horizons have not been enhanced, nor has the progressive realization of sexual equality satisfied women's desires for personal happiness. There is an increasing awareness that men and women must achieve new levels of mutual understanding if either is to realize their full potential.[86]

Men have nothing to gain and everything to lose from abusing or avoiding women. Most men do not desire to dominate women or to thwart their hopes for a full realization of all their abilities. But it is not sufficiently appreciated that men, like women, can suffer impairment of their personal identity. Like women, men can experience a deep frustration of their hopes for fulfillment. As men will not be impoverished by their acknowledgement of the dignity—and suffering—of women, women should not fear the consequences of a comparable rec-

84. See Patrick M. Arnold, *Wildmen, Warriors and Kings.*
85. Simone de Beauvoir, *The Second Sex,* chap. 16.
86. "How do we transcend the polarization between women and women and between women and men, to achieve the new human wholeness that is the promise of feminism, and get on with solving the concrete, practical, everyday problems of living, working, and loving as equal persons?" (Betty Friedan, *The Second Stage,* 41). Other feminists recognize the dangers of a "circular, self-confirming rhetoric" which traps the militant woman in an unsatisfying narcissism (Rosalind Delmar, "What Is Feminism?" in *What Is Feminism?* ed. Juliet Mitchell and Ann Oakley [New York: Pantheon Books, 1986], 27).

ognition. Mutual affirmation begins with an understanding that being either a masculine or a feminine person is a legitimate mode of human existence:

First and foremost there is the human person, masculine and feminine. . . . There is only one unique and identical essential condition for the person, the human person, which is applicable to both males and females, because the *personal substratum*, the plane upon which one is a "person," is more radical than the duality of the sexes.

[W]e can say that *on the personal* plane man and woman are *equally persons*, equally worthy and possessors, as human persons, of identical rights and duties. But one thing is the substantive plane of the "person" and another the plane of the sexual dimension. On this latter plane men and women are, respectively and reciprocally, neither superior nor inferior but simply different.[87]

Men and women are not just opposites of each other. They are equally human and, as a person, each is created for his or her own sake. But neither can fulfill themselves alone. Their growth, as an individual man or woman, is unlikely to occur without some meaningful contact with a person, or persons, of the opposite sex. Otherwise, reciprocal independence leads to reciprocal indifference. There must be appropriate encounters between the sexes which provide opportunities for mutual affirmation in the various venues of public and private life.

Every individual longs to be fully himself or herself in a way that does not diminish anything that is essential to their sense of personal dignity. This aspiration, which is a commonplace in the general literature on autonomy, is equally applicable to the desire to be either a masculine, or a feminine, person.

87. Pedro-Juan Viladrich, *The Agony of Legal Marriage*, trans. Alban d'Entremont (Pamplona: University of Navarra, 1990), 58–59. In his reflection *Mulieris Dignitatem*, John Paul II holds that the equal dignity of men and women is derived from their being both created in the image and likeness of God. In this Christian anthropology men and women, human to an equal degree, both possess reason and free will. Both are persons, created for their own sakes. But, as human, they are called to an interpersonal communion, in truth and in love, in a manner appropriate to all the social encounters in which they may be engaged, as either men or women.

While demanding as much, one must also be prepared to acknowledge in the other the mystery of sexual difference.[88]

Sexual reconciliation will not be easy; it will require much good will on both sides. Men and women must be also willing to know more about each other. And the way of knowing will be a way of questioning, of asking why, and how, we are different:

Man is unsettled by woman and woman by man. There is always this unsettlement by the opposite sex where there is the encounter of man and woman. Each is asked by the opposite sex: Why, *quo iure*, are you *de facto* so utterly different from myself? Can and will you guarantee that your mode of life which disconcerts me is also human? Can you show me this in such a way that I can understand it?[89]

The unsettled relations between men and women can be improved through a dialogue on difference, as well as by reciprocal recognition of an equal dignity. Through such a civil conversation we can overcome the past and begin to bring a new wholeness to our common life. The chapters that follow are a reflection upon such questioning.

88. Compare Letty M. Russell, *Growth in Partnership* (Philadelphia: Westminster Press, 1981).

89. Barth, *Church Dogmatics*, 167. See also the discussion, "The Limits of the Thinkable," in Andrea Nye, *Feminist Theory*, chap. 5. See also Drucilla Cornell and Adam Thurschwell, "Feminism, Negativity, Intersubjectivity," in *Feminism as Critique*, ed. Seyla Benhabib and Drucilla Cornell (Minneapolis: University of Minnesota Press, 1987).

2. REASON AND GENDER

1. *The Masculinization of Thought*

Of all the obstacles that limit the advancement of women, those touching upon knowledge and values are the most difficult to remove. Women seeking acceptance within professional and intellectual communities are often expected to exhibit qualities of thought and action that characterize the lives of men. And if their performance does not meet standards established by men, it is likely that nothing significant will be expected from them.

Knowledge is power, a power that is more than a means of understanding and controlling nature. In the context of sexual oppression, it is another way that men maintain their dominance over women. Here everything is at stake, because the capacity of every person to have a full human life depends upon their opportunities to develop and express the deepest potentials of the mind and heart.

In the early stages of feminism, attention was focused upon the improvement of the situation of women within a patriarchal culture. Reform was directed primarily toward political and legal emancipation. Now, the exclusion of women from full participation in the universe of moral and rational discourse activates a deeper aspiration for liberty:

The women's liberation movement is not only explicitly feminist in that it arises from a developed feminist consciousness, but it is much more inclusive in its agenda than was the women's emancipation movement of the early 1900s. The liberation which contemporary feminists seek is not merely freedom *from* marginalization, oppression, discrimination, and violence but freedom *for* self-definition, self-affirmation, and self-determination; in other words, the effective recognition of their full humanity as persons and the freedom to exercise that personhood in every sphere. Thus, the contemporary movement envisions not only political and legal rights for women equal to those of men but the liberation of women (and men) into the fullness of human personhood.[1]

When a woman lacks the independent capacity to assert her own positive truths and values, she is unable to contribute her insights and experiences to the various fields of human knowledge. This inhibition also affects relations between the sexes. When denied opportunities for higher forms of self-expression, women may, out of frustration, attack the modes of understanding upheld by men. Masculine claims of cognitive objectivity are then dismissed as spurious modes of knowledge. To some feminists, such uses of the intellect represent a "point-of-view-less-ness" that is nothing other than the limited and partial perspective of men.[2] Women hope to do away with philosophies of mind that maintain the dualism of subject and object, body and spirit, reason and emotion. Masculine attachment to an abstract universalism—which reduces reality to thought—excludes the experiential understanding of women from the development of human culture.

Within the women's movement there is disagreement over the relation between reason and gender. Some are convinced that the full attainment of equality will provide women with the opportunity to demonstrate that their own cognitive abilities and moral conceptions are substantially the same as those of men. Others see a danger in such an approach, because they

1. Sandra M. Schneiders, *Beyond Patching: Faith and Feminism in the Catholic Church* (New York: Paulist Press, 1991), 8–9.
2. In the legal literature, this opposition can be found in works such as Clare Dalton, "Commentary: Where We Stand, Observations on the Situation of Feminist Legal Thought," *Berkeley Women's Law Journal* (1987). See also Katharine T. Bartlett, "Feminist Legal Method," *Harvard Law Review* 103 (1990): 829, and Lynne N. Henderson, "Legality and Empathy," *Michigan Law Review* 85 (1987): 1574. For an important discussion of how perspectives are relational, see Martha Minow, *Making All the Difference* (Ithaca: Cornell University Press, 1990). In the philosophical literature the better opinion is that the standard of evaluation is not whether a work is masculine but whether it reflects a male bias which can be used to subordinate women. Alison M. Jaggar, "Feminist Ethics: Projects, Problems, Prospects," in *Feminist Ethics*, ed. Claudia Card (Lawrence, Kan.: University Press of Kansas, 1991), 90.

fear it would deprive women of the uniqueness of their feminine perceptions.[3] The problem becomes more complicated
when one considers how much matters of mind and spirit have
androgynous implications.

To the medieval philosophers, men and women were equal
with regard to reason. The subordinations of woman to man
arose primarily from bodily difference. As an immaterial power,
reason existed in the soul, and in the soul there was no sex.[4]
In this limited sense, human nature was complete in both men
and women. A related and somewhat different insight has
been developed within modern psychology. Jung and his followers assert that every person has both male and female com-
ponents in their psyche. There are primal patterns, or archetypes, of the unconscious, which attract the soul of every
human being. Included among these are two basic sexual
archetypes: the *animus,* or masculine spirit, and the *anima,* or
feminine spirit.[5]

The point of psychological androgyny is to show that although each person is predominately masculine or feminine,
he or she also possesses significant qualities of mind and heart
that are generally attributable to the opposite sex. At the level
of intense intellectual activity, it is difficult to determine which
disposition is operative. Coleridge believed that great minds
are androgynous. There is no doubt that the state of mind
needed for creative work is one of detachment from conscious
sexual identity.

3. See, e.g., Jean Bethke Elshtain, *Public Man, Private Woman* (Princeton:
Princeton University Press, 1981); Carol Gilligan, *In a Different Voice* (Cambridge: Harvard University Press, 1982).

4. Genevieve Lloyd, *The Man of Reason* (London: Methuen, 1984). See also
Genevieve Lloyd, "Augustine and Aquinas," *Feminist Theology: A Reader,* ed.
Ann Loades (Louisville: John Knox Press, 1990).

5. C. J. Jung, *Anima and Animus* in 7 Collected Works II, II. (Princeton:
Princeton University Press, 1977). These qualities are sometimes referred to
as parts of the self which we are prone to repress. See Rollo May, *Love and Will*
(New York: W. W. Norton, 1969), chap. 5. H. L. Mencken observed that "neither sex, without some fortifying with the complementary character of the
other, is capable of its highest reaches of human endeavor. . . . Here, as elsewhere in the universe, the best effects are obtained by a mixture of elements"
(*In Defense of Women* [New York: Octagon Books, 1977], 11–12).

It is difficult to determine the gender origins of any particular expression of intellectual life. However, as women take full advantage of their enlarging cultural opportunities, they should bring their own powers to bear upon the entire range of human experience. Those women writers who have noted the androgynous dimensions of mental life have at the same time insisted that the creative power of women is different from that of men. They feel that it is important to draw out and develop these differences rather than to stress the similarities of reasoning power and perception among men and women. Such distinctions not only insure the self-realization of women; they also force men to assume responsibility for their own distortions of reason which have been developed within a patriarchal culture.[6]

The belief that women lack the capacity fully to exercise the powers of human reason is a deeply rooted prejudice. From the beginning of Western culture, the separate creation of woman and her profound involvement with the reproduction of human life virtually excluded her from those higher intellectual operations that were thought to define human nature more fully. The predominance of reason was in the male, and masculine primacy was assured by contrasting the positive elements of thought with lesser qualities symbolically associated with women.

To be fully operative, reason must control passion and assert its superiority over mere sense perception. Where mind was, flesh was no more. Moral progress as well was gradually associated with the power of the mind to transcend nature and

6. "But this creative power differs greatly from the creative power of men. . . . [I]t would be a thousand pities if women wrote like men, or lived like men, or looked like men, for if two sexes are quite inadequate, considering the vastness and variety of the world, how should we manage with only one . . . ? Ought not education to bring out and fortify the differences rather than the similarities? For we have too much likeness as it is" (Virginia Woolf, *A Room of One's Own* [New York: Harcourt Brace, 1929], 152). A similar sentiment appears in a poem by Laura Riding entitled "World's End": "All is lost, no danger / Forces the heroic hand. / No bodies in bodies stand / Oppositely. The complete world / is likeness in every corner" (See Robert Graves, *Autobiography*).

all that is derived from the feminine dimensions of existence. Reason became the rational: a higher realm of thought characterized by the explication of universal principles and the logical order of ideas.[7]

The development of masculine conceptions of thought and action was accompanied by the articulation of gender distinctions that reinforced male dominance. Differences between reason and emotion were articulated over a wide range of human activities. It was acknowledged that the inwardness of women, with their interior knowledge and compassion for others, gave them a certain moral superiority, but their assumed incapacity for universal thought doomed them to an inferior status. Even their champion John Stuart Mill believed that women were more suited for public activities that did not require sustained reasoning directed toward the general good.[8]

René Descartes is a crucial figure in the development of this disparagement of the feminine. For him, abstract thought was the only sure means of increasing knowledge and advancing human understanding. The acquisition of knowledge was carefully distinguished from the arts of persuasion. Cognition was generated through the mind's conversation with itself. The struggle for clear understanding was not, as with the ancients, a conflict between different parts of the soul; with Descartes, there is a more radical separation between the soul and the body. The body is thought of as being opposed to reason. And the achievement of rational thought requires a complete transcendence of the sensual. Love, as a passion, is now distinguished from purely natural affection and becomes a desire to unite with what is good for the soul. For Descartes, true knowledge exists beyond the realm where woman is at home.[9]

With the emergence of rationalism the procedures necessary

7. Genevieve Lloyd, *The Man of Reason.* See also Carol McMillan, *Women, Reason, and Nature* (Princeton: Princeton University Press, 1982), chap. 1.

8. John Stuart Mill, "The Subjugation of Women," in vol. 21 of *Collected Works,* chap. 4.

9. Charles Taylor, *Sources of the Self* (Cambridge: Harvard University Press, 1980), chap. 8. Irving Singer, *The Nature of Love,* part 2 (1984), chap. 8.

for the modern development of science were being expanded into a general philosophy. Reason could operate only in a world uncontaminated by feeling. The conquest of physical nature was accomplished through this masculinization of thought. This approach was gradually extended throughout the whole field of human relations. The new world of objectivity was an *unheimlich* world, a state of homelessness. The real world of experienced life was being reduced to a construct of geometric relationships.[10]

A similar disposition to separate the world of mind from the world of nature appeared in the development of moral theory. To protect morality from individual caprice, it was thought that the ethical must be based upon the universal. The disparagement of the feminine was intensified. A woman's fulfillment of her roles as wife and mother gave her life a moral dimension, the significance of which was confined to the domestic. The biological characteristics of women connected their existence with the rhythms of animal reproduction, while the distinctively human world of reason and will was reserved for men. The specificities of maternal love were considered admirable but inferior, since they were qualities held in common with other animals. Knowledge derived from theoretical principles was to be the uniquely human form of philosophical and ethical understanding.[11]

Kant carried these dispositions toward moral generalization to a high level of articulation. He believed that in the development of ethical awareness there is a progression from subjectivity, which represents the immaturity of consciousness, to a public space of universal principles. Since morality is a form of self-legislation, adherence to generalized imperatives must be autonomously pursued. This pursuit requires a distancing of reasoning from emotion. As feelings are excluded from the

10. Karl Stern, *The Flight from Woman* (New York: Farrar, Strauss, and Giroux, 1965), chap. 11. Also see chap. 5, where Stern observes that after Descartes, "Methods became mentalities."
11. Carol McMillan, *Women, Reason, and Nature.*

ground of morality the separation between reason and nature is reinforced.[12]

Kant's moral philosophy was directed toward the articulation of rights that would assure the mutual external freedom of individuals. This requires a disinterested disposition, which allows the liberty of one to be impartially reconciled with the freedom of all. For Kant, the duties that the self owes to others are essentially duties that the individual owes to himself, and this lack of connectedness in Kant's theory has been a stumbling block for women. It is generally recognized that his approach is incompatible with those feminist views which maintain that some form of attachment to others is essential to any conception of the good life. What is not sufficiently appreciated is the fact that the Kantian tradition includes an attitude toward the meaning of life that is profoundly offensive to the sensibilities of women.

Kant gives a higher regard to the individual than to the community, and his view that the world is driven by discord introduces fundamental rivalry and competition difficult to reconcile with feminine values of relatedness and friendship. More importantly, the impulse toward transcendence that permeates his work creates an essential tension between his conception of ethics and a feminist vision of life. As a fundamental disposition, Kantian idealism is an aspiration of the masculine spirit to defeat the transience of nature and to challenge the power that the universe holds over the destiny of autonomous man. This elevation of existence above the contingencies of feeling and circumstance is meant to dignify man, but it excludes him from the pursuit of happiness. And it is this loss of happiness, with its sense of pleasurable existence, that is so objectionable to the feminine spirit.

12. R. J. Sullivan, *Kant's Moral Theory* (New York: Cambridge University Press, 1989). Kant was influenced by Rousseau, and it was Rousseau who expressed the idea that "the good man is moral not for the sake of eternal happiness but for the sake of morality itself, but he must be allowed to hope for eternal happiness when he sacrifices this worldly happiness to morality" (Bloom, *Love and Friendship*, 82–83).

From its beginnings, patriarchy was based upon man's obedience to a superior divine will. Submission to God's power over man also legitimized man's dominion over both women and nature. This act of primal obedience was detached from any explicit desire for happiness. Kant's ethic is a secular expression of the same attitude. Ethical life is now thought of as a pure form of duty; an expression of will through which man reveals to himself the unconditional value of moral obligation. In this striving for righteousness, neither self-love nor happiness is a legitimate motive for action. Respect for the moral law replaces both the desire for happiness and the human inclination toward the good.[13]

From a feminist perspective, the purpose of human action should be the realization of felicity rather than the surpassing of incarnated existence. This is not the same as an unrestricted hedonism. Women recognize that limitation and sorrow are unavoidable; the objective is, nonetheless, to live a harmonious life in which delight has supremacy over deprivation.[14] The masculine drive for transcendence, as perpetuated by masculine myths, is unacceptable to feminists because it requires a repudiation of happiness. Masculine heroes are lonely, homeless wanderers forever searching for abstract truth. This is the consequence of a quest for universal meaning, a quest that has become detached from all that is authentically human:

While it is true that man is fundamentally different from animal, there is something seriously misleading about the idea that reason is some sort of entity or faculty that is simply superimposed on his nature. For often the use of such terms as "reason," "intellectual faculty," or "consciousness" to denote man's distinctiveness leads to talk not about real human beings but about disembodied pure intelligence, so that reason becomes hypostatized, something existing by itself, outside any human activity or institution. . . . This is what happens when Kant, for example, puts forward his conception of morality.[15]

13. Jacques Maritain, *Moral Philosophy* (1964), chap. 6. See also C. F. Murphy, *Descent into Subjectivity* (1990), chap 4.

14. Marilyn French, *Beyond Power* (New York: Summit Books, 1985), chap. 4.

15. Carol McMillan, *Women, Reason, and Nature*, 12–13.

A feminist morality is embedded. It gives to the values of care, connectedness, and nurturance a preference over unconditional imperatives derived from a theoretical ethics. A morality based upon women's values is directed toward a *well-being* rather than realization of abstract perfection.[16]

Before exploring more deeply the ways that reason and morality as manifest in feminine experience differ from the vision of men, we should first consider some of the general consequences of the masculinization of thought. Recall our earlier remarks on the androgynous nature of ideas. We observed that at the most intense levels of creativity, distinctions of gender recede. What is accomplished by either a man or a woman begins to influence the whole of human culture. If we are aware of that expansiveness which inhers in thought, we may see how attitudes toward the meaning of mind and value originally promoted by men have influenced the outlook of both men and women as they have struggled to understand the meaning of personal existence in the modern world.

II. *Individualism and Equality in an Age of Abstraction*

The opposition between reason and nature developed by men within a rationalistic, patriarchal culture was motivated as much by a quest for identity as it was by a striving for power and domination. Where a culture is matricentric, not only does maternal influence dominate, but an abundance of positive, life-affirming values spills out into the wider society. Devotion to one's offspring, emotional connectedness, a spirit of equal care and responsibility; these and other feminine values make

16. Carol Gilligan, *In a Different Voice*. See also Marilyn French, *Beyond Power*, chap. 8. This contrast can also be seen in the so-called Kohlberg-Gilligan controversy over the proper domain of ethics. Perceptive scholars mark the contrast as one involving the demands of abstract justice (Kohlberg) and the requirements of the good life (Gilligan). See, e.g., Seyla Benhabib, "The Generalized and the Concrete Other," in *Feminism as Critique*, ed. Seyla Benhabib & Drucilla Connell (Minneapolis: University of Minnesota Press, 1987). In her essay "Impartiality and the Civic Public," in the same collection, Marion Young observes that "by simply expelling desire, affectivity, and need, . . . deontological reason represses them, and sets morality in opposition to happiness" (63).

an immense contribution to general human happiness. But there are also negative effects. A matriarchal *ethos* creates a bondage to blood—or soil—which can impede the development of individuality. To exist as a separate self, one must move beyond the circle of domestic warmth. For reasons that we have already considered, this impulse is strongly experienced by the male. As he seeks to find his manhood beyond the domestic circle, the male begins to realize new potentialities of reason as he moves into a broader universe.[17]

As these drives toward masculine fulfillment have been actualized within Western history, the results have been a mixed blessing. Feminists have recorded the destructive effects of this widening effusion of male energy, and they justifiably protest against the marginalization and subordination of women that has accompanied this prodigious struggle. But the development of Western civilization, even when conceived as a patriarchal system, has, in spite of its persistent violence, brought enduring benefits to all of humankind. Developments in science, the arts, economy, law and government, derived primarily from masculine initiatives, have enhanced the lives of both men and women. The overall utility of these developments may be endlessly debated, but controversies over the balance between destruction and creativity are necessarily inconclusive. Such debates also evade shared responsibilities for the failures of civilization. It would be more profitable to consider the extent to which the darker aspects of a male-dominated culture have become impervious to the distinctions of gender.

Significant ideas are androgynous. They can appeal, for good or ill, to either sex. And even when they originate with one, they can influence the conduct of the other. In a scientific age, the dominant abstract themes and ideals begun through masculine activity start to shape a generally receptive culture. The objectification of existence begun in the epoch of rationalism to serve the purposes of science also altered the nature of human relations. It became widely believed that all life

17. Erich Fromm, *The Sane Society,* chap. 3.

should be measured by the standards of autonomous reason. The human person, as well as inert things, were reified. Human association was often reduced to impersonal encounters between two abstractions who use each other for some instrumental purpose. In an objectified world there is a lack of connectedness and mutual respect. And very little is taken on trust.[18]

Where abstraction is ascendant there is a tendency, increasingly shared by both men and women, to regard a theory about oneself and others as more authentic than the actual situation of a growing or declining human relationship. Expertise abounds.[19] This giving-over of ourselves to abstractions is a vice that can distort feminine as well as masculine attitudes toward the existence of others. We are all prone to treat the other as an instance of a theory rather than as a unique person toward whom one has some form of specific relationship. Moreover, the proliferation of preformed ideas accentuates reliance upon stereotypes. Stereotypes are oppressive, but as forms of thought they establish a cognitive dependency that is accepted as often as it is imposed.

In women's views of men, as well as men's views of women, generalizations are given priority over what can be learned from specific encounters. This spirit of objectification is reinforced by the values of individualism. The ideals of personal autonomy formulated in the Enlightenment are usually thought to be incompatible with a feminist morality of relationships. However here, as with the whole rationalist agenda, there are androgynous intimations.

Individualism encourages a person to rise above all contingencies. Persons become "abstractions from the immediacy of

18. Ibid., chap. 5. The same analysis can be found in the novels of the late Walker Percy. For a discussion of his views, see Jerome Taylor, *In Search of Self: Life, Death and Walker Percy* (Cambridge, Mass.: Cowley, 1986). For a discussion of the importance of trust, see Annette Baier, "Trust and Antitrust," in *Feminism and Political Theory*, ed. Cass R. Sunstein (Chicago: University of Chicago Press, 1990), 279.

19. Carol McMillan, *Women, Reason, and Nature.*

physical being."[20] This theory of the individual as a complete being, capable of independent self-actualization, is no longer an exclusively masculine ideal. An ethic of self-interest, and a distancing of oneself from union with others, which began as a form of male self-assertion, has become gradually associated with the emancipation of women. Feminists may protest that their intuitions of connection are epistemologically antecedent and morally superior to the values of individualism, but at the same time they are strongly attracted to the idea of absolute personal independence.

The individualistic model of personal existence was initially held up as a standard of masculine self-determination. Man was an end in himself. At the time the ideal was formulated, women were excluded from the advantages of self-realization. Caught in the routine and drudgery of middle-class life, the life of a woman revolved around a circle of domesticity, and it was only within that sphere that she was allotted her opportunities for happiness. Unable to become a complete person, she eventually rebelled against the narrowness of her status and claimed for herself the same rights to self-realization as those that have been asserted by men.[21]

As women have advanced in the acquisition of an independent existence, they have begun to experience a tension between the goals of autonomy and the values of connection and commitment:

Feminism as an ideology developed in interaction with the development of individualism and cannot be understood apart from it. Feminist scholars have exposed the deceptions of individualism for women and have charted the ways in which women writers have wrestled with its demons. Today, the principal debates within feminism directly reflect the ways in which women, beginning in the eighteenth century, have attempted to claim the full status of indi-

20. Elizabeth Fox-Genovese, *Feminism without Illusions* (Chapel Hill: University of North Carolina Press, 1991), 227.
21. Betty Friedan, *The Feminine Mystique* (New York: W. W. Norton, 1963). Simone de Beauvoir, *The Second Sex*, ed. and trans. H. M. Parshley (New York: Alfred A. Knopf, 1952).

vidual without losing their identities as women. Feminists have nonetheless been slow to grasp the extent to which our specific ideas of
woman's nature derive from the discourse of individualism. . . .
   . . . To the extent that women have been "colonized" by the ideology of individualism, it has shaped their ways of thinking about
themselves and the world. . . . Born with the emergence of individualism, feminist theory has been torn between two illusions: the illusion that the abstract possibilities of "autonomous" individualism
could be fully realized for women (if indeed they ever have been or
could be for men); and the illusion that the individualist view of
woman-as-other can, by some miraculous transubstantiation be converted into a general and "feminist" law of female experience.[22]

There is more, of course, to this striving for self-realization.
A feeling of independence implies that one is a person. As persons, women refuse to be thought of as just the opposite of the
masculine. To be a woman must be something in itself. However, as the ideology of individualism becomes pervasive, it
can affect a woman's pursuit of her personal identity in a way
that endangers the vitality of distinctively feminine virtues.

A woman enamored of individualism can be drawn back and
forth between the poles of receptivity and assertion, self-
sufficiency and connection, as she moves out of a status of subordination into a liberating experience of personal autonomy.
This dialectic raises the further question of whether female
emancipation, insofar as it is inspired by masculine values,
will lead to a cessation of all sexual interdependence.

The relatedness of men and women is an aspect of their sexual polarity. Fundamental differences between them establish
elemental distinctions which, when they flourish, enrich both
personal and social existence. This basic diversity is threatened by any form of egalitarianism that would replace sexual
distinctiveness with an artificial common identity. For whenever either sex seeks to assimilate fully the ideals and values
of the other, that which draws them *to* each other is no longer
given its proper weight.

22. Elizabeth Fox-Genovese, *Feminism without Illusions,* 138. Compare
Diana T. Meyers, "The Socialized Individual and Individual Autonomy," in
Woman and Moral Theory, ed. Eva Feder Kittay and Diana T. Meyers (Totowa,
N.J.: Rowman and Littlefield, 1987).

A decline of difference also reflects the ambiguities that inhere in the concept of equality. The pursuit of moral and legal equality is an essential means for overcoming discrimination against women and creating the conditions necessary for them to achieve personal fulfillment. However, on the plane of philosophical reflection, broader considerations must be taken into account. In an age of abstraction, it is extremely difficult to articulate and apply an ideal of equality that will not destroy sexual uniqueness. An equality of sameness is oppressive because it denies the individual the opportunity to become either a masculine, or a feminine, person. This leveling is a consequence of social and political forces, but it is essentially rooted in the order of ideas.

I am not speaking against the equality of women; but the positive aspects of this tendency for equality must not deceive one. It is a part of the trend towards the elimination of differences. Equality is bought at this very price: women are equal because they are not different anymore. The proposition of Enlightenment philosophy, *l'ame n'a pas de sexe*, the soul has no sex, has become the general practice. The polarity of the sexes is disappearing, and with it erotic love, which is based on this polarity. Men and women become the *same*, not *equals* as opposite poles. Contemporary society preaches this idea of unindividualized equality because it needs human atoms, each one the same, to make them function in a mass aggregation, smoothly, without friction; all obeying the same commands, yet everyone being convinced he is following his own desires.[23]

Where significant distinctions between men and women are ignored, the freedom and dignity of women, as women, is compromised. That is why we have already insisted that, although men and women are equal as persons, they are sexually different. The challenge is to understand differences in such a way that diversity is not incompatible with an indis-

23. Erich Fromm, *The Art of Loving* (New York: Harper and Row, 1956), 15–16. Feminist legal theorists have insisted that the achievement of equal rights for women must include respect for legitimate differences. See Mary E. Becker, "Prince Charming: Abstract Equality," *Supreme Court Review* (1987): 201, and Martha Minow, "Foreword: Justice Engendered," *Harvard Law Review* 101 (1987): 10.

pensable equality. One must resist the leveling tendency. Where sameness prevails, the mutual attraction of the sexes is diminished and there is less possibility of a creative union that would reconcile the differences. The richness of gender diversity is then reduced to biological advantage or disadvantage, and the remaining variants are expressed in a competitive rivalry. Under these circumstances the lives of men and women never connect in any meaningful way.[24]

When equality is made absolute, personal existence is distorted. A conception of the individual as one who is capable of being completely self-actualized becomes a general humanistic aspiration. Autonomy is no longer a masculine property, since a woman's quest for an independent existence may be as ardently pursued as any man's longing for self-determination. This parallelism is not without reason; it is inexorably linked to the overcoming of male domination. If women had not made such demands for personal independence, they could never have overcome their oppression. Furthermore, the subjection of women has been facilitated by their own fears of self-assertion. When women become conscious of their personal dignity they can no longer live solely for others and never for themselves.

Men and women must struggle to determine for themselves the outer boundaries of the quest for individual self-determination. There is, however, a sense in which women have a natural advantage in the struggle to determine the limits of personal independence. However much they may be influenced by individualism, their self-consciousness also includes an awareness of vital, concrete responsibilities to persons

24. On the lack of connectedness between masculine and feminine, see K. Stern, *The Flight from Woman*. The relation between de-eroticization and the pursuit of abstract equality is a theme of Allan Bloom's book *Love and Friendship*. Whenever gender is referred to throughout these essays as a positive force, I am referring to gender as an element of self-identity and not as a conventional attribution of a role, or a simple anatomical fact. Gender is an endowment, capable of cultivation, which has an important bearing upon the development of personal character. See the excellent study by Steven G. Smith, *Gender Thinking* (Philadelphia: Temple University Press, 1992).

other than themselves. This sense of relatedness can be seen in the revival of interest in the experience of mothering. Contemporary women are beginning to recapture the significance of giving birth, and this renewal contains fresh opportunities for a deeper understanding of how reason is manifest in different aspects of human existence.[25]

III. *Natural Existence and the Restoration of Reason*

Masculine thinking has insisted upon a distinction between reason and nature, and it has assumed that intellectual knowledge cannot be obtained from activities such as procreation that have parallels in the animal world.[26] Because women relate to others with much passion, emotion, and intuition, they were presumably incapable of either logical reasoning or sustained thought. Feelings, and the family life based upon them, were considered to be forms of being that operated below the realm of reason. However, from a woman's perspective, birth—a supreme example of natural existence—is also central to the experience of being human. And, as a way of being human, it is also a way of being reasonable.

When freely chosen, the experience of being a mother is one of immense personal importance. The living out of that experience places great demands upon the rational as well as the emotional dimensions of human nature. The reasons for giving birth can be as rich and varied as the reasons men give for their own, often destructive, behavior. Hegel believed that, as mothers, women participated in the universal because the maternal disposition potentially embraced all children. However, modern women see value in the intensely personal experience

(handwritten margin note: mother immense exp.)

25. E.g., Sara Ruddick, *Maternal Thinking: Toward a Politics of Peace* (Boston: Beacon Press, 1989); Marta Weigle, *Creation and Procreation* (Philadelphia: University of Pennsylvania Press, 1989); Virginia Held, "Birth and Death," *Ethics* (1989): 99, reprinted in *Feminism and Political Theory,* ed. Cass R. Sunstein (Chicago: University of Chicago Press, 1990), 87; Jean Bethke Elshtain, *Public Man, Private Woman,* chap. 6; Carol McMillan, *Women, Reason, and Nature.* See also Lucinda Finley, "Transcending Equality Theory: A Way out of the Maternity and Workplace Debate," *Columbia Law Review* 86 (October 1986): 1118.

26. Carol McMillan, *Women, Reason and Nature,* chap. 1.

of giving birth to a unique, unrepeatable child. Here reason operates with particularity and it yields an experiential understanding.[27]

Giving birth and raising children has a moral as well as an intellectual significance. The experience engages an ethic of intimate relationships. Here the good is achieved not through conformity to universal standards but by the development of personal qualities needed to sustain the practices that surround and give meaning to the experience of mothering. Women set the values that inher in this experience against the more abstract excellences derived from an abstract male rationalism. The masculine sense of the good creates an opposition between reason and emotion and leads to an impoverished, limited view of human understanding. The reasonableness of maternal practices is also opposed to the masculine belief that the range of reason is exhausted in its theoretical expression.

The conviction that reason is operative within the maternal world is an attitude toward meaning which resonates with broader notions of truth. One of the most important developments in modern philosophy is a recovery of the value of knowledge based upon experience. The renewal has taken various forms. Wittgenstein's rejection of the idea of language as an exact calculus, and his discovery of meaning in the way that words are used in concrete life, is one example; the view that all knowledge is interpretation, as in deconstructionism and in some aspects of contemporary pragmatism, is another. These are among the various forms of antifoundational epistemology which women have found congenial to their own defense of reason.[28]

When reason is grounded in experience, truths, to the extent that they exist, are derived from practices rather than from some transcendent ahistorical position. There are no "whole-

---

27. Virginia Held, "Birth and Death."
28. For a general discussion of these influences upon feminism, see Carol McMillan, *Women, Reason, and Nature*, chap. 3. See also Katharine T. Bartlett, "Feminist Legal Methods," 829, and Martha Minow, "Justice Engendered," *Harvard Law Review*, 101 (1987): 10.

sale" constraints upon action that can be drawn either from the subject of activity or from the mind itself. Practices provide constraints, and they reveal the workings of the mind as it is engaged in the particularities of experience. This reasoning is a valid form of knowledge even though it does not aim at the formulation of a general theory or the explication of universal values.[29]

An understanding of reason as practice has an important relation to the maternal experience. The contexts of thought and action that are necessary to procreation and the raising of children reveal fresh aspects of reason and will as well as of imagination and compassion. The values called forth by parenting, and the mental attention it requires, provide opportunities for women to transcend their bondage to biological necessity. The experience also shows that women's possibilities of personal fulfillment are not limited to their engagement in the abstract activities which have been attractive primarily to men.

One objective of the reconceptualization of mothering is to elevate the experience above the demeaning associations connected with either a biological determinism or the assimilation of procreation to technological reproduction. Another purpose is the moral validation of an experience in which emotion is an overt element. In explicating these values, women writers have contributed to an aspect of philosophy that is, of itself,

29. Richard Rorty is the primary champion of this point of view. See, e.g., his *Consequences of Pragmatism: Essays, 1972–1980* (Minneapolis: University of Minnesota Press, 1982), which tries to defend the view that it is only through our vocabularies of action, or practice, that we can say something useful about truth. Such particular purposes have survival, or "coping," as their dominant objective. These *petits récits*, which make all knowledge "local" and "personal" tend to make the effective performance of tasks a supreme value. Skills, rather than the pursuit of ideals, becomes an educational goal (Jean-François Lyotard, *The Post-Modern Condition* [Minneapolis: University of Minnesota Press, 1984]). For a critical evaluation, see Michael S. Moore, "The Interpretative Turn in Modern Theory: A Turn for the Worse?" *Stanford Law Review* 41 (1989): 871. See also Charles Taylor, "Alternative Futures," in *Constitutionalism, Citizenship, and Society in Canada*, vol. 33, Research Project, Royal Commission for the Economic Development Prospects for Canada, Alan Cairns, Cynthia Williams, research coordinators (183).

gender-neutral. They have also revived some ancient truths about the relation between knowledge and virtue, truths that men and women whose allegiance is to abstraction are prone to forget.

To be able to do what is right in a practical situation one cannot depend only upon knowledge of general principles. Our actions may be guided by broad purposes, but they always become incarnate in the ways that we respond to the demands and details of what we are actually doing. To reason well within any practice requires an upright will and a willingness to transcend our egoism. The person who assumes such responsibilities is essentially related to others. Women, with their experience of mothering, have an intimate and subtle knowledge of these venerable truths. They understand that, although personal liberation is the object of moral life, it is not a self-assertive freedom but one achieved in love.[30]

By drawing upon the various revivals of practical reasoning that make thought immanent to action, modern women have joined forces with all who hope to overcome the accusation that knowledge that arises out of experience is somehow inferior to abstract reasoning. The dignity of the feminine is enhanced by disproving the opinion that reason is reserved for theorizing. However, it would be a mistake for women to embrace the attitude that the exercise of reason is confined exclusively to the domain of practices. Such a view would

---

30. Compare the discussion of moral education in Jacques Maritain, *Education at the Crossroads*, chap. 4, with the discussion of the myths of moral theory in Amièle Rorty, *Mind in Action* (Boston: Beacon Press, 1988), chap. 14.

In her book *Reproducing the World*, Mary O'Brien accentuates the difference between the male and the female approach to reproduction. "Man is related to his child only by thought, by knowledge in general, rather than by experience in particular—whereas motherhood is a unity of consciousness and knowing on the one hand and action (reproductive labor) on the other" (22). In her novel *The Women's Room*, Marilyn French exquisitely describes the love of a mother for her newborn child whom she has just taken into her arms: "What she was feeling, she knew, was love, a love blinder and more irrational than even sexual love. She loved him because he needed her. . . . He was helpless. . . . She knew that her life would from now on be dictated by that tiny creature, that his needs would be the most important thing in her life" (Marilyn French, *The Women's Room* [New York: Summit Books, 1977], 53).

be inconsistent with the emancipatory aspiration that seeks their full participation in all the possibilities of human culture.

In pursuing these reflections on reason and experience, I shall suggest that an understanding of thought that is *not* restricted to practices is much closer to the feminine dimension of existence than is usually realized. We shall see that there are connections between reason and intuition which, once understood, substantially enhance the possibilities for an expansion of the intellectual life of both men and women. The recovery of a broader sense of reason will also show that feminine objections to the masculinization of thought are justified on grounds that transcend traditional distinctions based upon gender. Finally, we shall observe how the exercise of reason is never completely separated from the distinctive ways that men and women interpret the personal meaning of human experience. To understand these themes one must distinguish the principles of traditional philosophy from those which govern the modern quest for knowledge.

At the heart of Cartesian philosophy, doubt replaced trust as the basis of inquiry. While the qualified suspension of judgment was necessary for the progress of experimental science, the new discipline required the self to distance itself from all experience and to transform it in thought. This constituted a fundamental change in the nature of reflective life as it had been understood both by the ancients and in medieval culture. Thinking became a penetrating restlessness, an uprooted and insatiable craving for knowledge. Closely allied with desires for power, this disposition disdains all affective relations with the world of nature. Furthermore, conflict is perceived as the basis of all relationships.[31]

Traditional philosophy is based upon wonder. It assumes a personal awareness that one does not fully understand what one encounters. It is also marked by a realization that what we

31. K. Stern, *The Flight from Woman*; Charles Taylor, *Sources of the Self* (Cambridge: Harvard University Press, 1986).

have taken for granted we do not adequately know. It is an awareness sustained by a sense of mystery.

> The innermost meaning of wonder is fulfilled in a deepened sense of mystery. It does not end in doubt, but is the awakening of the knowledge that being, *qua* being . . . is a mystery in the full sense of the word: neither a dead end, nor a contradiction, nor even something impenetrable and dark; mystery really means that a reality, the singular existing thing is . . . an inexhaustible source of light, and for ever unfathomable. And that is the fact that is experienced in wonder.[32]

What causes us to wonder is hidden. The uncovering requires a receptive attitude toward reality rather than a struggle with it initiated by an active will. What is awakened in us is a desire to understand, an open-mindedness toward what is fresh, new, and as yet unknown. This aspiration is not a wanton gaze intent upon satisfying its appetites or aversions. It also differs from the Kantian notion of the will as a desire that submits itself to the prescriptions of universal reason. Rather, the love of understanding is a spiritual capacity, which, realizing that it does not know everything at once, or perfectly, hopes to become more knowledgeable of the deeper world that lies behind immediate experience.[33]

32. Josef Pieper, *Leisure: The Basis of Culture,* trans. Alexander Dru (New York: Pantheon Books, 1952), 135. A similar idea is expressed by Gabriel Marcel, who refers to a primitive emotion of astonishment where "being, acknowledged as such grips the creature whom admiration stirs" (*Being and Having* [New York: Harper and Row, 1965], iii). The contemporary biologist-philosopher Leon R. Kass states emphatically that "the origin of philosophy is in wonder" (interview with Bill Moyers in *A World of Ideas,* ed. Betty Sue Flowers [New York: Doubleday, 1989], 366).

33. Josef Pieper, *Leisure: The Basis of Culture.* It should be noted that Mill's argument for freedom of expression relies heavily upon the incomplete nature of our knowledge and opinion. For a discussion of knowledge as a basic human good, see John Finnis, *Natural Law and Natural Rights* (Oxford: Oxford University Press, 1980), chap. 3. This approach is very different from either an idealistic philosophy which tries to govern reality from an eternal perspective or from a positivism which forces acceptance of the world as it is. But it also differs from a pragmatism which assumes that thought "can name the thickness of reality but it cannot fathom it" (William James, *A Pluralistic Universe* [1907], 112). Pragmatism shares with much of the modern ethos a belief that

The sense of wonder that sustains a philosophical spirit is essentially incomplete. This inconclusiveness is what distinguishes a philosophical approach to understanding from the objectives of science. The questions that science asks can all, in principle, be answered. Philosophy, by contrast, makes demands that are unrealizable because reality, in this life, can never be fully understood.

The pride of philosophers is usually attributed to the intellectual life; but as an authentic vocation, the search for truth requires much humility. A philosopher is a *seeker after knowledge* and a lover of wisdom. He or she desires to comprehend, as far as possible, the whole of reality.

To sustain a wondering attitude toward the real is not the same as pursuing a rationalistic interpretation of existence. The lure of abstraction can provoke the futile attempt to deduce understanding from a single principle, or a limited set of principles, which are assumed to possess decisive explanatory power.[34] Real knowledge, however, ranges both within and through experience in a quest for what is not fully possessed. Such a pursuit is sustained by expectation. It is open to what is not yet known, to fresh possibilities that will enrich both personal and social existence.[35]

Although reason is engaged in an exploration of experience, it is not limited to the world of the given. Nor could it be, if to reason is a profoundly personal act. Philosophy shares with all deeper human experiences a sense of disturbance; a feeling that what is immediate, or apparent, is not the final expression of being. This does not require a rejection of what immediately exists. There is not an opposition between what is experienced and what is thought about:

---

the mind is not devoted to understanding but should be used only to preserve life and increase comfort. These broader implications are explored in J. Huizinga, *In the Shadow of Tomorrow* (London: William Heinemann, 1936).

34. See the critique of rationalism in Carol McMillan, *Women, Reason, and Nature*.

35. Pieper, *Leisure: The Basis of Culture*. Compare Alfred North Whitehead, *The Function of Reason* (Boston: Beacon Press, 1929). See also Finnis, *Natural Law and Natural Rights*.

On the contrary, it is the same tangible, visible world . . . upon which a genuine philosophical reflection is trained. But this world of things in their interrelationship has to be questioned in a specific manner: things are questioned regarding their ultimate nature and their universal essence, and as a result the horizon of the question becomes the horizon of reality as a whole. A philosophical question is always about some quite definite thing, straight in front of us; it is not concerned with something beyond the world or beyond our experience of everyday life. Yet, it asks what "this" really *is*, ultimately. . . .

To philosophize means to withdraw—not from the things of everyday life—but from the currently accepted meaning attached to them, or to question the value placed upon them. This does not, of course, take place by virtue of some decision to differentiate our attitude from that of others and to see things "differently," but because, quite suddenly, things themselves assume a different aspect. . . . [I]t is in the things we come across in the experience of everyday life that the unusual emerges, and we no longer take them for granted—and that situation corresponds with the inner experience which has always been regarded as the beginning of philosophy: the act of 'marvelling.'[36]

Philosophy begins with an intuition: Whatever is, is. It rejects the rationalist assertion: I think, therefore I am. And it looks upon the world as Creation: an inexhaustible existence both magnificent and astonishing. Whatever is, is not just material to be used. The world, as a reality other than the self, has its own intrinsic value. It is not just an arena of human activity.

Philosophy does not equate knowledge with power, nor does it interpret the world merely to change it. It simply seeks to understand. And the simplicity of the encounter between the thinking person and being facilitates a distinctive form of human fulfillment. Philosophy suggests that the human happiness to be obtained from the use of reason consists in the pleasure experienced in "seeing what is and the whole of what is."[37]

The plenary exercise of reason resonates with the deepest meaning of liberty. Reason is the power that relates oneself to

36. Josef Pieper, *Leisure: The Basis of Culture*, 128–29. See also Jacques Maritain, *The Degrees of Knowledge*.

37. Pieper, *Leisure: The Basis of Culture*, 107. "The important theoretical experience leads necessarily toward the first principles of all things" (Allan Bloom, *The Closing of the American Mind*, 271).

objective being. As with Aristotle's *De anima*, it assumes that the soul is, in a certain sense, all. The range of one's relations defines one's world. The greater the capacity, the greater is the field of relations. The dignity of reason consists in the fact that it opens the human spirit to all that exists. In doing so, it makes possible the most extensive comprehension available to a finite being.

When one is reasoning to the full, one reaches a degree of reflection that characterizes the dignity of the human spirit. Here, at the highest natural form of inwardness, one is fully living in oneself; yet, one remains in contact with the world beyond the self. The qualities of independence and self-possession, which are basic aspects of human freedom, are now given a supreme expression.

The person who knows, deeply and comprehensively, is not the pure, detached spirit of German idealism. The knowing subject is a soul joined to a body, one in whom plant, animal, and spiritual life have been fused in a vital unity. Such a person does not reside in Olympian detachment above inferior modes of existence. He or she is a being in a world; one engaged in a personal quest for meaning through an encounter with an objective cosmos that manifests the amazing variety of existence.

This classical conception of philosophy has broad implications for the development of culture. But it also has an immediate relevance to the problematic relation between reason and gender. This traditional understanding of the life of the mind is far removed from the masculinization of thought that was the impetus behind rationalism.

Recall how rationalism developed in opposition to the feminine dimension of existence and held the most profound uses of reason to be the prerogative of maleness. The association of philosophy with wisdom, however, moves the desire for human understanding more in the direction of the feminine. The receptivity and connectedness that we have identified as aspects of authentic philosophy accentuate qualities of thought similar to virtues usually associated with the character of women. The intuition upon which the whole philosophical edifice is constructed suggests an even deeper relationship between thought and the feminine spirit.

We have already indicated how doubt, rather than trust, is a characteristic of rationalism. In this limited understanding of the nature of reason there are also a number of fundamental oppositions that express the hypermasculine mind's approach to reality. There are the familiar dichotomies between subject and object, abstract and concrete, reason and emotion. There is also a distrust of ways of knowing that involve an imaginative contact with reality. Here the conflict is between rationalism and the artistic temperament. It may take the form of an outright hostility to poetic sensibility or, as with John Stuart Mill, the strain may appear as a difficulty in understanding poetry as anything more than an effusion of sentiment.

These attitudes reflect a belief that the nature of the intellect consists exclusively in its power to grasp and articulate universal logical relations among whatever phenomena the mind may subject to inquiry. By contrast, poetry, and the arts in general, seek to find ways to express the singular that elude rational discourse. Heart speaks to heart in a conversation that struggles against any logically imposed, externally consistent order.[38]

Tensions between thought and imagination are inevitable, as is the case with all contrasts between reason and emotion. A suspicion of feeling may in some cases be well founded, since an excess of passion can set loose irrational forces which disperse the unities which could be gained by a concentration of thought. There is also the danger that the emotions may try to usurp the mind's legitimate authority. However, while feeling may, in particular circumstances, be opposed to thinking, reason and emotion are not essentially at odds. They could not be, for they are too closely related. For the intellect, in its most primeval operations, is grounded upon intuition:

38. Jacques Maritain, "The Pre-Conscious Life of the Intellect," in *Challenges and Renewals*, ed. Joseph W. Evans and Leo R. Ward (Cleveland: World Publishing, 1966). The relation between poetry and the maternal principle is an important aspect of the thought of Julia Kristeva. See Andrea Nye, *Feminist Theory*, chap. 5.

[R]eason possesses a life both deeper and less conscious than its articulate logical life. For reason . . . does not only articulate, connect, and infer, it also *sees*; and reason's intuitive grasping, *intuitus rationis*, is the primary act and function of that one single power which is called intellect or reason. In other words, there is not only logical reason, but also, and prior to it, intuitive reason.[39]

Any new aspect of being is first encountered through insight before it is discursively tested and justified. When reason operates in this perceptive manner, it acts closely with emotion and imagination.

The relationship between reason and intuition is such that a trust of, and connection with, the whole natural world is integral to the functioning of the mind. When this is acknowledged, we gain a richer understanding of the potentials of thought. We also change our perspective upon the relation between reason and gender. When human rationality was restricted to abstract ideas, a demeaning of the feminine was considered essential to progress in thought. This bias has had profoundly oppressive consequences. Women were led to believe that the important exertions of reason required attitudes of mind and heart that were inimical to their deepest sensibilities.

Invidious distinctions about reasoning powers have left some women inclined to claim for themselves only a small share of the powers of the human spirit. This may, in part, explain their attraction to the confining reasonableness of prac-

---

39. Maritain, "The Pre-Conscious Life of the Intellect," 34. The relation between intuition and thought should be compared with a related, but distinct, aspect of the emotional life. Feelings significantly influence the development of personality. The human subject feels as well as thinks: "It experiences emotions as coming from the depths of its 'I' . . . this 'self'-experiencing 'I' is not the pure 'I' for the pure 'I' has no depth. But the 'I' experienced in emotion has levels of various depths. These are revealed as emotions arise out of them" (Edith Stein, *On the Problem of Empathy,* trans. Waltraut Stein [The Hague: Martinus Nijhoff, 2d ed., 1970], 89). See also Max Scheler, *Formalism in Ethics,* trans. Manfred S. Springs and Robert L. Funk (Pittsburgh: Duquesne University Press, 1973). Diana Meyers observes that a coherent personality integrates emotional and intellectual life as essential aspects of a self-directed existence (*Self, Society, and Personal Choice* [New York: Columbia University Press, 1989], chap. 1).

tices. The affirmation of the contextual is, as we have said, a development of great importance. The danger, however, is that women will look upon all exertion of thought that passes beyond what is given as nothing other than an expression of masculine pride. Women may then limit themselves to ways of knowing connected with immediate experience.

Here, as elsewhere, we are faced with a problem of stereotypes. The masculine stereotype is of a manliness uttered through a striving for abstraction—a striving that masks a will to power. By contrast, the restriction of reason is the stigma of the feminine. Here the prejudice is that attention to the immediate constitutes the limits of female rationality. Some consider the reasoning power of women weak because, since present circumstances have such a hold on them, they miss the meanings to be derived from consideration of what is remote and universal.[40] This disdain for the reasoning power of women is not only insulting; it also reveals a lack of understanding of the relationship between intellect and intuition.

There is a polarity to human intelligence. Knowledge is both discursive and empathic. No hierarchy exists in the world of understanding; the two ways of comprehension must be combined in the pursuit of truth. Where ratiocinative and intuitive powers are both engaged, the potentials for comprehension are greatly enhanced. This is one path on the way toward a restoration of the feminine dimensions of human nature. Because of the richer interplay between reason and emotion expressed in her writings, it has been said that George Eliot had a deeper, and broader, grasp of the human condition than did her male counterpart, Henry James.[41] An intuitive sense of or-

40. "For it is just because their reasoning power is so weak that present circumstances have such a hold on them" (Arthur Schopenhauer, *The Pessimist's Handbook*, ed. T. Baily Sanders [Lincoln: University of Nebraska Press, 1961], 202).

41. Leon Edel, Introduction to Henry James, *Portrait of a Lady* (Cambridge: Riverside Press, 1956). For discussion of James's insights into the nuances of intimate life, see Martha C. Nussbaum, *Love's Knowledge* (New York: Oxford University Press, 1990). On the relation between discursive and intuitive ways of knowing, see Karl Stern, *The Flight from Woman*, chap. 3. Stern insists that

ganic life can lead a woman scientist to discoveries her male colleagues may be inclined to overlook. It is now acknowledged that a feeling for the concrete interconnectedness of existence gives novel direction to any field of inquiry. More competent than men with metaphors, women can artfully use images of growth and harmony to uncover the deeper meaning of all aspects of our common life.[42]

When reason, in itself, is seen in its relation to the feminine, the possibilities of intellectual life are greatly increased for women as well as for men. There can be no a priori limits to the capacities of women to participate in the most elevated forms of human culture and to do so without compromising their feminine character. Such involvement will realize the new demand for liberty to which we referred at the beginning of these reflections; an emancipation that is not just relief from oppression but also constitutes a freedom for the full expression of personality. To assist that process, we must not only end discriminatory practices; we must also overcome the false allocations of higher powers according to gender.

In the domain of the spirit we encounter the deep, and potentially androgynous dimensions of human nature. And we find a powerful weapon for the struggle against sexual dis-

---

one way of knowing is not superior to the other: "In fact, human knowledge seems to have the greatest chance to arrive at truth when the two methods are in perfect balance" (47). Stern's observation should be compared with that of H. L. Mencken, quoted in n. 5 above.

42. E.g., Martha Nussbaum on political life: "So you have the image of a person as like a plant-something that is fairly sturdy, that has a definite structure, but that is always in need of support from the surrounding society. The political leader in that image is like the gardener who has to tend the plant. The role of politics is to provide conditions of support for all the richly diverse elements in the full human life" (interview with Bill Moyers, *A World of Ideas*, 447–53). It has also been observed that Hannah Arendt, virtually alone as a woman political philosopher, made natality, or birth, a central feature of her thought (Bhikhu Parekh, *Hannah Arendt and the Search for a New Political Philosophy* [Atlantic Highlands, N.J.: Humanities Press, 1981], xi).

On feminine scientific discovery, see Evelyn Fox Keller, *Reflections on Gender and Science* (New Haven: Yale University Press, 1985); *Discovering Reality: Feminist Perspectives on Epistemology, Metaphysics, Methodology, and Philosophy of Science*, ed. Sandra Harding and M. B. Hintikka (Dordrecht: Reidel, 1983).

crimination. In matters of mind and heart the differences between men and women are much less than has been assumed.
When we see the intimate relation between reason and intuition we reduce the distance between masculine and feminine
ways of knowing. Yet, even when sexual difference is unob-
trusive, we cannot fully escape the influence of gender. Sexuality is not limited to the biological. It reaches the deepest
levels of personal expression, including those which engage
our minds and wills. At these levels, differences remain.

John Stuart Mill was of the opinion that the practical tendencies of women provided a healthy balance for the male proclivity toward excessive abstraction. While, for the most part,
women avoided the sustained mental labor necessary for speculation, their minds were more nimble than those of men and
less subject to excessive concentration. Mill did not look upon
women's abstention from theory as a matter of innate deficiency. Rather, he saw that it was related to the application of
their energies to more restrictive duties that were imposed upon
them by law and custom. Having been subjugated and confined
to a limited and limiting range of activities, a woman could not
fully appreciate the values of intellectual self-development.
Mill expected that as the education and general emancipation
of women progressed, both the mental powers and the moral
concerns of women should expand. They would then begin to
embrace "wider subjects of thought and action."[43]

Mill was also concerned over the limited influence that
women had in public life. The ending of discrimination against
them would lead to vast improvements for themselves and for
society. However, he worried that the tendency of women to
look upon public affairs from a domestic or family perspective
might limit their contribution to wider societal interests. This
lack of "a disinterestedness in the general conduct of life,"[44]
which Mill thought he perceived in the women of his time, is

43. John Stuart Mill, "The Subjugation of Women," in vol. 21 of *Collected
Works*, 327.
44. Ibid., 329.

a theme that reappears in the attitudes of some contemporary feminists, especially those engaged in legal studies.

In their critiques of the legal order, feminists often view the alleged objectivity of law with a profound suspicion. They adopt a posture of experiential particularity toward laws and practices, which, while purporting to be based upon disinterested criteria, are perceived by them as being oppressive to women.[45] The important values are those that women have developed through their own collective experience. Having been disadvantaged and marginalized in a masculine world, the radical legal feminist is not likely to be interested in the more general and inclusive concerns of the legal order.

In light of the injustices suffered by women under patriarchy, this attitude is understandable. No human being who experiences substantial discrimination within any society can be expected to take a great interest in that community's broadest problems. Nevertheless, the persistence of this restrictive attitude toward the scope of public life is troubling because it can renew doubts about the capacities of women which, in the past, have been a source of enmity in intellectual as well as

45. "Jurisprudence . . . as it has been taught in our law schools . . . [is] . . . a prototypically Enlightenment project, having to do precisely with the eternals of truth and justice, dependent precisely on the power and priority of reason. Jurisprudence generates sentiments and aspirations like those expressed in stone words engraved over the portals of Harvard Law School: 'Not under Man, but under God and the Law.' The problem was that when the men who ordered those words to be carved looked at God, they saw a man, and a man not unlike themselves. Women have long, if not always, held the suspicion, if not the knowledge, that what passed for point-of-view-less-ness was in fact His point of view. A point of view which did not always correspond to hers" (Clare Dalton, "Commentary: Where We Stand, Observations on the Situation of Feminist Legal Thought," *Berkeley Women's Law Journal* 3 [1987]: 1, 6). See also Martha Minow, *Making All the Difference*; Deborah L. Rhode, "The Woman's Point of View," *Journal of Legal Education* 38 (1988): 39; Robin West, "Jurisprudence and Gender," *University of Chicago Law Review* 55 (1988): 1; Lynne H. Henderson, "Legality and Empathy," *Michigan Law Review* 85 (1987): 1574; Joan C. Williams, "Deconstructing Gender," *Michigan Law Review* 87 (1987): 797–845; Katharine T. Bartlett, "Feminist Legal Methods," 829. While there is an extensive "standpoint" writing by women legal theorists, it remains a small percentage of all women's contribution to the law.

practical affairs. In the chapter that follows, these tensions will be explored in greater detail. But they also have a bearing upon these immediate considerations.

Traditionally, philosophers of law did not want to know whether individuals acted justly or unjustly in some particular case; they wanted to know what justice and injustice were in themselves.[46] Such inclusiveness reflected the impetus of reason in its search for the ultimate meaning of phenomena subject to its scrutiny. A radical feminist, even when she is concerned with the rights of all women, would reverse the inquiry. For her, the particular trumps the general. Mind and heart are concentrated upon the disadvantageous position of women, and that specific focus exhausts her attention. It is difficult to determine whether such concentration means to affirm an alternative truth about the nature of things or whether it is just a negative indictment of the masculine world.

Impassioned protest may reflect a conviction that all truth is ambiguous and has no meaning beyond specific circumstances. The changing nature of the life and circumstances of women may also explain a feminist insistence upon the indeterminance of all general principles.[47] The emphasis upon

46. See, e.g., the discussion in Part I of *The Republic of Plato*. In these dialogues "Socrates will speak to Athenians about their laws, and will ineluctably be drawn toward a quest for justice, the standard against which laws or practices are measured. . . . Justice . . . is in the first place to be found in the opinions of men. And the inadequacy . . . of opinions leads in turn to reflection on knowledge" (Allan Bloom, *Love and Friendship* [1993], 522).

47. Compare the observation of Simone de Beauvoir: "Woman does not entertain the positive belief that the truth is something *other* than men claim; she recognizes, rather, that there is *not* any fixed truth. It is not only the changing nature of life that makes her suspicious of the principle of constant identity, nor is it the magic phenomena with which she is surrounded that destroys the notion of causality. It is at the heart of the masculine world itself, it is in herself as belonging to this world that she comes upon the ambiguity of all principle, of all value, of everything that exists. . . . She knows that masculine morality, as it concerns her, is a vast hoax. . . .

"Not accepting logical principles and moral imperatives, skeptical about the laws of nature, woman lacks the sense of the universal; to her the world seems a confused conglomerate of special cases. . . . [O]nly immediate experience carries conviction." *The Second Sex*, chap. 21. George Sher has noted that

particularity in legal studies also suggests more pervasive differences between men and women over the relation between the general and the specific in broader areas of human culture. With that possibility in mind we shall pursue the remainder of these reflections on the relation between reason and gender.

IV. *Some Differences of Thought and Action*

Upon the realization of genuine social equality, women may become more fully committed to the general, as well as the immediate, problems of human culture. But the particular concerns that characterize the battles for sexual justice may reflect a deeper, more enduring feminine disposition. We cannot insist too much upon the fact that men and women are equal as persons. Yet we must also recognize that sexual identity influences, in some manner, all the manifestations of one's personal life—including those which engage the use of reason and the pursuit of values.

In matters of great personal importance, a woman will not commit herself to the supremacy of logic or to the pursuit of abstract perfection no matter how much these values have been purged of masculine dominance. Unlike the male, she is not disposed to transform her activities into objective categories. She would rather apply her intelligence and creativity to the improvement of the conditions of those around her. Nor is she inclined to detach herself from the personal significance of what she is doing. For her, abstract and concrete are indissolubly linked. A woman seeks a harmony in her overall existence.

A woman sees linkages between abstract idea and concrete

---

women may be more hesitant than men about the enforcement of principles because women are more aware of the qualifications which limit their application ("Other Voices, Other Rooms? Women's Psychology and Moral Theory" in *Women and Moral Theory*, ed. Eva Feder Kittay and Diana Meyers [Totowa, N.J.: Rowman and Littlefield, 1987]). The difficulties are also implicated in the conviction of some feminists that the existing structures of thought express a phallic language which forces women to pursue alternative modes of writing and speaking. See the discussion in Andrea Nye, *Feminist Theory and the Philosophies of Man*, chap. 6.

situation which elude the male. There are also advantages to her character which inevitably influence her attitude toward matters of both thought and action. Acutely aware of herself and of the circumstances in which she exists, a woman has the power to avoid the idealistic but often distracted behavior of her masculine counterpart. And her embeddedness in the world gives her an understanding of the concrete demands of moral life that is a vast improvement over the excesses of a male-centered rationalism.[48]

This important difference is best understood by reviewing the influence of rationalism upon ethical theory. The age of rationalism gave birth to modern science. When scientific method gained epistemic supremacy, unbiased certainty became the measure of human existence. There developed a disposition to insist that any significant reality must be subject to some exact, external observation. As applied to moral behavior, such procedures reduce the degree to which human action is presumed to be subject to personal agency. By way of compensation, the will is conceded a pure but arbitrary freedom. Volition, the remnant of personality, has an exaggerated but solitary status.

The antithesis between objective procedure and wanton will reflects a deeper opposition between reason and desire. The alliance of modern science with liberal theory accelerated the antithesis. Liberal psychology and political theory gave preeminence to individual self-interest, and this preference led to the conclusion that the individual's wants and aversions cannot be rationally justified. The good is reduced to the satisfaction of desire, while desire is understood as a collage of incoherent impulses, which must be controlled by impersonal rules and procedures. Reasons for action must be public rea-

48. Simone de Beauvoir, *The Second Sex*, chap. 21. Beauvoir insists that the qualities of women are not inherent, but arise out of the circumstances of their lives. However, the textual description is supported by other women writers of the first rank who view these dispositions as being more than transitory. See Gina Lombroso, *The Soul of Woman* (L'Anima Della Donna), book 3 (New York: E. P. Dutton, 1923); Simone Weil, *Waiting for God* (New York: Harper and Row, 1951), and Iris Murdoch, *The Sovereignty of Good*.

sons, but what is meant by reason is nothing more than a common power that exists within a uniform structure of the mind.[49]

In this conception of human action, the self is no longer conceived of as being a composite of reason and will. Nor is it embedded in nature. Rather, it is an empty, choosing, and desiring mechanism, which moves impulsively in and out of a world dominated by an impersonal logic. These instabilities encouraged the development of universal standards of morality, standards that overpower the self with their unconditional demands. Ironically, because such measures were conceived as some form of self-legislation, the will retained its position as the dominant quality of character.

Taken together, these conceptions of human motivation and action reflect some aspects of the masculine temperament, particularly that attraction to what is remote and distant. The disposition is also part of the male inclination to find identity and meaning in some form of separation. Women, by contrast, come to know themselves as they are known, particularly in relationships with others. Alert to the moral significance of concrete relations and circumstances, they take a special interest in ways of knowing that are connected with experience. For women, thinking is more a reflection upon what one is doing than a detached rumination upon the general significance of our actions.[50]

49. The opposition between the rational, thought of as conformity with scientific procedures, and the demands of moral autonomy are well represented in the works of B. F. Skinner. See, e.g., Skinner, *Beyond Freedom and Dignity*. The general problem is sketched in Iris Murdoch, *The Sovereignty of Good* (New York: Schocken Books, 1971). See also Alejandro Llano, *The New Sensibility* (Pamplona: University of Navarra, 1991).

50. See, e.g., Hannah Arendt, *The Life of the Mind*, which emphasizes the importance of thinking about what we are doing in order to avoid complicity in wrongdoing. In his review of Thomas Nevin's book *Simone Weil: Portrait of a Self-Exiled Jew*, George Steiner argues that although they wrote powerful works, Hannah Arendt and Simone de Beauvoir were neither of them, strictly speaking, philosophers. Simone Weil was, in his opinion, the only major woman philosopher. "At every possible point and beyond, Simone Weil chose thought against life, logic against the pragmatic, the laser of analysis and en-

The masculine spirit seeks to transcend what is given. Men take special pride in cultural achievements, such as impersonal contractual relations, which make it possible to project expectations from the present into a yet-unrealized future. For a woman, present time has a deeper significance. She will not be as interested as a man may be in passing beyond what is. For her, nearness activates ethical responsibility.

A woman sees that the will cannot do away with what is. She knows that there are duties that unavoidably present themselves to us and that demand our immediate attention:

The ideal situation . . . is rather to be represented as a kind of "necessity." This is something of which saints speak and which any artist will readily understand. The idea of a patient, loving regard, directed upon a person, a thing, a situation, presents the will not as unimpeded movement but as something very much more like "obedience." . . . Will continually influences belief, for better or worse, and it is ideally able to influence it through a sustained attention to reality. . . . As moral agents we have to try to see justly, to overcome prejudice, to avoid temptation, to control and curb imagination, to direct reflection. Man is not a combination of an impersonal rational thinker and a personal will. He is a unified being who sees, and who desires in accordance with what he sees, and who has some continual slight control over the direction and focus of his vision.[51]

Reason and the good make their claim upon the present. Yet the immediate is forever shifting. The potentialities for virtue are inexhaustible, because one moves from particular practices outward toward the "surprising variety of the world."[52] As contexts become more inclusive, a person becomes increasingly aware of the innumerable specific situations that lie beyond the self and call for its attention. In this encounter with expanding opportunity, there is no appeal to impersonal procedures. From a woman's perspective, these new possibilities

forced deduction against the fitful half-light, the compromise, and the muddle that allows the rest of us to carry on our existence" (*New Yorker* 68 [March 2, 1992], 86–91). Steiner's criteria for determining the rational reflect that reduction of philosophy to abstraction against which I am now protesting.

51. Iris Murdoch, *The Sovereignty of Good*, 40–41.
52. Ibid., 66.

for caring must be approached with loving regard rather than placed under siege by our willfulness.

Situated thinking may focus upon the needs of those who are disadvantaged in some specific way. However, such a deliberative attention is not meant just to bring relief to the oppressed. The deeper purpose is to reveal the difficult choices that one must make in various circumstances of personal, and relational, experience. Like Aristotle, women moral theorists reject the idea that there is always a single moral standard in terms of which all goods are commensurable. Nor do they believe that character is formed by habitual conformity to universal and abstract criteria. They affirm a qualitative heterogeneity of value, which constantly makes conflicting demands on our consciences.

The feminine sense of responsibility is directed toward an empathetic perception of circumstances rather than a habitual application of principle. This devotion concentrates upon the subtle nuances of the particular.[53] In specific situations, an attempt should be made to understand the feelings and circumstances of others rather than to judge matters in terms of our own self-interest. Through sympathetic attention one can try to see what others are experiencing. This form of responsibility is receptive rather than defiant in its attitude toward reality. But it is also careful to avoid the stereotypical view of women as persons who care only for others and never for themselves.[54]

Because women tend to accentuate attachment in their moral deliberations, they have been subject to the charge that their reasoning is inferior to more abstract and universal modes of thought. Such a charge, a residue of rationalism, is unjust, for any moral theory that emphasizes concern for others is clearly

53. Martha C. Nussbaum, *Love's Knowledge*, chap. 2. Jean Bethke Elshtain, *Public Man, Private Woman*, chap. 6. There is a good explanation of a feminist approach to legal practical reasoning in Katharine T. Bartlett, "Feminist Legal Methods," 829. I return to these questions in Chapter 3 of the present work.

54. For a reconciliation of the need for personal autonomy and self-respect with the care perspective, see the concept of responsibility reasoning developed by Diana Meyers in "The Socialized Individual and Individual Autonomy." See also Diana T. Meyers, *Self, Society, and Personal Choice*.

superior to one based upon fear of what others may do to oneself. The forms of practical reasoning advocated by women are distinguished by an engagement with circumstances rather than a detachment from them, and that is, for the most part, a distinct advantage.

The attention given by women to practical reasoning and the complexities of practical choice is, in one sense, a reaction against the excesses of abstract universalism promoted primarily by masculine thinkers. This is, of course, not merely a feminist response. Both men and women engaged in contemporary moral philosophy have drawn attention to the primacy that the demands of actual existence make upon our ethical natures. The restriction of moral reflection to the discovery of abstract and systematic normative structures is subject to common and widespread criticism.[55] And, while it is arguable that women have done a better job than their male counterparts in reconciling moral autonomy with connectedness to others, that does not suggest that men and women differ in their assessments of the nature of reason. However, some real and important differences remain which we must address if we hope to reconcile the masculine and feminine dimensions of existence. The differences in question here have to do with the problem of purpose.

In the modes of practical reasoning generally preferred by women, priority is given to the particular. By careful attention to what is given, one can discern a multiplicity of actual goods in specific situations—goods that are not timeless but rather embedded in concrete circumstances. Because of a caring response to these immediate realities, and the individuals encountered within them, one has reasons to act in a way that

---

55. See, e.g., C. L. Larmore, *Patterns of Moral Complexity,* (1987); N. Rescher, *Ethical Idealism* (Berkeley: University of California Press, 1987); E. F. Schumaker, *A Guide for the Perplexed* (New York: Harper and Row, 1977); E. L. Pincoffs, *Quandaries and Virtues* (Lawrence, Kan.: University Press of Kansas, 1986); and B. Williams, *Ethics and the Limits of Philosophy* (Cambridge: Harvard University Press, 1986).

is both integrated and selfless. Through such action one participates in the interdependence of the moral world.

This feminine vision of the nature of ethical action is at once elevated and restrictive. Consider, for example, the view expressed by Iris Murdoch:

> Right action, together with a steady extension of the area of strict obligation, is a proper criterion of virtue. . . . [T]he aim of morality cannot be simply action. Without some more positive conception of the soul as a substantial and continually developing mechanism of attachments, the purification and reorientation of which must be the task of morals, "freedom" is readily corrupted into self-assertion and "right action" into some sort of *ad hoc* utilitarianism. . . . With this picture must of course be joined a realistic conception of natural psychology . . . and also an acceptance of the utter lack of finality in human life. The Good has nothing to do with purpose, indeed it excludes the idea of purpose.[56]

One must agree with much of this perspective. In order to do what is right in a particular situation, any person, male or female, must have an upright will and be prepared to act with genuine love. And love "does not regard ideas or abstractions or possibilities, love regards existing persons."[57] A loving regard also accepts reality as it is rather than as what we would like it to be. And love also resists that grasping ambition to dominate external reality which too often characterizes a male approach to the natural world. Accepting the world requires us to look upon it as a habitat in which one lives but which one does not create. However, the difficulty with this otherwise admirable conception of virtue is that it restricts the good to what is immediate. It tends to overlook the extent to which an orientation toward the whole of existence—to what is beyond as well as what is present—is also an integral part of the moral life.

The development of virtue activates a multiplicity of values that are indispensable to an inclusive orientation toward the

56. Iris Murdoch, *The Sovereignty of Good*, 71.
57. Jacques Maritain, *Education at the Crossroads* (New Haven: Yale University Press, 1943), 95–96.

good. The appropriate integration of various goods makes up the character of a particular human person. The good person has a concern for interpersonal values; but that orientation does not exhaust the desire for the good. Not all values are interpersonal. Some of the most important, such as those related to truth, are impersonal by nature. Even life as a value has an abstract meaning, and, as an abstraction, it can come to the aid of the defenseless.[58]

A similar observation must be made about the weight to be given to what is immediate. The search for values reflects the soul's yearning for a complete life. Such longing cannot endure an absolute confinement. At some point reason rebels against given realities, no matter how broadly conceived, and begins to search for noncontextual values that may provide more adequate explanations of experience. In its pursuit of a fuller understanding, reason pursues ends that surpass what is bounded by either time or custom.[59]

Reason is now purposive, but in a way that goes beyond the designs of practical rationality. Instrumental reason illumines limited ends that are relevant to some pragmatic endeavor. In these circumstances, as we have seen, thought is never distinct from practice. The judgments that the mind makes are relative to specific situations and to the interests of a particular community of moral agents. If successful, reason is satisfied because the method works. But over time, rationalization gains

58. In her criticism of the pro-choice position on abortion, Elizabeth Fox-Genovese argues that it overlooks the relation between value and abstract thought. Elizabeth Fox-Genovese, *Feminism without Illusions* (Chapel Hill: University of North Carolina Press, 1991), chap. 3.

59. Alfred North Whitehead, *The Function of Reason* (Boston: Beacon Press, 1929). "Purposes are the mysterious pull of the future that really makes human life function. Human life, in many, many ways, is a desire for more life. When this desire fades or dies, we die" (Historian John Lukas, interview with Bill Moyers, in *A World of Ideas*, 446). This tendency toward the vertical may refer to temporal existence, but it also points to the ultimate destiny of the human person, which, in a Christian perspective, is a supra-temporal aspiration. This is what makes the human person superior to all temporal societies. See Jacques Maritain, *Challenges and Renewals*, ed. Joseph W. Evans and Leo R. Ward (Cleveland: World Publishing, 1968), chap. 16.

supremacy over objective value. End and means become in-
distinguishable. The method has become repetitious, incapable
of dealing with important questions, and a desire is aroused
for deeper explanations or justifications for action. The mind
rebels against the constrictions of established routine. Now
reason, disturbed, resists conformity to what already exists.
As it pursues deeper levels of meaning, it seeks to connect
what is immediate with what is beyond. Reason moves from
the practical to the speculative level of intellectual life.[60]

When reason acts pragmatically, it develops a method that
makes one aware of the detailed possibilities within a specific
practice. This is a significant accomplishment. But it ultimately
fails to satisfy. If a desire for a more complete understanding
breaks out, reason will rise above the established method. It
does so because it is no longer content with mere existence:

In this function reason is enthroned above the practical tasks of the
world. It is not concerned with keeping alive. It seeks with disinterested curiosity an understanding of the world. Naught that happens
is alien to it. It is driven forward by the ultimate faith that all particular
fact is understandable as illustrating the general principles of its own
nature and of its status among other particular facts. It fulfills its function when understanding has been gained. Its sole satisfaction is that
experience has been understood. It presupposes life, and seeks life
rendered good with the goodness of understanding. Also so long as
understanding is incomplete it remains to that extent unsatisfied. It
thus constitutes itself the urge from the good life to the better life.
But the progress which it seeks is always the progress of a better
understanding. . . .
There is a strong moral intuition that speculative understanding
for its own sake is one of the ultimate elements in the good life.[61]

Speculative reason is distinct from practical rationality because
reflection is not limited by some specific end. The mind now

60. Whitehead, *The Function of Reason*. Compare the observations on the
relation between instrumental rationality and the rationalization of public life
in Wendy Brown, *Manhood and Politics* (Totowa, N.J.: Rowman and Littlefield,
1988), chap. 8.
61. Ibid., 37–38. "The important theoretical experience leads necessarily
toward the first principles of all things and includes an awareness of the good"
(Allan Bloom, *The Closing of the American Mind*, 271).

moves through and beyond its absorption with immediate concerns and opens itself to a more inclusive existence.

Is this pursuit of higher purpose simply another expression of masculine *hubris*? We know from the legends of Faust that whenever an insatiable desire for knowledge is coupled with a refusal to accept persons or things as they are, the results can be disastrous. A realist appreciation of these dangers may partially explain the tendency of thoughtful women to take a skeptical view of the speculative inclination when it moves beyond immediate experience.

A woman's sense of what it means to be a natural being may lead her to remind men that, like women, they are "steadfastly bound, through all time to facts that know no movement and do not change: birth, suffering, and death."[62] The higher reaches of mental activity may be acknowledged, but with a warning that reflection cannot avoid our rootedness in the present or the extent to which even the most noble projects are bounded by our mortality. Such warnings must be taken seriously. But we must also take seriously the disposition toward an elevation of life—a disposition which, unavoidably, draws us toward abstract understanding.

The search for the good of understanding depends upon the collaboration of reason and intuition. It also engages virtues of the heart. The quest for the fullness of knowledge is a form of love. As an "agitation" of the soul it manifests a desire for the good and for happiness that is of much greater value than any pure intellectual detachment. Reason is, itself, a passionate faculty. Reason assimilates the creative power of eros in order to bring forth what it is appropriate for the soul to conceive in the order of knowledge and virtue. Such an enrichment justifies the progression from the particular to the general, whether the pursuit be of the good or of the beautiful.[63]

The inclination toward wholeness is part of the cultivation

62. Carol McMillan, *Women, Reason, and Nature*, 155. See also Simone de Beauvoir, *The Second Sex*, Part 7.

63. See the discussion of Platonic philosophy in Genevieve Lloyd, *The Man of Reason*.

of life. It moves the human spirit through what is immediate, past the narrow scope of critical analysis, toward a liberation of the imagination in meditation and conversation. In so doing

it excludes nothing; its virtue is to comprehend—in both senses: to understand and to take in the fullest view. Both are actions of the mind-and-heart, and therefore charged with the strongest feelings. Indeed, both interior monologue and spoken dialogue aim at discerning which feelings and what degree of each belong to an idea or image. This is how culture reshapes the personality; it develops the self by offering the vicarious experience of art and thought; it puts experience in order.[64]

Reason, intuition, and emotion collaborate in bringing the self to a greater understanding of itself and of its world. In this enlarged perspective, we transcend distinctions of gender which set up an opposition between thought and feeling. Feminine and masculine powers are now fully engaged. In the domain of thought and action, an integrated vision of empathetic thought reduces the distance between the worlds of men and women. We begin to create the conditions that will make it possible for them both to participate fully in the development of human culture.

The distinctive functions of thought and the cognitive theories developed to explain them are not divisible according to gender. For example, feminists are attracted to pragmatism, although its major advocates have been men. Contemporary women have shown less enthusiasm for speculative reason, which they often perceive to be a means adopted by men to perpetuate female subordination. It is impossible to forecast how much this attitude might change over time, as gains are made in equality of opportunity. If we remain aware of the fact that reason has much closer affinities with the feminine spirit than is usually recognized, we may be justified in expecting a greater participation of women in all the reflective endeavors

64. Jacques Barzun, *The Culture We Deserve* (Middletown: Wesleyan University Press, 1989), 20–21. Compare Northrop Frye, *The Educated Imagination* (Bloomington: Indiana University Press, 1964).

of human culture. Expansion will occur as the antagonism between abstract righteousness and the aesthetic disposition are gradually eliminated.[65] In any event, it is important to understand that the search for ends and purposes that lie outside the boundaries of immediate experience is not necessarily a sign of either masculine, or feminine, depravity.

At the present stage of human development, the speculative uses of reason are more likely to be found among men rather than women. Women are more inclined to look for the good in interpersonal contexts and to use abstract thought for the purpose of making self-understanding more widely available. Their appropriation of abstract theory is often motivated by a desire to correct some form of perceived injustice.[66] Women also tend to be attracted to the stabilities that can be gained from habituation to establish practice, while men are more likely to search for novel meanings over a much wider range of human experience.

In a humanism of equality, men and women will develop ways of thinking and acting that, respectively, they find to be most congenial. But they need not move in opposite directions. If women, in matters other than those in which they are directly concerned, took a greater interest in the life of reflective thought, the benefits to society, as well as to themselves, would be considerable. Conversely, if men would pay greater attention to the context of their lives, cultivating the practical habits and virtues that are indispensable to moral growth, their contributions to general well-being would increase significantly.[67]

65. In his study of Kierkegaard, Karl Stern explains how the great Danish thinker found it impossible to reconcile the love of beauty with a commitment to righteousness. Unable to see the aesthetic as anything more than hedonism without responsibility, Kierkegaard invented an ethic which was "fleshless and without beauty" (*The Flight from Woman*, chap. 10).

66. See, e.g., Susan Moller Okin, *Justice, Gender, and the Family* (New York: Basic Books, 1989); "Reason and Feeling in Thinking about Justice," *Ethics* 99 (1989), 229.

67. Compare Llano, *The New Sensibility*, with Romano Guardini, *The Virtues*, trans. Stella Lange (Chicago: Henry Regnery, 1967). The same need to

We may begin to summarize these reflections by recalling that when rationalism dominated Western culture, the domain of thought was reserved for a disengaged reason that built up, within itself, an abstract order of ideas. The speculative uses of the mind were primarily directed toward the development of mathematics and logical thought. This evolution was essential to technological development, but it also broke all substantive links between the mind and nature.[68] As the life of the mind was increasingly directed toward the control of what was not itself, it lost that receptivity to being which is the beginning of wisdom.

There was also a rejection of all teleological explanations of human life. Horizons of higher purpose were closed so that the human subject could be absolutely self-defining. Autonomous, he would devise his own ends rather than find fulfillment in a good that lay beyond himself. This objective led to further distortions. In ethics, a theoretical disposition displaced that practical orientation that had traditionally marked the world of action, and abstract normativity was directed toward an elaboration of rights rather than a pursuit of the good.[69]

These general developments, which are derived from the masculinization of thought, provide a background for an understanding of the objectives of the emancipation of women. Their revolt is not only against the discriminatory laws and practices of a patriarchal system; it is also a demand for the freedom to exercise their own unique dispositions of thought and action in all aspects of our common life. Women hope to bring a feeling intelligence to bear upon the problems of human society and, in so doing, to overcome that disparagement of natural existence and common experience that is the heritage of rationalism.

---

reconcile the concrete and the abstract can be discerned in the field of spirituality. The soul has a need for attachment and rootedness in a local environment, but also a need of relatedness to the whole (Thomas Moore, *Care of the Soul* [New York: Harper Collins, 1992], chap. 10).

68. Charles Taylor, *Sources of the Self*. See also D. Kolb, *The Critique of Pure Modernity* (Chicago: University of Chicago Press: 1987).

69. I explain this development in *Descent into Subjectivity* (Wakefield, N.H.: Longwood Academic, 1990).

A feminist attack upon ways of knowing upheld by men has been an important part of this liberation. The assault upon all that is abstract, disengaged, and controlling has humbled masculine pride. But it has also led to a reconsideration of the nature of reason, both in itself and in its relation to the other vital sources of action. Overcoming the dualities imposed by the masculinization of thought, we are now in a position to understand some of the deeper harmonies of human nature, which, it properly nurtured, can greatly enrich the lives of both men and women.

The potentials of comprehension that lie within the depths of each individual contain subtle links between reason and intuition, logic and the imagination, the general and the particular. They include both a sense of righteousness and a sensitivity to the beautiful. All these qualities of heart and mind are, for each human being, aspects of existence that are vitally and intimately intertwined. And although these potentials, which reflect the best of the masculine and feminine ways of existing, are part of a general human endowment, they do not cancel the basic distinctions between the sexes.

Enlargement of understanding should not be seen as a call for an androgynous humanism. For while it is true that sexual distinctiveness recedes as mental and moral life expands, the tension between the masculine and the feminine modes of being is never entirely eliminated. Nor would it be desirable if the differences between the sexes were to completely disappear from the field of culture. For "it would be a thousand pities"[70] if the creativity of men, as well as that of women, did not remain in some way unique. No one can be completely manly, or womanly, yet all aspire to be the best they can be as either a masculine or a feminine person. In a spirit of sexual equality men and women will draw upon their specific resources—those which make them distinguishable from each other as well as those held in common—and give their separate testimonies as to what it means to be fully human.

70. Virginia Woolf, *A Room of One's Own*, 152.

3. PUBLIC AND PRIVATE

I. *The Decline and Fall of Aristotelian Manliness*

Throughout the political history of the West there has been a separation of the public and private spheres of human existence. The distinction between the two realms has been most sharply maintained within the Aristotelian tradition, which insists that the distinctiveness of political life depends upon its liberation from the rhythms of necessity that characterize the domestic world. The *polis*, with its public space, is thought of as presenting opportunities for a form of life higher than what can be achieved in the unfree realm of the *oikos* or household.

For Aristotle, the public world was the place where men could reveal the excellences of their character and develop their personal virtues. They could achieve fame and immortality in public service, although their participation in such life was always accompanied by the risk of violent death. Women were excluded from participation in civic life. The domestic world they inhabited, along with slaves, was associated with a lower order of values. This household world was expected to serve the higher purposes of the male-centered political realm. The sharpness of the distinction drawn between public and private life in the ancient world set in motion forces that have led to a confining oppression of women. The feminist movement for emancipation from the bondage of patriarchy is directed toward the correction of this injustice.[1]

---

1. Hannah Arendt has been the principal modern exponent of the Aristotelian conception. See, e.g. *The Human Condition* (Chicago: University of Chicago Press, 1958). See also Melvin Hill, ed., *Hannah Arendt: The Recovery of the Public World* (1979) and B. Parekh, *Hannah Arendt: The Search for a New Political Philosophy* (New York: St. Martin's Press, 1981). The classical conception is also

In the conception of the ancients, the political ideal was of achievements higher, on a scale of values, than those associated with the mere fact of existence. By engaging in civic affairs men sought not just to live, but to live well. They hoped to experience a fullness of being beyond the satisfactions that private life could provide.[2] While this aspiration toward the ideals of a higher civilization has had an important bearing upon the course of Western history, it has had to compete with less exalted visions of human nature. By the time of the Renaissance, the objectives of political action had been substantially modified in order to account for a more realistic, and less exalted, conception of civic development. These changes, which have substantially influenced the course of Western history, also manifested a darker vision of masculine potential.

Male identity has always been problematic. Beginning with a separation from the maternal influences of the home, it develops through some contentious involvement with a broader, external, world. Men are drawn to some form of combative behavior—destined to struggle, in some way, with their external environment. Within the male there is also a kinship between force and order. Machiavelli developed a theory of politics upon these powerful masculine dispositions. He viewed man as an impulsive creature, intent upon mastery and conquest. Ambition and avarice were the principal motivations for participation in public life. And a craving for power and control, rather than the pursuit of some public good, became the dominant objective of political action.[3]

sustained in the writings of Leo Strauss. See, e.g., his essay "On Classical Political Philosophy," in *What Is Political Philosophy* (H. Gilden, ed., 1975). Important feminist critiques of the Aristotelian view include Wendy Brown, *Manhood and Politics: A Feminist Reading* in *Political Theory* (Totowa, N.J.: Rowman & Littlefield, 1988); Gerda Lerner, *The Creation of Patriarchy* chap. 10 (New York: Oxford University Press, 1986); and Jean Bethke Elshtain, *Public Man, Private Woman* (Princeton: Princeton University Press, 1981).

2. Aristotle, *Politics*, Book 7.

3. Leo Strauss, *Thoughts on Machiavelli* (Glencoe: Free Press, 1958); Federico Chabod, *Machiavelli and the Renaissance*, David Moore, trans. (1958). Jacques Maritain, *Man and the State* (Chicago: University of Chicago Press, 1952). See

The Machiavellian conception of political existence demeaned the classical ideals concerning the higher ends of human action. This narrowing of the objectives of politics was continued by later thinkers, such as Hobbes, who emphasized the isolation of the individual and the more destructive aspects of human encounter. Political theory became oblivious to higher ends, and organized life, as the domain of male action, became increasingly a place for the release of a *libido dominandi*. The criteria for public association came to depend upon elementary distinctions between friends and enemies.[4]

And the subordination of women was reinforced. The few women, such as Elizabeth of England and Isabella of Spain, who reached the heights of power were extraordinary exceptions. Generally, women were excluded from public life. They were considered not only inferior but also dangerous. The masculine drive toward power could be frustrated by the capacity of women to prevent men from realizing their ambitions. Woman, symbolized as Fortune, represented all that was unreliable and capricious. If men were to gain glory, it was important for them to keep women under subjection and to prevent them from participating in public life.[5]

---

also, Wendy Brown, *Manhood and Politics*, chap. 5. For a more recent assessment of the developments from Machiavelli to Hobbs, and beyond, see Alan Bloom, *Love and Friendship*, esp. chap. 6.

4. "He who seeks the salvation of the soul, of his own and of others, should not seek it along the avenue of politics, for the quite different tasks of politics can only be solved by violence" (Max Weber, *Politics as a Vocation*, trans. H. H. Gerth and C. Wright Mills [Philadelphia: Fortress Press, 1965], 52). The writings of Robin West provide good insights into these developments. See, e.g., "Jurisprudence and Gender," *University of Chicago Law Review* 55 (Winter 1988): 1; "Taking Freedom Seriously," *Harvard Law Review* 104 (1990): 43. For the basic distinction between friends and enemies, see Carl Schmitt, *The Concept of the Political*, trans. G. Schwab (New Brunswick, N.J.: Rutgers University Press, 1975). Schmitt, whose philosophy was influential in the Third Reich, considered the political to be a practical concept which does not require any moral evaluation of otherness. For a general study of these developments and their bearing upon issues raised by feminism, see Thomas Fleming, *The Politics of Human Nature* (New Brunswick: Transaction Books, 1988).

5. Wendy Brown, *Manhood and Politics*; Hanna Pitkin, *Fortune Is a Woman* (Berkeley: University of California Press, 1984). Pitkin views Machiavelli as

In the development of Western culture the rationalizations
for not allowing women to participating in civic affairs soon
took the form of a dubious exchange of power. We have already
seen how the practical authority a woman might exert at home
was thought by philosophers such as Rousseau and Kant to
legitimate her submission in matters of public importance. But
no matter how extensive was their domestic power and influence, such an absolute exclusion of women from the *polis*
would, over time, become intolerable. As we have seen, they
no longer accepted a male-imposed confinement to household
existence. As persons, they could no longer believe that sensual satisfaction, or even personal love, was the highest value
to which they could aspire.

The rebellion against domestic restriction was also caused
by an increased awareness of the interrelationship between the
public and private realms. To men, women posed a danger to
the *polis*; women would now repay the compliment. They could
no longer endure the threats to the continuities of life posed
by the increasingly destructive behavior of men in the public
arena. Protest against exclusion was being accompanied by a
damning assessment of the consequences of male control of
the *polis*:

The male element is a destructive force, stern, selfish, aggrandizing,
loving war, violence, conquest, acquisition, breeding in the material
and moral world alike discord, disorder, disease and death. . . . The
male element has held high carnival thus far, it has fairly run riot from
the beginning, overpowering the feminine element everywhere,
crushing out the diviner qualities of human nature until we know but
little of true manhood and womanhood, of the latter comparatively
nothing, for it has scarce been recognized as a power until within the
last century. . . . The need of this hour is . . . a new evangel of wom-

---

seeking to revive Roman virtues of decisive action. Looking back to Rome (but
not to Greece), he saw that: "Here was an uncorrupted community of real
men, competent to take care of themselves without being dependent upon
anyone else, sharing in a fraternal, participatory civic life that made them self-
governing. Nor was their public spiritedness a spineless, deferential uniform-
ity; in their domestic politics, as in their relations abroad, they were strong
and manly: fighters . . ." (*Fortune Is a Woman*, 48).

anhood, to exalt purity, virtue, morality, true religion, to lift man up into the higher realms of thought and action.[6]

This critique by a nineteenth-century suffragette pillories the political record of Machiavellian man. The quotation also reflects a belief that if governments became more responsive to women, there would be a marked improvement in the conduct of political affairs. At that time, those who suffered exclusion benevolently sought to influence the direction of the existing system. In the present phase of women's liberation, however, the premises are different. Now the demand is for the freedom of women to participate fully in the public sphere. There will no longer be a submission to the governance of men.

In the last quarter century there has been a remarkable increase in the number of women who have gained positions of responsibility and authority in all aspects of social and political life. As this process continues and remaining discriminatory barriers are removed, men and women will increasingly be required to work together to address the complex problems of contemporary existence. The quality of that collaboration will depend largely upon the fundamental attitudes that each takes toward the other. Men must renounce the prejudice that women are not capable of deliberation and action in matters of public importance. Men must also overcome their fear that women pose a threat to the accomplishment of political projects. The attitudes that women have toward men are also important—as important as the views that men have of themselves.

For some radical feminists, the masculine is an obsolete life form that should be banished from public affairs. Many others have less extreme views, but they are nevertheless persuaded that the male pursuit of power and prestige, and the subver-

6. Elizabeth Cady Stanton, quoted in Jean Bethke Elshtain, *Public Man, Private Woman* (Princeton: Princeton University Press, 1981), 232. See also Zillah Eisenstein, "Elizabeth Cady Stanton: Radical-Feminist Analysis and Liberal-Feminist Strategy," in *Feminism and Equality*, ed. Anne Phillips (New York: New York University Press, 1987), 77.

sion of politics to those ends, has not produced lasting benefits
for humankind. The fault is seen to lie in the elementary constituents of masculinity. Men compete, rather than collaborate.
Worse, their achievements always seem to require the defeat
of another. And their inveterate quest for immortality leads
them to strive toward transcendent ends that overlook the important contingencies of temporal life. The male is contemp-
tuous of feminine values, and, when he is in positions of
power, he acts in ways that too often lead to the destruction of
all the goods that women cherish.[7]

In Machiavellian thought, and indeed throughout Western
history, political man has tried to overcome the fact that he is
a creature of necessity. Even more than the threat of enemies,
he feels menaced by the elementary natural realities of birth
and death. As a result, "both individual men and the 'collective manhood' of the polis acquire a fragile, restless, anxious,
or overwrought character."[8] This image of troubled men is not
merely a construct of feminist ideology. The flight from the
feminine has been well documented in the psychological literature.[9] There can be no doubt that the masculine pursuit of
public glory has been at the expense of the feminine orienta-

7. Marilyn French, *Beyond Power* (New York: Summit Books, 1985); Elizabeth H. Wolgast, *The Grammar of Justice* (Ithaca: Cornell University Press, 1987);
Wendy Brown, *Manhood and Politics*. See also Susan Moller Okin, *Women in
Western Political Thought* (Princeton: Princeton University Press, 1979); Jean
Bethke Elshtain, *Public Man, Private Woman*, chap. 5. Compare the message to
women published by the Council Fathers at the conclusion of the Second Vatican Council. Acknowledging their "love of beginnings," the Fathers urge
women to exercise a supreme authority over matters of life and death: "Reconcile men with life and above all, we beseech you, watch carefully over the
future of our race. Hold back the hand of man who, in a moment of folly, might
attempt to destroy human civilization" ("Closing Messages of the Council,"
in *The Documents of Vatican II*, ed. Walter M. Abbott [New York: Herder and
Herder, 1966]).
8. Wendy Brown, *Manhood and Politics*, 27.
9. E.g., Rollo May, *Love and Will* (New York: W. W. Norton, 1969); Karl
Stern, *The Flight from Woman* (New York: Noonday Press, 1965). These observations are confirmed by the assessments of foreign critics. In his book *American and Chinese* (3d ed. [Honolulu: University of Hawaii Press, 1981]), the
anthropologist Francis Hsu, recognizes, from a Chinese perspective, the striving insecurity of the American male.

tion toward existence. The striving has also led men to un-
derestimate their own potentials.

Some believe that the deficiencies men display in public life
might be corrected if men were willing to accept the feminine
dimensions of their own personalities. Such a view of reformation is not restricted to ardent feminists. The decline of paternal influence in modern society (discussed in chapter 1) has
led some men to the conviction that their personal lives must
be built upon feminine qualities of character. Others, equally
disturbed by public disorder, would not abandon their maleness, but they would seek fulfillment in private rather than
public life. Such men would connect more deeply with their
families and personal friendships, distancing themselves as far
as possible from the burdens of civic association.[10] Still others
feel that they are obliged to renounce the whole patriarchal
structure of law and civilization and replace it with a culture
grounded firmly upon female values.

From the evidence of archaeological discoveries and the recovery of mythical traditions, we have reason to believe in the
spiritual authority of women within some earlier societies. In
communities influenced by some form of matriarchal pagan-
ism, reproductive values and the joys of fertility apparently
took precedence over norms derived from male dominance.
Since the subsequent masculine control of history has led to
women's exploitation and oppression, some men are persuaded that principles of fairness require that the male abjure
his quest for public power and authority and instead adopt the
life-sustaining world views of women. Once religiously ven-
erated, women and their values should now have social and
political prominence.[11]

This attitude suggests a psychological inversion. Previously
men formed women in a masculine image. Men who now
desire complete transformation would surrender their mas-

10. This position is defended in Charles Larmore, *Patterns of Moral Complexity* (New York: Cambridge University Press, 1987).
11. J. C. Smith, *The Neurotic Foundations of Social Order* (New York: New York
University Press, 1990).

culine identities and realign themselves with a feminine
ego-ideal. Such a renunciation seems to some the only way of
shifting the axis of human personality and culture away from
cycles of violence and subjection and of moving public life toward the superior feminine values of love, mercy, and compassion.

The devaluation of the masculine parallels the general advance of women. When a culture is patriarchal, women are
submissive. Under oppressive circumstances, a woman who
gives herself up to the image of herself that men have created
demeans her own existence. Thus, to gain her personal identity she must overcome the impositions of patriarchy. As as-
saults upon masculine power expose the destructiveness of
male-centered politics, this revelation of masculine failure has
also convinced some men that if the planet is to survive they
must surrender their own egos to matriarchal archetypes. The
nurturing spirit of the feminine, with its sense of connection
and reconciliation, is seen as possessing more humanistic
value than masculine acts of will and violence. Networks become more attractive than hierarchies.

The disposition to abandon maleness has the advantage of
highlighting the mistakes of the past and pointing to a more
integrated vision of the future. But it fails to attribute any positive significance to masculinity. One's conception of maleness
has important consequences for the quality and direction of
public life. Prevailing stereotypes of the male as a violent and
exploitative creature make it extremely difficult to articulate
any attractive or confident images of manhood.

The critiques of maleness have brought the darker side of the
masculine into clearer focus, but they have left an incomplete
picture of male identity. In particular, a pessimistic assessment
does not account for the ways in which men have assumed a
positive responsibility for public affairs. A more balanced assessment would recognize that men's involvement in civic life
has been life-giving as well as destructive. At the same time,
it must be recognized that uncomplimentary assessments of
the masculine record have a factual basis. A protest against

that history, by both men and women, must be taken seriously if we hope to make any progress in rehabilitating the public world.

11. *Toward the Reconstruction of Masculine Identity*

During the course of Western history, political action has been understood increasingly in terms of volitional factors that reflect the desires of men for domination and control. As a major field of masculine activity, political life has become a struggle for survival, status, and power. These combative forms of public engagement have had a profound influence upon men's conceptions of themselves and of what they are capable of achieving. Satisfied with a limiting view of their character, men have become resigned to a life in the polis that renounces any orientation toward higher ends. Wisdom no longer bears a vital relation to the overall purposes of masculine existence.

The determination to make the will the decisive attribute of masculine character has impeded the development of civilization. When not preoccupied with violent encounters, men have made command and subjection the decisive measures of social relations. As for intellectual life, they have placed knowledge at the service of power.

The forceful dispositions of men have influenced higher disciplines that have an important relation to practical life. Our reflections in Chapter 2, "Reason and Gender," showed the masculine quest for righteousness is oblivious to the feminine desire for felicity. Ethics becomes repressive when its demands become disassociated from the pursuit of human happiness. Under the regime of masculine imperatives, the good becomes a doctrine of duties rather than something that points to personal or social fulfillment. As injunctions and prohibitions proliferate, even the exercise of spiritual authority takes on some aspects of an imposed, inhuman order—becoming like William Blake's grotesque image of Urizen.[12]

12. There is an interesting study of this development in John Finnis, *Natural Law and Natural Rights*, chap. 2 (Oxford: Oxford University Press,

Archetypical paradigms of the patriarchal ethos evoke images that justify and deepen masculine authority. The commanding position of men in human culture has been aligned with themes of paternal supremacy whose origins were either a father-god, some form of monarchical authority, or the tradition of *pater familias*. This trilogy contains, in imaginative form, the principal rationalizations for male domination.

When expressed in mythical form, patriarchal paradigms reach the deepest springs of human action. Myths are powerful because they penetrate to layers of consciousness that lie beneath the level of immediate experience. Those myths concerned with father figures are relevant to an understanding of the masculine because they provide men with an opportunity to gain a deeper understanding of their own personal identities. Once assimilated, such stories can become inner exemplars which guide individual development.

Myths derived from stories of royalty are especially important. The image of sacred kingship, symbolized by the sun, was once a source of enlightenment for all men living within a particular kingdom. The king shared a common humanity with his subjects but the crown, ratified by God, gave the monarch a special dignity. At this level, in relation to his male subjects, "what he was had greatly to do with what they were, as in all fatherhood."[13]

1980). See also Charles Taylor, *Sources of the Self* (New York: Cambridge University Press, 1980), chaps. 9–15. Taylor makes some comments about Montaigne which are relevant to these reflections. The French thinker struggled to liberate self-understanding from the burden of the universal demands of moral experience which are so often interpreted in a tyrannical way. For a study of the image of Urizen as "Lord of the World of Man" who "is strong, sad, and cruel" see Harold Bloom, "States of Being," in *Blake: A Collection of Critical Essays*, ed. Northrop Frye (Englewood Cliffs, N.J.: Prentice-Hall, 1966).

13. *Of America, East and West* (New York: Farrar, Straus & Giroux, 1984), 24. Cf. Aristotle, *Politics*, bk. 1, chap. 12, 1259b15: "A King ought to be naturally superior to his subjects and yet of the same stock as they are; and this is the case of the relation of age to youth and of parent to child." The textual quote, from the writings of Paul Horgan, refers to Spanish kingship at the time of the discovery of the Americas. For the interrelation of religious belief and ideals of fatherhood, see Sigmund Freud, *Moses and Monotheism*, trans. Katherine Jones (New York: Vintage Books, 1939).

The myths and stories of kingship are valuable because they contain ideals of masculine life more varied, complex, and elevated than those which associate maleness with brute force and violence. The king established order; but it was an order that depended more upon his presence than upon the direct application of his power. The unity established by this personal sovereignty made possible a general tranquility. The king established a cosmos where there had been chaos.[14]

The good king recognized and affirmed those who were subject to his authority. Of course, not all kings were good. Some blessed and encouraged; others cursed and repressed. But the image has been tarnished as much by changes in the nature of government as it has by the character flaws of particular monarchs.

With the rise of democracy, monarchy as a political institution has been either eliminated or stripped of its former powers. However, as kings have disappeared, so also have dignified conceptions of manhood. Rapacious images of the warrior have all too often filled the vacuum left by the fall of regal images. Stories of kings and of their merits and accomplishments traditionally helped to sustain positive images of maleness. The eclipse of monarchy has led to a visual impairment which, when coupled with other influences, has contributed to the enfeeblement of the masculine character. Now there is a loss of all enlarged visions of manliness within the general culture; a dearth of positive archetypes might remind men of their deeper value as spiritual creatures.[15]

14. Basic studies of mythology can be found in the books of Joseph Campbell. See, e.g., *The Hero with a Thousand Faces* (New York: Pantheon, 1949) and *The Power of Myth* (New York: Doubleday 1988) (with Bill Moyers). See also Robert Moore and Douglas Gillette, *King, Warrior, Magician, Lover: Rediscovering the Archetypes of the Mature Masculine* (San Francisco: Harper and Row 1990); Robert Bly, *Iron John* (Reading, Mass.: Addison Wesley, 1990), chap. 4; and John Weir Perry, *Lord of the Four Quarters* (New York: G. Braziller, 1966).

The importance of positive images is stressed by Robert Bly in *Iron John* and by Sam Keen in his *Fire in the Belly* (New York: Bantam Books, 1991). See also Patrick M. Arnold, *Wildmen, Warriors, and Kings* (New York: Crossroad Press, 1991).

15. Arnold, *Wildmen, Warriors, and Kings*. See also Walter J. Ong, *Fighting*

The prevailing images of maleness—pride, lust, and aggression—are demeaning stereotypes, which men have great difficulty of overcoming. The desire to maintain a separate gender-type compounds the difficulty. While men may affirm some of the feminine aspects of their personalities, they will also try to develop the uniqueness of their being. The recovery of the masculine can occur only through an exploration of the ambivalent ambitions that lie within the soul of every man as he is drawn toward engagement with the world around him.

Men are impelled to risk their identity in some public place. They may be motivated by some search for power or fame; they may also be inspired by a self-denying effort to effectuate a moral vision. It is impossible to determine a priori what, in a particular instance, is the dominant motive for masculine action. Only a simplistic reductionism would eliminate all possibility of a positive alternative to an otherwise destructive, or malicious, intent.

The male's encounter with the external world is inevitably marked by some form of combat. Mythological images of the man as a warrior have a wide-ranging and enduring influence upon the masculine imagination. In time of war, soldiering becomes an ideal; in peace, the athlete is given pride of place. Although directed primarily toward physical combat, these archetypes of struggle have a bearing upon cultural as well as militant attainments. The need for contest—spiritual as well as physical—is deeply embedded in the male psyche.[16]

---

for *Life* (Ithaca: Cornell Univ. Press, 1981); David D. Gilmore, *Manhood in the Making* (New Haven, Yale University Press 1990). The late Walker Percy described the status of the male in modern culture as being one in which "most males seem content to be portrayed as drudge and boob, a nitwitted Dagwood who leaves everything to 'Mama'" (Walker Percy, *Signposts in a Strange Land,* ed. Patrick Samway [New York: Farrar, Straus and Giroux, 1991], 21). An important attempt to recover a sense of spiritual dignity can be seen in Thomas Moore, *Care of the Soul* (New York: Harper-Collins, 1992). Women writers have also seen the need to distinguish what belongs to masculine character from what constitutes male domination. See, e.g., Margaret Mead, *Male and Female* (New York: William Morrow, 1949).

16. Karl Bednarik, *The Male in Crisis,* trans. Helen Sebba (Westport: Green-

The violence that has marred this century makes it difficult to assign any positive value to the initiatives of men. Women are uncomfortable with male contentiousness. However, conflict is, in some measure, normal to men and it can be expressed in verbal as well as physical combat. The clash of ideas is not necessarily directed toward evil ends.

The absence of challenge and struggle can also encourage aggression. It is often forgotten how much modern, organized, belligerence has been facilitated by male passivity. Large-scale warfare is made possible when groups of men allow themselves to become pawns in struggles for power, subjecting themselves to the manipulation of influential military and political figures. And soldiers often fulfill, in virtual anonymity, a mechanical function as they participate in technologically managed wars of mass destruction.[17]

In spite of those qualifications, it must be recognized that a tendency to fight is a part of masculine psychology. The instincts associated with combativeness are probably based upon the masculine inclination toward spatial expansion. Men are inclined to gather, defend, and expand territories; this basic instinct is quickly assimilated to other endeavors subject to their control. The status they seek, particularly approval from women, is often associated with such energetic accomplishments. The significance of this tendency toward enlargement cannot be fully understood in terms of a desire for conquest.

The searching activity of men, with its sense of risk and adventure, has been an aspect in the creation and development of countless civilizations. Similar observations can be made about what is commonly called the entrepreneurial spirit. Fierce competition is often a necessary aspect of the creation of wealth, and, as with other forms of masculine action, the motives for economic engagement are various. Trade and in-

---

wood Press, 1970). This emphasis can be found in cultures whose heroes are warriors. See, e.g., Richard Fletcher, *The Quest for El Cid* (New York: Alfred Knopf, 1990).

17. Bednarik, *The Male in Crisis.* See also the authorities in n. 15, supra.

vestment can be initiated for reasons which range from raw greed to a sincere effort to achieve an abundant prosperity for the general community.

The anthropological dimensions of manliness reveal dynamics of virility that are manifest in advanced as well as developing societies. All societies devise ways of restraining and channeling male energies. Images of what it means to be a man set standards of accomplishment which are largely the result of cultural influences. Some contain societal expectations of appropriate masculine performance in service to the community. These may range from primitive forms of bonding to more elaborate structures of conformity imposed by a broader society. While widely diverse in their expression, modes of manliness are designed to correct self-absorption, restrain violence, and resolve the inevitable tension between the demands of instinct and the tasks of civilization. The inherent vocation of the male, however, is to change, rather than to accept, what is given.

Combativeness is, of course, often a sign of male immaturity. Yet all men have an acute sense of opposition, which may bring them into conflict with their environments. The opposition may be expressed by way of athletic contests, adversarial social relations, or, more subtly, in forms of philosophical comprehension based upon rigorous division and distinction. The agonistic posture that men display in social life has been a major target of feminist criticism. Many women find the masculine disposition toward differentiation to be not only a source of their oppression but also the manifestation of an attitude toward life which is fundamentally at odds with a feminine conception of harmonious and humane existence.

The male propensity to destructive physical combat, together with the personal violence they have inflicted upon women, is justly condemned as a paramount example of masculine immaturity. At the same time, it is impossible to understand the basic dispositions with which men approach public life if one looks upon all contentiousness as inherently evil. Every male desires some battlefield. He delights in danger; but he also senses the value of the struggle to realize some purpose greater than himself. The adversarial temperament has, admittedly, violent implications; but it operates across a wide range of social activities, from organized sports to spirited academic and political debates. The dedication and disciplined service to an end required by these activities may be abused or distorted; however, any attempt to displace them entirely weakens the vitality of social existence. A wrestling with life is unavoidable, even when the action is not physical in nature. Intellectual combat, for example, not only clarifies the search for truth, it also helps to insure that citizens resolve differences according to law. A tradition of lively argument is indispensable to the progressive development of all the arts and sciences.[18]

The process of rehabilitating maleness includes a frank recognition of the extent to which men are responsible for a social world filled with violence and oppression. Men now struggle to articulate more positive and constructive standards of maleness. They also hope to preserve a degree of virility that can lead to powerful, though nonviolent, responses to the challenges of public life. As this reconstructive process continues, it is important to gauge how women will respond to this reformation of masculine identity.

18. Ong, *Fighting for Life*. See also Bly, *Iron John*, chap. 6. Psychologists have pointed to the harm that students can suffer in a contentious classroom setting. However, Bly argues: "[T]he disappearance of fierce debates is a loss. When the playful verbal combats disappear, then warriorhood becomes reduced or restricted to wrestling, football, the martial arts, guerrilla warfare, blood-and-guts movies" (*Iron John*, 164). Bly and others interested in myths see a progression from the combative stance of the warrior to the adoption of dispositions associated with kingship. This is confirmed by experience. One thinks of the careers of soldier-statesmen such as George Washington, Dwight Eisenhower, or, more recently, the dramatic peacemaking actions of Nelson Mandela in South Africa. Changes in the lives of Nobel Peace Prize awardees Yitzhak Rabin and Shimon Peres of Israel and P.L.O. chairman Yasir Arafat are also notable. The lack of such progression may be evidenced by an inordinate attraction to athletics, innocent in itself but having ominous implications, since, as Freud observed, those who love sports love war (*Moses and Monotheism*, Part III, 2.4).

Feminists are divided in their attitudes toward power and uncomfortable with the effort needed to sustain it. Some hope to eliminate fierce energy from public life and replace it with a diffuse caretaking rooted within female experiences of nurturing. Others are more concerned about how power is to be used. They recognize the importance of struggle to the performance of any public action, but they oppose the use of power to create, or sustain, hierarchies. They will also carefully assess the value of what one is laboring to achieve. Wherever interests are publicly contested the worry is over whether the results will advance, rather than interrupt, the continuities of human existence. Feminists acknowledge the need for courage; they respect bravery only when it sustains life and does not unnecessarily risk death. The general hope is that in a post-patriarchal world, human action will be directed not just to overcoming necessity but also to drawing new possibilities from it.[19]

This new sensibility denies the classical distinction between public and private life, and sees in the reproductive labor of women, with its effusion of connected care, a new paradigm for the reconstruction of the world beyond the household. An intimate experience of human continuity not only brings new life into the world; it also assists personal and social maturity. The experience of procreation is of inestimable value even though it does not exhaust the capacities of women to influence the broader world and gain personal distinction in public activities.[20]

Thoughtful feminists recognize the importance of allowing domestic values to be given their appropriate range of influence:

[W]e can learn from childrearing as a mode of creative work in which an experience of continuity and creative transformation of the world

19. Jean Bethke Elshtain, *Public Man, Private Woman*; Wendy Brown, *Manhood and Politics*.

20. Virginia Held, "Birth and Death," in *Feminism and Political Theory*, ed. Cass R. Sunstein (Chicago: University of Chicago Press, 1992), 84. Compare Carol McMillan, *Women, Reason, and Nature*.

are simultaneously featured. . . . We can engage with environment and our bodies as if they were organic and sentient rather than passive matter awaiting our imposition of form. We can learn to develop new modes of life out of historically given ones, rather than staging coups or seizing history by force, impetuousness, or rape. We can find continuity in long labors of love in which we are truly invested and represented rather than once-only deeds that record a performance rather than a person. We can prove and distinguish ourselves through our cares rather than by risking our deepest attachments. . . . We can achieve recognition for work rather than ownership, for devotion and not only daring, for ingenuity or imagination and not only audacity.[21]

This feminist political perspective is not a form of separatism which condemns the world beyond the home. Women now search for personal meaning within broader communities than the family, while not at the same time ignoring the total context of their lives. No longer shut up in the domestic sphere, they are entering into the dialogue of collective identity which occurs within the world of public action.

Feminism is bringing to end a process by which men defined the role that women should play in the various arenas of common existence. The movement has shown that women, like men, are entitled to be fully human; equally engaged in the highest achievements of economic, political, and intellectual life. Where men were once privileged to experience personal fulfillment beyond the home, now both men and women shall be free to decide, on their own, who they are and what goals they wish to pursue.[22]

Men and women now encounter each other as free persons searching for new ways of fulfillment. In this reconciliation of the public and private spheres, women are beginning to accept the masculine aspects of their own personalities while preserving their uniqueness as women. Men are also moving toward an understanding of their own imperfect existence. By enlarging the images of manliness, they hope to overcome vi-

21. Wendy Brown, *Manhood and Politics*, 205–6.
22. This is a major theme in the writings of Susan Moeller Okin. See, e.g., *Justice, Gender, and the Family* (New York: Basic Books, 1989).

olent stereotypes without, at the same time, adopting new patterns of passivity.

Two different gender dispositions: one emphasizing personal bonds, the other impersonal ends, must be given room for expression in the field of public action. It remains to be seen whether all these developments will proceed in a spirit of mutual respect and recognition. The public life of the future must not be distorted by any kind of gender stereotypes. For a civilization of sexual equality to emerge, there must be the cooperation of men and women acting together under circumstances in which the distinctive contributions of each are freely and reciprocally acknowledged.

III. *The Challenge of Feminist Jurisprudence*

Every struggle for emancipation eventually asks the legal order to legitimate its aspirations. It is, therefore, quite natural that the reform of law has been a major objective of the women's movement. In the Anglo-American world, the formal barriers to the legal recognition of women as independent persons have been removed, yet women are still deprived of the full equality under the law to which they are entitled. In theory, as well as practice, feminists are actively working for the realization of a legal system that is "unharmed by patriarchy."[23] They hope to correct all injustice based upon gender and bring both the law and legal institutions more closely into harmony with the values and goals of women.

A feminist jurisprudence has deconstructed the established myths of liberty, equality, and the rule of law, in order to uncover their gender bias. Women scholars have shown how valued conceptions of personal freedom often reflect the masculine pursuit of an isolated autonomy—an individual independence that is disconnected from deeper values of personal and social responsibility. Feminists have also exposed the way in which principles of legal equality discriminate against women

23. Heather Ruth Wishik, "To Question Everything: The Inquiries of Feminist Jurisprudence," *Berkeley Women's Law Journal* (1985): 64, 66.

when law is enforced without regard for distinctive feminine experiences. Throughout the entire field of legal studies, there has been an attempt to describe the causes and consequences of the subordination of women.[24]

To develop strategies for changing the patriarchal assumptions upon which such oppression rests requires an *interested* inquiry into the legal system. In a feminist legal method, careful analytical attention is given to a myriad of distinctive situations in which, under existing law, the subordination of women is perpetuated. Each situation is unique; its full specificity cannot be anticipated in advance. The nonconsensual aspects of sexual abuse cannot be understood without examining the trauma from the point of view of the person adversely affected. The same may be said of the harm done by pornography, or the discriminations experienced in the pursuit of employment opportunities. Concentration upon the particularity of injustice, and an insistence upon the multiple perspectives that impinge upon a given legal question, are the primary characteristics of an evolving feminist approach to law. By taking account of all indices of oppression, this effort has led to some important reforms. Yet it reflects an attitude toward the meaning and purposes of law whose general value is more problematic.

In their pursuit of legal reform, feminist scholars have sought to explain their particularistic orientation by drawing upon various modern philosophical developments. They are

24. Anne C. Scales, "The Emergence of Feminist Jurisprudence," *Yale Law Journal* 1373 (1986): 95; Joan C. Williams, "Deconstructing Gender," *Michigan Law Review* 87 (1989): 797; Deborah L. Rhode, "The Woman's Point of View," *J. Leg. Ed.* 38 (1988): 39; *Justice and Gender* (Cambridge: Harvard University Press, 1989); Herma Hill Kay, "Models of Equality," *Univ. Ill. L. Rev.* (1985): 39; Catherine A. MacKinnon, *Toward a Feminist Theory of the State* (Cambridge: Harvard University Press, 1989); Martha Minnow, *Making All the Difference: Inclusion, Exclusion, and American Law* (Ithaca: Cornell University Press, 1990); Katharine T. Bartlett, "Feminist Legal Methods," *Harv. L. Rev.* 103 (1990): 829; Lynne Henderson, "Whose Nature? Practical Reason and Patriarchy," *Cleve. State L. Rev.* 38 (1990): 169; Robin West, "Jurisprudence and Gender," *Univ. of Chic. L. Rev.* 55 (1988): 1. See also *Feminist Jurisprudence*, Patricia Smith, ed. (New York & Oxford: Oxford University Press, 1993).

attracted to pragmatism, which stresses the contextual basis of knowledge. This use of pragmatism facilitates the desire to make legal as well as moral judgments relative to a particular situation and the interests of the parties involved. Perspectivism has also been influential. The importance of a point of view places an emphasis upon the subjectivities of textual interpretation. Feminist jurisprudence also finds some justification for its methods in Aristotelian forms of practical reasoning.

In the previous chapter we observed how, in the area of practical reason, women are particularly sensitive to the need to do what is right in a specific context. And, whenever values are opposed, difficult decisions must be made. If one follows the tradition of Idealism, the tendency in such situations is to give preference to a particular value and then to weigh the alternatives with reference to that unique value's preeminence. This approach rests upon the belief that responsible choice requires the reduction of existential complexity to some uniform measure of judgment. An Aristotelian approach to practical experience rejects the idealistic solution, and does so in a way that is appealing to feminist jurists.

For Aristotle and those who follow his method, there is an explicit recognition of the divergence of values that inhere in any important practical situation. This complexity does not allow for the maximization of a single value. To be reasonable in resolving particular conflicts, one must fairly deliberate over the independent significance of all discordant values. Each separate value is an element of the good life which must be recognized for what it is, in itself, as a distinct part of a composite whole.[25]

Some feminists describe their approach to legal issues as a novel form of Aristotelian practical reasoning. Their subtle

25. Martha C. Nussbaum, *Love's Knowledge*, chap. 2. The fundamental reference is to *Nicomachean Ethics*, Bk. 6. See also Gadamer, *The Idea of the Good in Platonic-Aristotelian Philosophy*, trans. P. C. Smith (New Haven: Yale University Press, 1986); R. Beiner, *Political Judgment* (Chicago: University of Chicago Press, 1983); Charles E. Larmore, *Patterns of Moral Complexity*. Compare N. Rescher, *Ethical Idealism: An Inquiry into the Nature and Function of Ideals* (Berkeley: University of California Press, 1987), chap. 3.

awareness of the dilemmas and oppositions that inhere in specific situations, and of the need to reconcile such differences, gives their approach to legal controversies a place in traditions, a place in the Aristotelian tradition, which shows a respect for value divergence.[26] Undoubtedly, there are similarities. However, there is a tendency in feminist legal writing to avoid the heterogeneous character of conflicting values in controversies in which women have an intense interest.

In the controversies that touch upon their personal privacy feminists are not inclined to give all the diverse values their proper weight. For example, in the debates over abortion, the majority of feminist legal scholars fiercely defend freedom of choice; but they do not acknowledge the heterogeneities implicit in these tragic conflicts. Feminist jurists have explained with great eloquence the intrusive nature of an unwanted pregnancy and they defend with equal ardor the right of a woman to make her own decisions in a matter of such intimate concern.[27] But, with rare exceptions, these writings give little recognition to the independent value of the fetus. Nor do they acknowledge the societal interest in the protection of the unborn.

The argument of feminists that the complexities of the abortion problem demand deference to the discretion of the pregnant woman deserves more respect than it usually receives.

---

26. E.g., Katherine T. Bartlett, "Feminist Legal Methods." Compare Martha Minow, "Feminist Reason: Getting It and Losing It," *Journal of Legal Education* 38 (1988): 47. I apply these insights to the legal process in "Dialectical Reasoning and Personal Judgment," *University of California at Davis Law Review* 26 (1993): 623.

27. "[T]he danger an unwanted fetus poses is not to the body's security at all, but rather to the body's integrity. Similarly, the woman's fear is not that she will die but that she will cease to be or never become a self" (Robin West, "Jurisprudence and Gender," *University of Chicago Law Review* 55 (1988): 1, 59–60. See also Francis Olsen, "Unraveling Compromise," *Harv. L. Rev.* 103 (1989): 105; Joan Williams, "Abortion, Incommensurability, and Jurisprudence," *Tul. 2 Rev.* 63 (1989): 1651. For a criticism of the emphasis upon autonomy, see Elizabeth Fox-Genovese, *Feminism without Illusions.* See also Andrew Kaufman, "Judges and Scholars: To Whom Shall We Look For Our Constitutional Law," *J. Legal Ed.* 37 (1987): 184. The most recent Supreme Court decision, reaffirming the right to choose an abortion, subject to certain qualifications, is *Planned Parenthood of Southeastern Pennsylvania v. Casey,* 112 S.Ct. 2791 (1992).

There is something offensive about coercion being directly applied in a matter of such intimacy. Furthermore, those who are
opposed to abortion also fail to acknowledge the complexities
of the problem on the plane of law and politics. Whatever may
be the response of personal conscience, *as a matter of public law
and policy* the question cannot be resolved by the selection and
enforcement of a single value. In political fora, the opposing
parties defend their positions with uncompromising rigor;
within the law, however, the interests of both the pregnant
woman and the fetus must be given their due recognition.
Here the decisions are not reducible to the decisive influence
of a single principle. The conflicting interests must be given
their separate, independent, value.[28]

The abortion controversy also draws attention to some of the
epistemological premises of radical feminist reasoning. An un-
expected pregnancy dramatically accentuates the degree to
which the fortunes of women are subject to the power of male
sexuality. One faced with the dilemmas that such a pregnancy
imposes is quite understandably not inclined to believe that
the question can be resolved by reference to any impersonal
and objective criteria. It is arguable that here, if anywhere, the
positional nature of truth should be vindicated. The one who
truly knows what is at stake is the one who is undergoing the
experience; preference to her judgment may be required, not
only because of considerations of privacy, but because the matter is, in principle, subjective by its very nature. But this subjectivity, which accentuates immediate experience, overlooks
the abstract quality of objective principles:

The main difficulty with this position lies in its repudiation of any
attempt to define life in the abstract. For, if a rigid and abstract def-

---

28. Compare Laurence Tribe, *Abortion: The Clash of Absolutes,* with Martha
Nussbaum, *Love's Knowledge.* Nussbaum points out that in the Aristotelian
tradition there is a picture of choice as a quality-based selection among goods
that are plural and heterogeneous, each being chosen for its own distinctive
value: "To value each separate constituent of the good life for what it is in itself
entails, then, recognizing its distinctness and separateness from each of the
other constituents each being an irreplaceable part of a composite whole"
(56–57).

inition of life embodies dichotomous male thinking, it also embodies the highest standard of civilization—the great respect for human life in all its diversity—that human beings have been able to devise . . .

The second difficulty with this position lies in its assumption that one individual can determine another individual's desires. . . . To say . . . that we have a right to decide which living being would and would not want to live under which conditions is to assume precisely that arrogant disregard for another's subjectivity for which feminists condemn men's attitudes toward women.[29]

A charge often made against men is that, being absorbed in abstraction, they do not fully understand the harms experienced by women. However, the observation quoted above— by a woman writer—suggests that, if personal experience becomes legally decisive whenever there is an opposition of values, it will be impossible to maintain that balance between public and private life which is so essential to the fabric of general order.[30]

The opposition between abstract and concrete values that inheres in the conflicts over abortion reappears throughout the entire legal process. Men aspire to objectivity, and this disposition is reflected within the whole of legal culture. Some feminists see it as evidence of the male ambition to dominate and control. The law, as established by men, is interpreted as an expression of will, producing legal methods and procedures that are both hierarchical and authoritarian. This distanced le-

29. *Feminism without Illusions*, 84.
30. The tendency of some radical feminists to make the situation of the women decisive is not only incompatible with an Aristotelian notion of complexity; it also ignores the context in which practical reasoning and judgment occur: "[W]e must insist that Aristotelian practical wisdom is not a rootless situational perception that rejects all guidance from on-going commitments and values. A person of practical wisdom is a person of good character, that is to say, a person who has internalized . . . certain ethical values and a certain conception of the good human life. . . . If there were no such guidelines and no such sense of being bound to a character, if the 'eye of the soul' saw each situation as simply new and non-repeatable, the perceptions of practical wisdom would begin to look arbitrary and empty" (Martha C. Nussbaum, *The Fragility of Goodness* [Cambridge: Cambridge University Press, 1986], 306). For a discussion of how radical feminism, like the so-called 'recovery' movement, assumes that there are no objective measures of suffering, see Wendy Kaminer, "Feminism's Identity Crisis," *Atlantic* (October 1993), 51, 66–67.

gal regime, it is argued, ignores the plight of women. It also disregards others similarly disadvantaged by existing law.

Critical studies of existing legal structures have shown how a presumed objectivity can actually favor existing divisions of power and sustain hierarchies which obstruct the development of personal and social identities.[31] These studies raise important general issues of injustice, which are beyond the scope of the present study. But they provoke a reconsideration of the value of the quest for objectivity as a characteristic disposition of the male gender.

The male propensity toward abstraction is difficult to comprehend. It is impossible to determine how much of the general attraction of men to abstract reasoning is innate, and to what degree it is caused by cultural influences. Some factors can, however, be identified. We have already noted how the inclination toward impersonal goals is a recurrent aspect of masculine engagement in public life. Objectification is a related phenomenon. In the pursuit of scientific, economic, or political achievements, men translate their activities into some objective form, which continues to exist independently of the original action. Cultural creations become self-contained: transcending the individual, they perpetuate themselves according to their own immanent principles. Propensities toward reification reflect the specialization of complex societies. They are more compatible with a masculine than a feminine temperament.[32]

Because of his impersonal orientation, the male can participate in objectified practices without undergoing any threat to his personality. Without experiencing a challenge to his self-

31. The work of Roberto Mangabeira, which is critical to this development, shares many of the concerns of radical feminism. See my study, *Descent into Subjectivity* (Wakefield, N.H.: Longwood Academic Press, 1990), chap. 3.

32. Georg Simmel, *On Women, Sexuality, and Love,* trans. Guy Oaks (New Haven: Yale University Press, 1984). See also, Walter Ong, *Fighting for Life,* chap. 3. A characteristic of this disposition may be seen in the description of Ronald Reagan by his close associate, James Baker. Reagan was, according to Baker, "the kindest and most impersonal man I ever knew" (Peggy Noonan, *What I Saw at the Revolution* [New York: Random House, 1990], 150).

identity, he can, with good conscience, approach his work with genuine detachment. The male is, as we have already pointed out, prone to see the significance of his life in terms of contact with an external domain. This is his mode of inhabiting and perfecting our common world. For a woman, by contrast, it is more difficult to sustain distinctions between objective and subjective existence. Less able to endure the separation of the self from its objects, a woman is not as easily distanced from the specific activities in which she is engaged. What she does is more intimately related to who she is. In this, she has an advantage. Since her nature is more integrated, the various parts of her life are not easily separated from the whole of her existence.[33]

In the development of any cultural activity where men have predominated, objectivity is not asexual. But if it is "biased," it is so in the sense that the process of establishing normative structures that outlast their creators is a distinctly masculine mode of being. These forms of impersonal creation are relevant to the accusations which radical feminists make about the legal system. The objectification of the legal process is not inherently unjust. Nor is it, necessarily, the manifestation of a masculine desire to dominate women. And although it is more compatible with a masculine temperament, it is not an exclusively male mode of dealing with public experience. Here, as with all qualities of mind, there are androgynous implications.

It may be objected that even if the tendency men have toward objectification is not designed to perpetuate female oppression, it is, nonetheless, an example of that masculinization of thought we have already noted as being a deplorable consequence of rationalism. The modern legal systems of the West were significantly influenced by the Enlightenment; furthermore, it may be remembered the Enlightenment proclaimed that authentic thinking always occurs beyond experience. Rationality was understood as an activity of the mind with itself,

33. Simone de Beauvoir, *The Second Sex*, Part 7.

and this attitude influenced vast domains of human activity. In science and culture, including law, one was encouraged to leave the given world and reconstruct it within.[34] The habits of mind engendered by these ideals undoubtedly contribute to those attitudes of disengagement and distancing which feminists working within the law find so objectionable. However, if one takes account of the whole legal tradition, one will discover much closer connections between reason and experience.

From its beginnings, Western legal science has been based upon a dialectical mode of reasoning. Moving back and forth between theory and detail, it is a process in which inductive logic predominates over deductive reasoning. Throughout this history, the thinking of lawyers and judges has always been more practical than speculative.[35] Nevertheless, there has also been a tendency toward generalization and abstraction so persistent and pervasive that it can not be attributed solely to the influence of rationalism or the ideals of the Enlightenment.

Since the time when legal studies assumed an independent significance in Western history, there has been a palpable effort to identify and define jural elements that, being repeated in particular instances, suggest that they share similar features. This led jurists of both the continental and common law traditions to articulate general conceptions, rules, and standards that might provide a more comprehensive understanding of the legal process as a whole. Those who have borne responsibility for the development of the legal order have sought to discover deeper reasons for specific legal doctrines. They have also tried to assess the significance of jural events under generally viable standards of practical reason. In light of feminist attacks upon legal objectivity, it is worth exploring

34. Charles Taylor, *Sources of the Self* (Cambridge: Harvard University Press, 1980). See the fuller discussion in Chapter 2 of the present work.
35. Charles M. Radding, *The Origins of Medieval Jurisprudence* (New Haven: Yale University Press, 1988); Harold J. Berman, *Law and Revolution* (Cambridge: Harvard University Press, 1983), chap. 3; Roscoe Pound, *Law Finding through Reason and Experience* (Athens: University of Georgia Press, 1960).

whether this abstractive orientation has humanistic value, or whether it simply provides a further example of the lamentable tendency of men to try constantly to transcend the natural contexts of existence.

In law, as in any field of culture, the pursuit of higher, more general, purposes reveals that search for deeper meaning which we have already identified as an essential aspect of reason. It is, simultaneously, part of the personal quest for the good. Juridical reason is not indifferent to the substantive content of thought, because it is determined to apprehend the various aspects of the good that lie within its range of inquiry. This is a questioning which has important practical consequences when one turns from thought to judgment.

The impulse toward transcendence in juridical thought manifests a conviction that the enduring values of a legal order must be given priority over the more subtle aspects of specific occasions. The balance to be struck between the general and particular, in any specific instance, is controversial, and the matter does not, of itself, have any gender significance.[36] As might be expected, women jurists have usually sided with those who give preference to the factual over the normative in the resolution of legal controversies. The more interesting question is whether women should automatically align themselves with every attitude toward law which, by its obstinate preference for experience, inevitably restricts the range of reason. It is a question which bears directly upon the quest for the complete emancipation of women in the world of common action.

A primary purpose for removing the barriers to women's participation in public life was to make possible their complete involvement in all aspects of human culture. This ideal bears especially upon those activities that evoke the highest poten-

36. The writings of Frederick Schauer address this controversy. See *Playing by the Rules* (New York: Oxford University Press, 1991). See also "Rules and the Rule of Law," *Harv. Journal of Law & Public Policy* 14 (1991): 645. See also Schauer, "Formalism," *Yale Law Journal* 97 (1988): 509 and "The Jurisprudence of Reasons" (Bk. Rev.), *Michigan Law Review* 85 (1987): 847.

tialities of human nature. As we have already emphasized, there must not be any a priori limits to the powers of understanding which women, as well as men, might bring to bear upon the more complex problems of civilization. With that objective in mind, it is well to remember that the supreme accomplishments of any culture include an effort to subject the world to the order of reason. And reason has a range which an obsession with particularity is unable to comprehend.

Whenever mind is alert and active, it becomes dissatisfied with various ways of merely coping with experience. Reason then expresses itself as a desire for a deeper, fuller intelligibility. In the previous chapter, we explained some of the roots of this basic inclination. We showed how any attempt to grasp the whole order of things brings together, in concert, the powers of intellect and intuition. One manifestation of this spirit within the legal process can be seen in forms of reasoning designed to trace the interconnectedness of the concepts which inform all significant juridical relationships.

An acute sense of injustice may ferret out subtle discriminations, but too great a pursuit of the particular often mixes ideological conviction with the administration of justice. The effort to acquire a more adequate comprehension of the law arises out of a conviction that law is intelligible in itself and not subservient to any external purposes.[37] Those who embark upon such an intellectual journey gain the satisfaction of perceiving the basic and diverse goods that justify the autonomy of the legal process and give jural life its richness and variety. They also gain the power to confront the future with a confidence born of liberation from detail.

The tendency of men to subordinate experience to rules, and to rise from rules to principles, appears in different ways throughout the entire legal process. Feminist jurists look upon this orientation with skepticism. They believe that an appeal to abstraction provides men with a means of avoiding the emo-

37. Ernest J. Weinreb, "Legal Formalism: On The Immanent Rationality of Law," *Yale L.J.* 97 (1988): 949; Summers, "Theory, Formality, and Practical Legal Criticism," *L.Q. Rev.* 106 (1990): 407.

tional dimensions of existence. Adherence to the rule of law may be advanced as a noble ideal; it can also encourage proclivities toward detachment and control which continue existing patterns of gender oppression.[38] These objections have some merit. But it is also important to account for the values that sustain the search for broader standards of meaning.

Consider impartiality. Impartiality entails the development and application of neutral principles to legal conflicts. This is done in order to assure that important judgments rest upon some foundation greater than the personal preferences of a particular judge. For law to be something more than pure power, the justifications offered for specific decisions should rely upon reasons that transcend the immediate result.[39] This obligation to adhere to the impartial articulation of principle may frustrate the desire of an individual judge to do what he or she thinks justice requires in a particular circumstance. But the frustration may be understandable when the specifics of a given situation are considered with reference to the purposes of the legal system as a whole.

To act upon principle is to act for reasons that apply to all who are similarly situated. Such an ideal transcends particular contexts, but it does not require an indifference to them. It is not illogical for a pattern of decisions to be both contextual and principled. Women may be more hesitant than men to evoke principles as reasons of judgment, as they are usually more aware of how abstract standards are subject to various quali-

38. See, e.g., Lynne H. Henderson, "Legality and Sympathy," *Michigan Law Review* 85 (1987): 1574. But see Toni Massaro, "Empathy, Legal Storytelling, and the Rule of Law," *Michigan Law Review* 87 (1989): 2099, for a critique of Henderson.

39. Judicial decisions make value choices which must be defended by criteria which distinguishes these functions from expressions of pure power. They must be principled: "A principled decision . . . is one that rests on reasons with respect to all the issues in the case, reasons that in their generality and their neutrality transcend any immediate result that is involved" (Wechsler, "Principles of Constitutional Law," *Harvard Law Review* 73 (1959): 1. Professor Henderson refers to this as an indication of the flight to abstraction. See further Kent Greenawalt, *Law and Objectivity* (New York: Oxford University Press, 1992).

fications.[40] If the law is to be fair to all affected by its power, it must reduce some contingencies to rules, which, by their normative force, restrict the intensity of inquiry into the details of a perceived injustice.

The general use of a legal standard that gives preference to the general over the particular is one manifestation of the principle of equality. Feminists have shown that when equality disdains difference, injustice is the result.[41] But neither women nor men can afford to ignore how, in general, broad standards assert the supremacy of reason over experience. These values may require the uniqueness of a given situation to give way to wider, more comprehensive norms, whose purpose is to justify the legal order as a whole.

The abstract, generalized, quality of legal normativity contributes to a culture of enduring standards and also promotes consistent and impartial justice. But it must be admitted that these justifications do not fully address the concerns that modern women express about the ultimate purposes of a legal order. Feminist practical reasoning recognizes the importance of both contextualization and abstraction, but resists the idea that legal norms should ever be given a hierarchical predominance in the administration of justice. Feminists advocate a more open-ended approach, not only to remove oppression, but also to allow adequate scope to the deeper levels of affection that are engaged in all important human relationships. To them, jurisprudence is patriarchal because it is abstract and because it does not make adequate use of the values woman can bring to the administration of justice.

The rule of law may have replaced the Hobbesian state of nature, but men continue to relate to each other with fear and suspicion. Their stance of individual isolation provides a foun-

40. George Sher, "Other Voices, Other Rooms," in *Women and Moral Theory,* ed. Eva Feder Kittay and Diana T. Meyers (Totowa: Rowman & Littlefield, 1987).
41. Alison M. Jaggar, "Sexual Difference and Sexual Equality" in *Theoretical Perspectives on Sexual Difference,* ed. Deborah L. Rhode (New Haven: Yale University Press, 1990), 239.

dation for an ostensibly rational system of legal rights and duties; for women, however, this structure is seriously deficient because it ignores the importance of a positive relation to others:

> Women's concept of value revolves not around the axis of autonomy, individuality, justice and rights, as does men's, but instead around the axis of intimacy, nurturance, community, responsibility and care. For women, the creation of value, and the living of a good life, therefore depend upon relational, contextual, nurturant and affective responses to the needs of those who are dependent and weak, while for men the creation of value, and the living of the good life, depend upon the ability to respect the rights of independent co-equals, and the deductive, cognitive ability to infer from those rights rules for safe living. These two "official" stories sharply contrast.
>
> . . . Women value and have a special competency for intimacy, nurturance, and relational thinking, and a special vulnerability to, and fear of, isolation, separation from the other, and abandonment, just as men value and have a special competency for autonomy, and a special vulnerability to and fear of annihilation.[42]

Men look upon the legal order as a civilized realm of liberty; women insist that to the extent that law prefers autonomy over relatedness, it becomes a means of displacing responsibility for the realization of justice. The appeal to neutral principles can mask an atomistic conception of social life in which isolated individuals, demanding their rights, avoid the deeper obligations that arise out of the interconnectedness of our common plight.[43]

Women want to keep law from being an impersonal mechanism whose only purpose is to regulate abstract relationships between antagonistic, separated egoists. Women also bring to the administration of justice an imaginative and emotional understanding of the harms experienced by the more vulner-

---

42. Robin West, "Jurisprudence and Gender," *Univ. Chic. L. Rev.* 55 (1988): 1, 28. For a Chinese appraisal of the American male's fear of others, and of lasting obligations, see Francis L. K. Hsu, *American and Chinese*, 3d ed. (Honolulu: University of Hawaii Press, 1981), chap. 11.

43. Carol Gilligan, *In a Different Voice* (Cambridge: Harvard University Press, 1982). But see Seyla Benhabib, "The Generalized and Concrete Other," in *Feminism as Critique*.

able members of the community. In empathy, a certain sympathy is operative, through which one tries to understand the predicament of another in a unique, particular situation. Such a project does not, of itself, offend standards of impartiality, for its purpose is to understand rather than to identify with a painful experience.

Within feminist jurisprudence there is also a discernible shift from entitlements to responsibilities. For many women, justice is more a response to a wrong than it is an affirmation of right. This sense of injustice manifests a person's capacity for righteous indignation. Such women see less room for "neutrality" because, for them, the doing of justice is connected with a passionate desire to correct any wrongdoing that is revealed, in context, through a sympathetic understanding of a specific injury. As the center of gravity shifts to the situation, antecedent measures of legality, and right, do not have the same significance they possess in a male-centered jural world.[44]

Injustice frequently causes suffering, but not all suffering springs from injustice. Woman, however, does not make this distinction; in the feminine code everything that can cause suffering to others, and can be avoided, is unjust; everything that can give happiness without harming anyone is just, and consequently legal. To woman all actions that caused unhappiness and need not have done so, even if they were authorized or imposed by law are a source of regret and re-

44. This is a pervasive theme in the works of women who are legal scholars. See, e.g., the authorities cited supra, n. 24. For a fuller development, see Elizabeth H. Wolgast, *The Grammar of Justice* (Ithaca: Cornell University Press, 1987). Similar themes can be found in the field of political theory. In her study of Adam Smith, Patricia Werhane observes: "[W]e truly project ourselves into another experience, according to Smith, in order to understand—although not experience—what another person is feeling rather than merely to relate that situation to our own. Sympathy is the comprehension of what another feels or might feel in a situation, but it is not an experimental or sentimental identification with that feeling. With the help of imagination, sympathy is the means through which we place ourselves in another's situation and conceive of what another feels, experiences, or is capable of feeling in a particular situation or set of circumstances" (Patricia H. Werhane, *Adam Smith and His Legacy for Modern Capitalism* [New York: Oxford University Press, 1991], 33). See also Edith Stein, *On the Problem of Empathy*, trans. Waltrant Stein, 2d ed. (The Hague: Martinus Nijhoff, 1970).

morse. . . . Woman makes no distinction between a mean action and a violation of the law.[45]

This desire to correct all wrongs and heal all wounds also reveals a difference in the way that women understand social relations. A woman prefers to treat others as though they were neighbors rather than strangers, and she is impatient with legal doctrines, such as those holding no duty to rescue someone toward whom there is no special duty, because such doctrines emphasize the distance between individuals.[46] This attitude, which is part of a deeper desire to close the gap between the public and private worlds, is deserving of respect. But it must also be noted that there are limits to legal connectedness that are not simply male expressions of mutual fear.

Law aspires to do equal justice between persons. Thus it must treat individuals as being, in important respects, distinct from one another. Justice is the giving to another what is his or her due; without some separation, we cannot determine what is owed:

Private law focuses upon the immediate transaction between the parties, and the juridical construal of this transaction filters away their loves and hates, hopes and despairs, needs and apprehensions. Con-

45. Gina Lombroso, *The Soul of Woman* (New York: E. P. Dutton, 1923). Cf. Christine Hoff Summers, "Feminism and Resentment," in Symposium, Feminist Theory Reconsidered, in *Reason Papers* No. 18 (Fall 1993). Summers recognizes the relation between righteous moral indignation and resentment, but insists that they are, to some degree, distinguishable. Resentment "rationalizes, justifies, and fosters in women a wholesale rancor. It has little to do with moral indignation. Resentment may begin in and include indignation, but it is by far the more abiding passion" (2).

46. A desire to bring principles of care and concern to tort law can be seen in the writings of Leslie Bender. See, e.g., "Feminist (Re) Torts: Thoughts on the Liability Crises, Mass Torts, Power and Responsibilities" *Duke L. J.* (1990): 848; "A Lawyer's Primer on Feminist Theory and Tort," 38 *J. Legal Ed.* 3 (1988). Compare the discussion of "Who Is My Neighbor" in Donoghue v. Stevenson (1932) A.C. 562, 580. (Lord Atkin).

A similar issue is the balance to be struck between justice and mercy. "[J]ustice is an authentic virtue in man. . . . Nevertheless love is 'greater' than justice. . . . The primacy and superiority of love *vis à vis* justice . . . are revealed precisely through mercy . . ." (John Paul II, *Dives in misericordia,* encyclical of November 30, 1980).

versely, when a certain aspect of solidarity, such as love, is thought to be the defining feature of a relationship "the King's Writ does not seek to run." . . . Private law treats the parties as mutually external, postulating only the recognition of others as others and not the sharing of a life of passion.[47]

This observation about the limits of the private law of torts, property, and contract has much wider implications. There are some general limits to the range of affectivity in the overall ordering of legal and political life. Generosity is in short supply in societies that are so large and complex that they cannot be effectively governed by standards applicable to face-to-face encounters. The passions that directly motivate personal action are not suitable to the broader requirements of social union. A natural, affectionate concern for others does not have the range or extension necessary for enduring social stability. The mutual advantage of all must be protected by rules that, although are not always compatible with particular interests, will over time promote a general good.[48]

IV. The Ambiguities of Public Life

The misunderstandings between men and women concerning the boundaries of law turn in part upon the qualities of

47. Ernest J. Weinrib, "Enduring Passion" (Bk. Rev.) *Yale L. J.* 94 (1985): 1825. (While this observation is made in a critique of the passional dimension of critical legal studies, it has an obvious relevance to the present reflections.) If law must distance itself from the intensity of intimate life, it is equally true that reliance upon legal rights may not advance the development of healthy interpersonal relations. See John Hardwig, "Should Women Think in Terms of Rights?" in *Feminism and Political Theory*, ed. Cass R. Sunstein (Chicago: University of Chicago Press, 1990), 53. See also Martha Minow, *Making All the Difference* (Ithaca: Cornell Univ. Press, 1990), chap. 9. Minow points out that rights are means of interpreting communal experience; they can never fully express individual experience.

48. Hume, *A Treatise of Human Nature*, Bk. 3, Pt. 2, 1–3. See also "An Inquiry Concerning the Principles of Morals," chap. 2, in Hume's *Moral and Political Philosophy*, ed. H. D. Aiken (1972). Annette Baier's writings on the virtues of trustworthiness reveal both the possibilities of extending personal virtues from private to public life and a sensitivity to the limits of such an extension. See her paper "Trust and Antitrust," in *Feminism and Political Theory*, ed. Cass R. Sunstein (Chicago: University of Chicago Press, 1990), 279.

character that are engaged as one moves from realms of intimacy to the broader world of impersonal relations. One important consequence of the women's movement has been to demonstrate the personal nature of human action in every aspect of common life. Feminism has contributed to the revival of interest in how individual choices are explicable in terms of virtues and vices. But there are deeper complexities. The tension between nearness and distancing—which we explored in our reflections on gender—gain renewed importance as one tries to articulate the distinctiveness of public life. Differences between men and women at this level are not limited to what is explicable by biological or anthropological reflections. They also depend upon one's conception of the nature of the world beyond the home.

In their struggle to lessen the distance between the public and private spheres, feminists hope to heal the division between those who sustain life and those who try to transcend the elementary obligations of existence. Drawing upon their own experience, feminists see the public world as a place where we are engaged with necessity. Here, we must deal with the stubborn actualities of our bodily being as well engage ourselves in the pursuit of abstract values. They insist that reproduction and life maintenance are intrinsic elements of the common good. Having those values in mind, they are vehemently opposed to the Aristotelian separation of the public and private realms.

Feminists are also searching for a more meaningful and personal conception of political activity. They demand new standards of public action to replace the masculine warrior mentality, which, unfortunately, continues to bring so much suffering and destruction to the human family. There is a preference for models of behavior that will release the creative aspirations of the human spirit while sustaining the harmonies and continuities of existence. Women look for new ways of collective being—ways graciously developed rather than forcibly imposed.

The failure of the Aristotelian tradition to grasp either the intrinsic value of family life or its public importance was a fundamental error, which must be admitted by all who are otherwise attracted to the classical conception of political existence. But the desire to maintain some distance between the public and private worlds has been based upon reasons other than an indifference to reproductive values. The primary concern has been to keep the *polis* sufficiently independent of other concerns to give adequate scope to all the possibilities of human action.

To the ancients, the household was controlled by higher powers, which determined the ends to be pursued. The elementary tasks of creating and sustaining life were imposed from without by the gods. "Nature," wrote Aristotle, "by this cycle . . . fulfills her purpose of perpetuating existence."[49] What made public life distinctive was the fact that its *telos*, being virtually indeterminate, could be freely developed. The men who were engaged in public life could collectively decide upon the general terms of coexistence and, in so doing, realize a freedom higher than what one could hope to achieve within the world of domesticity.

This elevation of public over private life is justly condemned by women for its discriminatory premises and its exclusionary effect.[50] However, it must be pointed out that a continuing desire to maintain the special character of public life does not logically entail a denial of the importance or significance of the

49. The *Oeconomica* 3, in vol. 23 *Aristotle*, G. Cyril Armstrong, trans., (Cambridge: Harvard Univ. Press, 1969).

50. Drawing upon themes of sociobiology, Thomas Fleming would make the family the basic sexual unit and restore the subordination of women to men within families and communities. This "natural law" of male domination would be carefully balanced by an obligation to care for women and children. Thomas Fleming, *The Politics of Human Nature* (New Brunswick: Transaction Books, 1988). This thesis is effectively refuted by Elizabeth Fox-Genovese. She points out that, should we reach a point in human development where men were effectively obligated to support the women and children for whom they are responsible, there will no longer be ". . . any biological justification for depriving women of the full development of their demonstrable capacities for social, political, and culturally useful labor of all kinds" *Feminism without Illusions*, at 50.

domestic realm. Aristotelians who continue to insist upon the distinction between public and private life are opposed to other aspects of social existence that obstruct that human flourishing which the *polis* is meant to achieve.

Classical theory dimly perceived the presence of a social world, a place of human activity that existed somewhere between the public and private spheres. Society, as a distinct reality, was at first only dimly perceived. It developed slowly, and as it did, it gradually drew to itself economic activities that had originally fallen within the scope of domestic activity. In modern life, the social realm is an arena dominated by economic considerations—the production and consumption of goods and services, repeated in cycles of inexorable necessity. To modern Aristotelians, this endless expansion of the socio-economic sphere endangers the exceptional nature of the public world and the opportunities for personal fulfillment which involvement in that broader world would otherwise provide.[51] One consequence of this unfolding of necessity is the prominence given to social values in the field of political action. The good of life is increasingly limited to sheer existence. The highest good—beyond technological development or financial growth—is whatever makes life easier or longer. Private concerns are the substance of the general welfare, because the economy is as much a political as it is a social activity.

Social security—which, broadly conceived, embraces all the vulnerabilities of human existence—has become an integral part of the political programs of all modern governments. These values are not to be scorned, especially when they hold out a possibility of reasonable well-being to those who would otherwise be destitute. The common interest in material welfare is what makes the economic dimensions of social existence the concern of modern public policy. The difficulty is that whenever relations of exchange and consumption predominate, the imperatives of immediate need not only drive public policy, they also determine the nature and duration of what-

51. Hannah Arendt, *The Human Condition*, chap. 2 (1958). See also, "What Is Freedom?" in *Between Past and Future* (1961).

ever union exists among peoples. As the public become consumers rather than citizens, they develop a sense of togetherness in which the central trait is that of simply being alive and, hopefully, sharing in a common prosperity.[52]

Where problems of survival gain political priority there is still some opportunity for the realization of higher ends. Principles of commutative justice regulate the reciprocities of exchange. By, for example, insisting upon the good faith performance of valid contracts, these principles affirm the good in a way that surpasses the basic desire for self-preservation.[53] And the application of standards of equality to the needs of those who are either disadvantaged or suffer discrimination elevates any society whose horizons would otherwise be limited to material ends. However, when the socioeconomic dynamic eclipses the political, there is a loss of the deeper forms of human connectedness which are the foundations of enduring community. There are few opportunities for persons to come together to discuss and resolve the permanent problems of public life— problems that include but also surpass the elementary requirements of existence.

The importance of public life and its priorities may be glimpsed through the difficulties now being experienced by the European community. The initial Danish rejection of the Maastricht treaty has forced thoughtful Europeans to consider

52. "Society is the form in which the fact of mutual dependence for the sake of life and nothing else assumes public significance and when the activities connected with sheer survival are permitted to appear in public." *The Human Condition* at 46. Habermas, in his analysis of the institutional structure of modern societies, would align the family and the public sphere while joining the capitalistic economy and administrative state within the systematically integrated domain of material reproduction. This has been challenged by feminists as exaggerating the differences between the family household and the economy. Like the workplace, the family is a domain of ". . . labor, exchange, calculation, distribution and exploitation . . ." Nancy Fraser, What's Critical about Critical Theory?" in *Feminism As Critique*, 31, 37.

53. This is the essential theme of Robert Nozick's neo-Lockean social philosophy. See: *Anarchy, State, and Utopia* (1974). Compare, F. A. Hayek, Legislation and Liberty, in 2 *The Mirage of Social Justice* (1976). For an attempt to establish the ethical value of wealth maximization, see Richard A. Posner, *The Economics of Justice* (1981).

whether the integration of diverse economies is, of itself, sufficient to the establishment of a durable society. Where primary loyalties are to existing nation states, any attempt at more inclusive union would require something more than material unification. Attention must also be given to problems of coexistence that are of a more constitutive than economic nature. In some appropriate fora, questions of political structure and authority will ultimately have to be addressed by all who hope to overcome basic instabilities. There must be some deliberation and decision over other fundamental questions of a common life that have heretofore been avoided.[54] These foundational questions relate to a different order of values than those associated with sheer existence or with material comfort and prosperity.

There are other examples in contemporary life that dramatically demonstrate how the range of the political cannot be limited to the socioeconomic sphere. The breakup of the Soviet Union and the transformations in South Africa reveal how fundamental matters of governmental structure and political concord have priority over matters of exchange and consumption. The genocide in the Balkans and in Rwanda remind us of how important it is for individuals to transcend elementary attachments and relate to each other as citizens rather than as tribal rivals struggling to survive. And the process of building democratic institutions, in Haiti and elsewhere throughout the

54. See generally, John Pinder, *European Community* (New York: Oxford University Press, 1991). For editorial opinion on the consequences of the Danish vote, see: Julia Anguita, *Renegociar Maastricht*, El Pais, 12 de Junio, 1992, p.12. Compare: Conor Cruise O'Brien, "Toward European Disunion," *Harpers* 285 (July 1992), 18. It is important to compare, and distinguish, the conception of political life being developed in the text from what Habermas designates as "communicatively achieved" modes of social integration. We agree with feminists who insist that family life should aspire to such freely exchanged ideas of coexistence rather than rely upon a presumed normativity of shared values which often reflect inequalities of power. See Nancy Fraser, op.cit., supra. As for the realm of public discourse much of what Habermas says about the importance of open dialogue confirms our textual argument. However, Habermas may be interpreted as postulating an unacceptable opposition between reason and desire. See the important challenge of Iris Marion Young, "Impartiality and the Civic Public," in *Feminism as Critique*.

globe, reaffirms the value of learning to live together in a common world—a fundamental theme in classical political philosophy.[55]

These deepest dimensions of political existence reveal a desire for permanence that is deeply rooted in the human heart. The prayer of Aeneas, that the gods "grant us a walled home of our own, a place for tired men, a future and continuing city,"[56] reflects the aspirations of all who commit themselves to the establishment or flourishing of some commonwealth. Because of these aspirations, which surpass contingent necessity, the scope of public life can never be reduced to purely private concerns.

Preserving the uniqueness of the public world is a goal more humanistically compelling than any hypermasculine desires for fame and glory. Mixing metaphors, one might suggest that the political world has its own "household" values, and that they are, in important respects, different from those which characterize life in the domestic realm. The *polis* is, or should be, a place where citizens make a home for themselves during their life on earth. A public realm arises whenever men and women move beyond the family circle and meet in a space where, acting together (or through those whom they have authorized), they consider, argue, and resolve problems that are common to all. In such gatherings, regard is directed toward modes of living together, which give any society its fundamental character. Those who participate act out of a desire to preserve what has preceded them and to create something that will endure beyond their passing.[57]

55. In an ongoing political regime, a larger outlook arises whenever fundamental matters of pluralistic concord have to be resolved. The Supreme Court refers to our Constitution as "a covenant running from the first generation of Americans to us and then to future generations. It is a coherent succession . . ." *Planned Parenthood of Southeastern Pennsylvania v. Casey*, 112 S.Ct. (1992): 2791, 2833.

56. Virgil, *The Aeneid*, Bk. III, C. Day Lewis, trans; (New York: Doubleday & Company, 1953).

57. For discussions of the dimension of permanence in the thought of Hannah Arendt, see B. Parekh, *Hannah Arendt and the Search For a New Political*

The purpose of joint action in public space is to overcome elementary discord and establish the means for peacefully reconciling the conflicts that inevitably arise in the course of a shared social existence. The field of action is more difficult and challenging than any imagined dialogue or hypothetical agreement. While this articulation of the public world may arise in the continuous development of a particular political community, its meaning is much deeper than conventional politics. There is no elementary division between friends and enemies. Speaking and acting is not limited to protecting or advancing specific interests. Nor is "consciousness raising" or seizure of power the overarching objective. The political, in the sense intended here, refers to all efforts, in public, to establish by persuasion and dialogue the objective conditions for a stable common life.[58]

There is nothing in this conception of a public life that is opposed to the interests of women. In fact, it opens new opportunities for them. And it has a meaning for men as well. This elevated sense of the political calls upon them to reassess their conception of virility and to cease looking upon the public world as a field of perpetual enmity and primitive competition.[59] The separation of the public from the private world in the sense intended here also does not exclude values connected with reproduction or economic necessities. But it recognizes that living creatively is more important then just existing. In its advancement toward a richer "intellectual and

---

Philosophy, Ch. 6 and Peter Fuss, "Hannah Arendt's Conception of Political Community," in the Recovery of the Public World.

58. See L. Strauss, "On Classical Political Philosophy," in Political Philosophy (H. Gilden, ed. 1975). Survival in a time of oppression is treated as an accomplishment by some feminist writers, e.g. Ruth Ginzberg, "Philosophy Is Not A Luxury," in Feminist Ethics, Ch. 8.

59. This is beginning to be seen as a challenge to maleness: "The challenges seem overwhelming, and we are understandably tempted to retreat into professions and corporations that swallow us, into private pleasures and high consumption. But lets call it what it is: moral cowardice, abdication of responsibility, voluntary myopia. . . . The historical challenge for modern man is clear—to discover a peaceful form of virility and to create an ecological commonwealth, to become fierce gentlemen" (Sam Keen, Fire in the Belly, 121).

emotional life, building collective existence, inventing new possibility, stretching horizons"[60] it is an ideal of community that should appeal to all persons of good will.

Feminists who recognize that the scope of public action is not limited to matters of reproduction or life maintenance have been as much concerned about the personal qualities of those engaged in public activities as they have been about the objectives they might pursue. Under conditions of masculine dominance, fear and suspicion have been the operative motives for political engagement. When women were excluded from participation, they looked upon men in public life as "the successors of the early warriors . . . around the campfire plotting the next day's attack."[61] Feminists wish to bring values of mutual trust into the public world so that caring and connectedness can replace more destructive forms of human encounter. This drawing of the political toward the personal is a vast improvement over a politics of violence and enmity, and it constitutes a decisive repudiation of the Machiavellian and Hobbesian conceptions of public affairs. An emphasis upon interpersonal contact and affirmation also corresponds with important developments in the forms of civic action that have emerged in response to the demands of democratic life.

In modern societies, public space is often occupied by inert bureaucracies, leaving the social world to be dominated by impersonal market mechanisms. The sterility of these landscapes is inhospitable to our deepest needs for human connection and fulfillment.[62] The steady increase in voluntary organizations is an attempt to humanize these otherwise hopeless spheres of

60. Wendy Brown, *Manhood and Politics*, 206–07.
61. Attributed to Eleanor Roosevelt, in Blanche Wiesen Cook, Vol. I, *Eleanor Roosevelt 1884–1933* (New York: Viking Press, 1992), 367. Her review of the lives of great men led Virginia Woolf to conclude that, with the exception of literature, "All the other professions according to the testimony of biography, seem to be as bloodthirsty as the profession of arms itself . . ." *Three Guineas* (New York: Harcourt, Brace, and World, 1938), 63.
62. Compare the appraisal of the world of Max Weber in Wendy Brown, op. cit., Ch. 7.

social action. Neighborhood groups, public service associations, and nongovernmental bodies, operating on both the national and international plane, testify to a new surge of civic vitality and concern. These activities enrich the social world and lessen the distance between public and private life.[63]

Civic associations attract persons who desire to move beyond the circle of their immediate concerns and make a positive contribution to the general good through some form of engagement with fellow citizens. These organizations cannot be classified under criteria based upon a traditional public/private dualism. Though they are independent of public authority, they do not serve purely private interests. And, while they are committed to some general good, they do not act as agents of the state. Their relevance to these reflections upon feminism lies in the forms of friendship upon which they rely.

Associational activity is intensely personal. To achieve its objectives, civic organizations depend upon voluntary, spontaneous, shared commitments among members who are devoted to some explicit public good. Openness and mutual trust are the primary means for developing a cohesive spirit among those who participate. Through the application of such personal qualities, a certain unity is formed—a solidarity that is a social expression of love.[64] Such organizations do not pursue wealth or power; nonetheless, involvement in them brings great personal advantages. When one is engaged with civic associations, the wider world beyond the home is less alien to the individual self. The development of shared values in a context of interpersonal connectedness provides practical relief

63. Alejandro Llano, *The New Sensibility,* Alban d' Etremont, trans. (Pamplona: Universidad de Navarra, 1991). For a discussion of the importance of chosen connection with others, beyond one's "community of origin" and the importance of such broader relationships to personal self-identity, see Marilyn Friedman, "Feminism and Modern Friendship: Dislocating the Community," in *Feminism and Political Theory,* Cass R. Sunstein, ed. (Chicago: Univ. of Chicago Press, 1992), 143.

64. See the critique of Roberto Unger in C.F. Murphy, *Descent Into Subjectivity,* Ch. 4. And see the observations of Pope John Paul II on the relation between mercy and love in *Rich In Mercy,* supra.

from the more abrasive aspects of commerce or conventional politics.

The forms of friendship that vivify associational activity defy comprehension within classical categories of human association. They lessen the distance between public and private, since they are aspects of personal relatedness that are closer to the vitalities and intimacies of family life than to the qualities of character required to meet the more demanding aspects of political existence. Yet, since they are of great importance to the purposes of civilization, they are of a public nature. By contrasting these two forms of engagement, we may be able to comprehend some further differences between a masculine and feminine approach to general coexistence. As connectedness to others is an important theme in contemporary feminist thought, it is important to explore the nuances of relatedness one must take into account if one wishes to understand fully the broadest potentialities of human action.

In the classical view, politics calls together for some public purpose a multiplicity of actors, each of whom is a unique individual. The lack of familiarity among the participants is what distinguishes the political, in its highest forms, from other types of public association. Here, the distinct identity of each, and the unique contribution which they alone can make to the deliberations, is what makes such a coming together an opportunity for the flourishing of personal virtue as well as the promotion of the commonwealth.[65] For there to be constructive coaction among those who are otherwise unconnected, a certain amity must exist among those directly involved in such general deliberations. Otherwise, dialogue cannot proceed in an atmosphere of mutual respect. However, unlike the closeness between persons which characterizes civic association, regard for one's peers in the public context is derived from the distance that the reality of their differences places between them.[66]

65. Hannah Arendt, op. cit.
66. Compare the critique of Roberto Unger's conception of political life in *Descent Into Subjectivity.*

There are other differences. The social connectedness that develops in civic associations allows one to deal, in an interpersonal way, with those with whom one is not in conflict. Political friendship, however, is union without intimacy. Requiring only a common commitment to the broadest principles, it is open to the many. Considered as a personal quality, this *philia,* or complex form of civic friendship, is extremely difficult to develop. It requires one to accept the difference of the other while, at the same time, being willing to collaborate with him or her in a joint effort to bring some permanence to a fragile but common life.[67]

The emphasis that *philia* places upon interpersonal distance rather than nearness touches upon other important questions relevant to a dialogue with feminism. Feminists contend that love, more than any other value, is what is missing from the male-dominated public world.[68] If the absence of love is seen to lie in an indifference to the plight of the marginalized, oppressed, or the disadvantaged, such criticism is a valuable antidote to the quest for a political achievement devoid of compassion. But if love is seen in relation to the qualities of personal character necessary to sustain the most enduring forms of public association, its delineation will be more subtle and complex.

The demands of essential political life run counter to the desires for intimacy. Yet "what does not reach out to order the world does not love."[69] Beyond the associational activities that connect private with public action, there are other ways of expressing a concern for others who are not otherwise close to us. We can direct our empathetic capacities toward those with

67. Hannah Arendt, *The Human Condition,* 243. For a general discussion of her views of intimacy in public life see Ronald Beiner, *Political Judgment,* Ch. 6. See also Richard Sennett, *The Fall of Public Man,* (1977); Allister Sparks, "The Secret Revolution (Letter from South Africa)," *New Yorker* (April 11, 1994), 56.

68. Feminists insist that public communication aims not only at a shared understanding but is also motivated by "the desire to love and be loved." Iris Marion Young, "Impartiality and the Civic Public," in *Feminism as Critique,* 57, 72. See also Robin West, supra.

69. Martha Nussbaum, *The Fragility of Goodness,* 199.

whom we have no established bonds of civic or social friendship. The development of a harmonious multiracial society, for example, cannot be achieved through exclusive reliance upon legal rights and abstract ideals. It will also require qualities of interpersonal acquaintance which, until now, have been virtually untapped. However, it should also be recognized that there are modes of civic friendship and civility whose flourishing depends upon more distanced relations among individuals who desire an ordered social life. And these relations, even when impersonal, also deserve to be characterized as aspects of love.

The broader sense of political life, which we have been trying to elucidate, sometimes requires a willingness to cooperate on public affairs with persons for whom one may feel no particular affection, and under the constraint of disinterested responsibility. The struggle to create with others a home for all during their life on earth, "to unite people, rather then divide them,"[70] demands qualities of concern that, in their variety, allow ample scope for all the compassionate qualities that make us—male or female—authentically human.

We cannot afford to view public life as an arena that brings to light in simplistic contrast the destructive potentials of the one gender and the nurturing qualities of the other. The regeneration of civic life will require us to respect rather than oppose each other, acknowledging our differences of moral and aesthetic expression as well as our needs for both distance and intimacy. We can then creatively join the tendencies toward transcendence with that affective particularity which alone makes life worth living.

70. Barbara Jordan, *Speech to the Democratic National Convention*, New York City, July 13, 1992.

4. LOVE AND MARRIAGE

1. *The Happiness of Love*

At first glance, love between the sexes does not appear to be an appropriate subject for reflection. Love engages deep feelings and emotions that are, in many respects, refractory to thought. There is also the matter of privacy. As it falls within zones of intimacy, love strives to be as immune from the intrusions of reason as it is from the power of the state. This aversion to theorizing about love reveals how intensely personal are the sexual relations between men and women. It also explains why most understanding of the subject is autobiographical in nature. Better to have knowledge based upon the experience of a "heart-felt mind" than the arid speculations of abstract philosophy.[1]

What we know of love has been, and will remain, primarily experiential. But here, as elsewhere, we should be wary of any inclination to limit the range of reason. Since the time of Plato, philosophers of major stature have considered the question of love worthy of profound reflection, and there is nothing in the contemporary relations between men and women that would justify the abandonment of such mental effort.[2] Quite the con-

1. See the reflections on masculinity in Sam Keen, *Fire in the Belly* (New York: Bantam Books, 1991). See also Gloria Steinem, *Revolution from Within* (Boston: Little Brown, 1992). For an academic attempt at intellectual comprehension see Alan Soble, *The Structure of Love* (New Haven: Yale University Press, 1990).

2. Allan Bloom, *Love and Friendship* (New York: Simon & Schuster, 1993). An understanding of the importance of reflection upon the meaning of sexuality appears in the Spanish literature. See, e.g., Pedro-Juan Viladrich, *The Agony of Legal Marriage*, trans. Alban d'Entremont (Pamplona: Universidad de Navarra, 1990), and José Ortega y Gasset, *On Love*, trans. Toby Talbot (New York: Meridian Books, 1957). See also Robert Johann, *The Meaning of Love* (Paulist Press, 1966), and Denis de Rougemont, *Love Declared*, trans. Richard Howard (New York: Pantheon, 1963). For an understanding of love as an emotional

trary. The crisis of sexuality, and the related problems of marriage and the family, reach the heart of our collective experience. We cannot allow these vital areas of life to continue along their present course of disintegration without an attempt at rational comprehension. There is also the issue of power. Without the guidance of reason, the quality and duration of intimate relations between the sexes will be determined by novel patterns of oppression and abuse. Mutual life without reason has a way of becoming a struggle of wills.

Some philosophers who have sought to bring heterosexuality under the domain of the rational have felt obliged to posit an opposition between reason and feeling. For Kant, categorical norms should purify the will and release it from the control of sexual passion. There is much to be said for this point of view, particularly when such precepts provide a measure of protection against sexual exploitation. But such a defense of human dignity comes at a high price. Any system of thought that establishes an intrinsic antagonism between reason and feeling ends by disparaging or ignoring some vital aspect of human nature.

Rationalism misunderstands the erotic dimension of existence. To the mind striving for abstract certainty, eros is nothing more than arbitrary and wayward sexual desire, a desire that has no independent meaning. Its value, to the degree it has any, depends upon its normative regulation. It is tempting to describe such an attitude as puritanical, a characterization perhaps justified by the definition of the puritan as one who fears that somewhere, someone might be happy;[3] for while eros is linked to sexual expression, at a deeper level it expresses the indelible constant inclination of the human person to pursue a life of joy and fulfillment.

As a natural urge toward a complete life, eros is an inherent

---

state which cannot be conceptualized, see Paul Tillich, *Love, Power, and Justice* (New York: Oxford University Press, 1954), chap. 1.

3. Puritanism is "the haunting fear that someone, somewhere, might be happy" (H. L. Mencken, *'Sententiae', A Book of Burlesques*, 1920) quoted in the *International Thesaurus of Quotations*, 763.

part of human nature. "By nature the creature endowed with reason wishes to be happy and therefore cannot wish not to be happy."[4] There is an obvious quality to such an observation, yet it has never been easily assimilated to a reflective outlook. Resistance is not limited to those who prefer the joys of thought to those of sensuality. More important difficulties arise when it is recognized that the human happiness for which eros yearns is the happiness of love.

The elementary urge for fulfillment that constitutes the erotic is self-serving. Yet, as a quest for the good of life, it includes a desire for closeness and community with others. The possible joy of receiving what we love, awakened by the senses, is an experience that arises most intensely in encounters between men and women. Such encounters are sexual, but the paramount attraction, which draws us beyond ourselves, is the beauty and goodness we see embodied in a person of the opposite sex.[5]

Eros and sexuality are intimately related, but they are not synonymous. In modern life, the erotic dimension has been identified with an instinctual desire that has as its object an increase in excitement and the release of tension. The predominant emphasis upon gratification confuses pleasure with happiness. Much of the confusion is traceable to the influence of Freudian psychology.

Freud understood that the sheer satisfaction of libido is ultimately self-defeating. He came to realize that eros represents a life force that surpasses, and is often in conflict with, sheer genital instinct. However, given his inherent pessimism as well as his attraction toward mechanistic explanation, he could not grasp the deeper purposes. For Freud and those subject to his influence, eros could be nothing more than a deep instinctual force driving us, as it were, from behind toward some in-

4. Thomas Aquinas, *Contra Gentiles* 4, 92; quoted in Josef Pieper, *About Love*, trans. Richard and Clara Winston (Chicago: Franciscan Herald Press, 1972), 71. Compare the review of the ancients in Allan Bloom, *Love and Friendship*.
5. Pieper, *About Love*. See also Irving Singer, *The Nature of Love*.

explicable destiny. He did not comprehend its possibilities for either human happiness or personal freedom.[6]

We have already observed how the refusal to give eros its due is based more upon an uneasiness with the primacy of the desire for happiness than with a distaste for the physicality of copulation. Opposition hardens when the happiness of love is conceived as something the individual needs but cannot demand. Better to cultivate a stoical self-sufficiency than be constantly aware of a fundamental dependency. Better still to make the self the cause, rather than the object, of love.

It is commonly agreed that love based upon qualities or performance falls below the ideal of unselfish love. Yet when we think of being loved ourselves, we would prefer to be loved for our achievements or the qualities of our character, rather than for the mere fact that we exist. We do not want—no matter how much we need—undeserved love.[7] There are good reasons for such resistance. Unqualified love is always in danger of overvaluing its object and the recipient may justifiably fear the growth of false expectations. No one wants to be considered as being better than he, or she, actually is. Yet it is also possible that the lover perceives potentials of which the beloved is unaware. Like it or not, it is only by being loved without reserve that one can freely become what one is.[8]

The most cogent arguments against being a recipient of love come from the superiority of loving over being loved. The giving of selfless love is obviously better than the selfish need to be loved. Moreover, a craving for the contentment of love is clearly a sign of human weakness. Real need is also devalued whenever eros is reduced to genital sexuality. If all we want from the other is physical satisfaction we shall fail to recognize

6. Rollo May, *Love and Will* (New York: W. W. Norton, 1969), chap. 3. Freud does not deserve all the blame. With Nietzsche the will to power predominates and, as Allan Bloom observed, modern thought, being generally preoccupied with lower motives, cannot understand the deeper delights of lovers (*Love and Friendship*, Epilogue).

7. C. S. Lewis, *The Four Loves* (Glasgow: William Collins & Sons, 1960), chap. 1.

8. Pieper, *About Love*, chap. 3. See also, Ortega y Gasset, *On Love*.

our deeper indigence. It is when authentic needs are mutually acknowledged that wanting to be loved has a genuine value.

There is a further reason to be wary of too much emphasis upon selfless love, for it can mask a deeper egotism. Those who think too highly of themselves have a strong desire to be always in a position of giving rather than receiving in matters of love. The quest for absolute independence is a less obvious defect than passive sensuality; it is, nonetheless, an essential mark of human pride. Those who exaggerate their self-sufficiency reveal the unfulfilled nature of their own lives.[9] They forget that they, too, are finite creatures; like the rest of humankind, they can fully exist only when, in some important way, they are being confirmed by the love of another.

Wanting to be loved is not essentially selfish, since the ability to love presupposes the experience of being loved by another. The two conceptions—loving and being loved—may be reconciled by saying that love, although primarily needful, *develops* through unselfish acts. The transition is from need to bestowal. However, this transition to the happiness of unselfish love may be impaired because of another factor that is closely related to need. It is often forgotten that we cannot love others unless we properly love ourselves.

The low self-esteem of many contemporary men and women has contributed a great deal to the chaotic nature of the love between the sexes. Lack of self-esteem suggests the absence of self-approval. For whatever reason, we have become unable to affirm ourselves. We have lost the ability to say to ourselves, "It is good that you exist."[10] As persons who hope to love, we

9. The excessive self-love of Kierkegaard is discussed in Pieper, *About Love*, chap. 5. On Kierkegaard's pride of self-sacrifice, see K. Stern, *The Flight from Woman*, chap. 10. See also Martin Buber, "The Question to the Single One," in *Between Man and Man*, trans. Ronald Gregor Smith (New York: MacMillan, 1975). Buber's essay is a critique of Kierkegaard's rejection of Regina Olson.

10. Pieper points out that the lack of self esteem is also based upon the absence of love from others. ". . . Above all, the ability to love, in which our own experience achieves its highest intensification, presupposes the experience of being loved by someone else . . ." *About Love*, 29. In *Love and Friendship*, Allan Bloom emphasizes the disparagement of eros in Christian thought. It

must find ways of existing for our own sakes. We must all learn to accept ourselves as we are, not as we might become.

Self-esteem also has a gender component. Sexual stereotypes can weaken an already fragile self. In this regard, our self-conceptions may be enhanced by new understandings of women as women and of men in their manhood. While each of us is a distinct individual with a particular and unique history, we are also either masculine or feminine persons. Our ability to love any person of the opposite sex depends, in part, upon our ability to affirm ourselves as having either a masculine or feminine disposition, together with all the powers and needs that are part of such sexual identity. When gender is cleansed of oppressive social conventions, it enhances personal self-esteem in ways that can positively influence the quality of heterosexual relations.

There is a further implication of self-esteem which bears upon the giving of our love. Here self-esteem becomes self-respect. While we may recognize our need to love, we may rightly withhold ourselves if our inherent dignity would be placed in jeopardy in a specific encounter.[11] We can act toward others only as we would act toward ourselves. Being one with ourselves is, in this sense, more important than becoming one with another. Yet, in spite of these qualifications, it is of supreme importance to understand that the joy of love exists only when we are together with those whom we love.

Love is magnetic. When a man and a woman are in love, each is drawn out of themselves by what they see in the other. As sexual attraction intensifies, it is practically impossible to distinguish what is receptive from what is outgoing. But to keep these emotional dynamics in perspective, it must be emphasized that love between the sexes involves a union that is more than physical. An authentic lover craves more than sex-

---

is, perhaps, ironic that the works of Pieper, upon which these reflections depend so heavily, are the works of a Catholic philosopher.

11. Martin C. D'Arcy, *The Mind and Heart of Love* (New York: Meridian Books, 1956), 323–25.

ual pleasure. Moreover, where consummation is easy, it loses its significance. Eros, awakened by the senses, can be betrayed by sensuality. In "consumer" sex, one is being used for the ends of the other. Both are frustrated, because neither finds that deeper union with another person that is the object of the erotic inclination. To be compatible with human dignity, sexuality must be integrated with the whole of interpersonal existence.[12]

Eros is more attentive to the awakening of desire than to its satisfaction. With the aid of the will, eros keeps human love from acting in isolation from deeper desires for happiness. Eros also calls the person to that self-forgetfulness that brings lasting joy. Love deepens as one begins to love the other, not for what one needs, but for what the other is. The desire for happiness is not satisfied by receiving constant approval, but by an affirmation directed toward another.

The common idea that personal well-being depends upon a proper balance between subjective feeling and objective experience is especially relevant to the development of love. Needed love, unrequited or lost, causes much sorrow; the happiness of love consists of the joy which accompanies our giving. This is why to love someone is more valuable than even loving ourselves. We participate in that fullness promised by eros when we join with and rejoice in the happiness of another human person. Where sexual love is mutual and totally committed, each loves the other not *as* they love themselves but rather with the love *of* themselves.[13]

Eros draws us out of ourselves, arousing yearnings for happiness that we are powerless to resist. However, eros opens up possibilities that it cannot, of itself, fulfill. Eros may direct us to whatever goodness or beauty is embodied in the other

---

12. Rollo May, *Love and Will*, chap. 2; Pieper, *About Love*, chap. 9.

13. The joy of love is transitive, linked with a direct object. "To love always implies to love *someone* or *something*. And if this element is missing in a definition, it has failed to hit its target" (Pieper, *About Love*, 77). This is contrary to Sartre's view that to love is to have the other in oneself or to give the other safety in terms of my freedom. Compare Jean-Paul Sartre, *Notebooks for an Ethics*, trans. David Pellawer (Chicago: University Chicago Press, 1992), vol. 1.

but it cannot bring about the interpersonal fulfillment it encourages. As love deepens, there is a reaching out for union.
The achievement of that union and the happiness it implies
will depend, to some extent, upon unconscious forces: the
character of the parties involved and all the innumerable factors of disposition and environment that make up the gravi-
tational field of love. But it will also depend upon choices,
freely made, by both lovers.

It is difficult to determine the extent to which love is voluntary or involuntary. When we speak of "falling in love," we
mark the influence the loved one has upon the lover. Here love
is *in* the lover but not *by* him. One specific person stands out,
at a closer distance, than all the others. As the world becomes
more reduced and concentrated, the unique other becomes a
constant presence and focus of the lover's attention. Such romantic involvement is extolled in popular culture, but its re-
lentless demands can be harmful both to the lovers and those
to whom they are otherwise responsible. The requirements of
the wider, objective world are neglected as lovers fall deeper
into an emotional entrapment that excludes or distorts the rest
of life.[14] The absorption of love is difficult to resist, because it
corresponds to some of our deepest inclinations. But it cannot
be reconciled with our sense of human dignity and the way
that such dignity guards our inner freedom.

Lovers paralyzed by love are persons no longer in charge of
their wanting and in danger of descending into a more destructive state. When falling in love does not move to a more stable
form of intimacy, it can quickly turn to hatred. Eros, as a positive, life-giving force, is caught in a struggle with inclinations
toward death. But hatred is its more immediate adversary.
Love and hate are active emotions; both are turned toward another. But, while love turns toward its object to affirm it, hatred
seeks to deny its value. Hatred is lethal; its intent is to extin-

14. See, Ortega y Gasset, *On Love*, chap. 1. Romantic excess can be contrary
to eros as well as other values because it can destroy the deeper longings of
the soul. That is why eros is not limited to the embrace by a man and a woman
who intensely desire to be together. See Bloom, *Love and Friendship*.

guish the other. In hatred, only a separation will bring satisfaction. Love, by contrast, is satisfied only with union.[15]

Love seeks a union that, although inherently sexual, hopes for more than physical satisfaction. The union sought must meet the deeper needs of the person. We have seen how these include the need to love, as well as to be loved. Love has its stages. Those who *fall* in love may come *to be* in love. Lovers are then mutually involved in a more extensive physical and emotional adjustment, which begins to move the relationship beyond the vicissitudes of romance.[16] If love is to be complete, it must reach a higher stage of development. The desires for happiness aroused by eros seek a form of sexual coexistence that can satisfy the deepest needs of interpersonal union and affirmation. What is required is a form of sexual relation that, as a lasting, mutual bond makes possible the constant affirmation of another who is the object of one's love. This is possible only when love is transformed in marriage.

II. *Mutual Consent to Lasting Love*

To act in favor of a person by a commitment of enduring love, and to remain firm in that commitment, is an awesome responsibility. But it is the only way for a man and woman—

15. Ortega y Gasset, *On Love*. When eros is rejected, it can be replaced by a love conceived as the fulfillment of a command. Tillich, *Love, Power, and Justice*, chap. 2.

16. Compare Irving Singer, *The Nature of Love* (Chicago: University of Chicago Press, 1985), vol. 3, chap. 10. Singer distinguishes between romantic and marital passion. The sense in which he uses the expression "being in love" is meant to apply to the latter form of relationship, in response to the claims that romance is incompatible with marriage. The tension between romance and married love is explored in Denis de Rougemont, *Love in the Western World*, trans. M. Belgion (New York: Pantheon Books, 1956).

Being in love also engages the dynamics of initiative and response. In a Christian anthropology the initiative of bestowing is a masculine action. If the feminine accepts the gift of love, she will respond with the gift of her own person (John Paul II, *Mulieris Dignitatem*, chap. 7). The failures of masculine initiative are amply recorded in the psychological literature. The frustration and unhappiness of women are caused more by the denial of love by passive men than by their injustice or their tyranny (Karl Menninger, *Love against Hate* [New York: Harcourt, Brace, 1942], chap. 3).

who are persons, not just male and female beings—to love each other fully. Love, deeply experienced, is a reaching out toward the abundance of being that is the intimate and existential reality of a particular person of the opposite sex. In the unitive love of marriage, the sexual and the personal are reconciled. By founding a permanent union, the lovers express their desire to give to each other what belongs essentially to themselves. By self-donation they become fully present to each other in a way that makes it possible for them to develop a society of their love.

Committed love transcends fleeting encounters or the merely conventional "relating" to one another. It makes possible what can never be obtained by factual cohabitation. Those who make marriage vows have accepted an invitation to surpass contingency and the provisional nature of merely romantic entanglement. To realize the promise of eros, a particular man and woman decide upon a common future. What they are now as individuals is not what they will be as a couple. Yet, by a present act, they willingly donate their separate prospects to create a shared destiny. The achievement of that future will depend upon the fulfillment of mutual promises cleansed of qualifying conditions.

Married love is a commitment to exclusivity and permanence; a bonding "till death do us part." The magnitude of the obligation demands, by way of proportion, a genuine, uncoerced, choice. Through a better understanding of that choice—both its liberty and its intentions—we may overcome a fundamental obstacle to the establishment of enduring love between men and women. This requires more careful attention to the nature of our willing.

The will seems to have little to do with the experience of love. We may recognize the will as a controller of passion, but we have difficulty in seeing it as an active, constructive, force in the dynamics of love. The instinctive and compulsive aspects of sexual activity are well known, and, as such psychological understanding increases, it becomes harder to attribute any positive causal influence to volition. We may see that some choice is operative when we select one person, out of many possibilities, as a mate, but we are not inclined to recognize that the will can have a decisive influence upon the quality or duration of that love.[17]

In earlier chapters we saw how exaggerated assertions of will, particularly in its masculine, individualistic form, have had disastrous consequences both for women and for the development of human culture. In the domain of the sexual, the position of the will is more ambivalent. In a patriarchal society, it made its presence known through the domination of wives by their husbands. Yet, as we have seen, under modern domestic conditions the desire for supremacy can become the aspiration of either men or women.[18] We are all tempted to give expression to our impulses to control; we must resolve the tension between love and power. We have yet to realize the happiness the will can create through its power to affirm the well-being of another.

Our changing understanding of the role of the will in the general culture may beneficially affect its relationship to heterosexual love. With the advance of science and technology, we came to think of our encounter with the natural world as one in which, from some independent perspective, we disposed of that world as we wished. But as our ecological conscience has developed, we protest against this unlimited domination of creation. We have come to understand the global environment as a habitat in which we live but which we do not create, and whose independent reality we must respect. Rather than imposing our sovereignty upon nature, we are trying to enter into some harmony with its inherent order.[19] Our approach to human heterosexual love should employ analogous concepts of interdependence.

Disenchanted with traditional connections between love

17. Rollo May, *Love and Will*, chap. 7.
18. See the exploration of the mutuality of oppression in chapter 1 of the present work.
19. See Alejandro Llano, *The New Sensibility*, trans. Albon d'Entremont (Pamplona: Universidad de Navarra, S.A. 1991).

and marriage, Western culture has become attracted to the unlimited possibilities of sexual experimentation. With some justification, we look upon conventional norms as obstacles to creative freedom and as unresponsive to our needs or interests as persons. But here, as with the environment, an absolute liberty, which treats natural reality as infinitely malleable, leads to a fundamental imbalance that is in the end dehumanizing.[20]

The crisis of sexuality is usually attributed to the flaunting of established norms. But it is only partially related to the willful disregard of moral principles. Paradoxically, the urge to innovate is a sign of vitality as well as a mark of disintegration. It embodies the aspiration of the human spirit to find meaning and freedom within the most elementary dimensions of existence.[21] Still, while variations in sexual relations may suggest the fertility of choice, the search for novelty also reveals the painful distance between our desires and our understanding of the means appropriate to their fulfillment. We miss these connections because we fail to see the natural value of married love and do not comprehend the power of our wills to bring the benefits of permanence into the orbit of our sexual lives.

If reason cannot establish a lasting bond between a man and a woman, the imagination might compensate for what nature does not provide. Marital commitment then becomes a way of civilizing sexual desire. This was the approach of Rousseau. He thought that love is imaginary; a mutual illusion. The problem was to educate a man to believe that a woman whom he idealizes will satisfy his longing for sensual happiness.

The will was important to Rousseau's conception of married love. however, for him, the will was not a natural faculty. It had to be built up, by the deceptions of romance, so that sexual longing could be directed to an enduring attachment. The cultivation of an erotic imagining of a woman would lead a man to believe that the object of his affections would bring him com-

---

20. Compare Pedro-Juan Viladrich, *The Agony of Legal Marriage*, trans. Albon d'Entremont (Pamplona: Universidad de Navarra, 1990).
21. Ibid.

plete sensual satisfaction within a permanent and exclusive union.[22]

The woman must be free to choose whom she will marry. Then, through the exchange of vows, the parties will make a binding but self-imposed commitment to each other. The obligations which they assume are meant to assure mutual respect while, at the same time, preserving moral freedom. But the duties of marriage impose a heavy burden. The whole seriousness of life is invested in the Rousseau compact. Its obligations are onerous, because the marriage bond creates a dualism between happiness and morality.[23]

In contemporary life the impotence of the will appears to be a more pressing problem. A person may wish to avoid the instabilities of sexual experimentation but he, or she, also does not want to submit blindly to traditional forms of married life. Psychologically, the will suffers a paralysis. It is caught between the sexual forces that constitute the "vicissitudes of instinct" and the harsh demands of an authoritative superego that would impose its standards of righteousness upon us.[24] Accustomed to think of the will as a faculty that expresses our power over nature, we have yet to understand how the exercise of our freedom can bring us fulfillment within an intimate but natural order of existence.

The structure of marriage is not created by the will of the partners, yet their consent is essential to its coming into being. One must freely accept this objective order, in a manner compatible with one's dignity. A free person cannot allow himself or herself simply to be swept away by the impulses of nature. Nor can one blindly submit to a conventional form of existence. An unconditional, lifelong commitment must be in harmony

22. Allan Bloom, *Love and Friendship*, Part 1.
23. The weight of these responsibilities makes Rousseauan marriage "bear a very heavy burden" (ibid., 118).
24. "Depth psychology has discovered a side of human existence which should not be covered again by idealistic or moralistic fears and postulates. The *appetitus* of every being to fulfill itself through union with other beings is universal and underlies the *eros* as well as the *philia* quality of love" (Tillich, *Love, Power, and Justice*, 32–33). See also, Rollo May, *Love and Will*, chap. 7.

with our deepest aspirations, as human persons, to choose freely what will promote our happiness.

The consent to marriage is expressed in a wedding ceremony through an exchange of vows. From a juridical perspective, the event may be viewed as a matter of contract, but there are difficulties with this approach. Feminists are concerned that the pact will give direct, legal validity to relations of dominance and subordination already operative within the larger society. Their concern is shared by others. John Stuart Mill's renunciation of whatever legal powers he would attain through his marriage to Harriet Taylor dramatically illustrates the hegemonic potentials of such a contractual regime.[25]

Further problems arise from the refinement of the understanding of contract as a general legal practice. Under modern law, contracting parties are able to agree between themselves as to the content and duration of their mutual obligations in a virtually unlimited manner. These capacities are applied, with some success, to prenuptial agreements. Yet it is not possible to reconcile the transformation of status that arises from the mutual exchange of the marriage vows with the standard theory of contract. Some see the difference to lie in the speech act that is at the heart of the wedding ceremony. There, both the man and the woman engage in a "performative utterance" and, "by virtue of saying the words, the standing of the man and woman is transformed. In the act of saying 'I do' a man becomes a husband and a woman becomes a wife."[26] There is

---

25. Mill objected to the prevailing conception of marriage which, by confirming masculine dominance, gave one party a legal power over "the person, property, and freedom of action of the other." A condition of his engagement to Harriet Taylor was that "she retains in all respects whatever the same absolute freedom of action, and freedom of disposal of herself and of all that does or may at any time belong to her, as if no such marriage had taken place, and I absolutely disclaim and repudiate all pretension to have acquired any *rights* whatever by virtue of such marriage" ("On Marriage" [1851] in *Collected Works of John Stuart Mill*, ed. John M. Robson [Toronto: University of Toronto Press, 1984]). See further, Carole Pateman, *The Sexual Contract* (Stanford: Stanford University Press, 1988), chap. 6.

26. Carole Pateman, *The Sexual Contract*, 164.

further difference between marriage and other modes of agreement. The general principles of contract do not require that one should account for the substantive attributes of the parties; but, in the marital pact, sexual differences are integral to the nature of the agreement. The reason these differences are essential can be seen in the purposes of the exchange.

The "I do" of the wedding ceremony is a public action by which the parties reciprocally donate themselves to each other with the purpose of creating a conjugal bond between them. They accept each other, as they are, with respect to everything that pertains to the unity of life they have established. The consent, if freely given, creates a bond of justice. As spouses, they are no longer just emotionally linked. Each owes himself or herself to the other with respect to the union they have created out of their mutual love. Obligated with respect to what is conjugal between them, they are bound to mutual duties, which, having assumed, they must perform. The "I do" is a transitory act. But the marriage union, once established, exists independent of the wills of those who brought it into being.[27]

The transformative union that arises out of the mutual exchange gives an enduring and exclusive quality to the spousal relationship. Neither party, however, loses their separate selfhood. As persons, they remain as subsistent beings each having his or her own unique ends. They are not instruments for the realization of each other's ends. Nor is their inherent dignity subservient to the ends of marriage. But they have given themselves to one another, as husband and wife. And they have committed themselves, together, to an unknown future.

While they have entered a relation that makes demands

---

27. Viladrich, *The Agony of Legal Marriage*, chaps. 4 and 5. In the development of these distinctions it is important to keep in mind the distinction between the natural and the legal. Marriage, as a natural phenomenon, is a society or community of life. In legal history, the jural reality was conceived as a substantive unity which assured the supremacy of the husband and the subordination of the wife. Modern law, in the pursuit of spousal equality, emphasizes the independence of the partners rather than the community of life between them. Mary Ellen Glendon, "Marriage and the State: The Withering Away of Marriage," *Va.L.Rev.* 62 (1976): 663, 701.

MARITAL OBLIGATIONS

upon them, they are not being blindly submissive to some superior power. The fulfillment of marital obligations is often experienced as a mechanistic imposition, without reason and without vision, serving to realize purely functional ends. What is essential about marriage is reduced to its most general aspects and then imposed upon individuals of whom no more is expected than passive acceptance. These impositions are at war with the individual desire for a self-directed life. To resolve these difficulties eros must come to the aid of morality.

The decision which the lovers have made in the marriage ceremony corresponds with their inherent inclination toward the joy of interpersonal fulfillment. They have been drawn into a unity that harmonizes with the way that they, as lovers, are naturally predisposed. Through the marriage vows, they have converted their mutual love into love itself. But committed love entails responsibilities. The duties of marriage are not derived from the wills of the parties; neither, it must be added, does their binding force come from the law, or from the conventions of society. The origins are ontological, from the order of being. The free decision of the man and a woman, and that alone, causes these higher directives to enter into their world.

MARITAL CONSENT

The marital consent by which a man and a woman freely give themselves to each other is a uniquely autonomous act. For to choose to dispose of oneself is a supreme expression of personal freedom. At the same time the act is not willful. There is not a sovereign disregard of natural realities. The parties are not imposing *their* wills on something that stands in the way of their happiness; they are acting in accord with objective realities that are designed to assure that happiness. They are agreeing to renounce their absolute independence so as to pass to a community of life which they shall live as a husband and as a wife.

Through this decision to live a conjugal life, the love between a man and a women moves to its highest experiential level. In this relation of espousal, one does not pursue an imagined ideal; each takes the other's good—as either this imperfect man or this imperfect woman—as one's own. The will has not been displaced by erotic sensibility, but the possibilities of mutual affirmation inspired by eros now have an appropriate field of action. The conjugal love of marriage moves the desires of the parties beyond sentiment and, while fully sexual, it breaks the hold which libido and instinct would have over the designs of sexual attraction. This is the authentic freedom of love:

> We should make no mistake about it: by "freedom of love" we do not mean that he who loves is not bound by anything, or that love is something fatal, inconsistent, fleeting, unstable, arbitrary and un-responsible. The freedom of love is the freedom of the voluntary act. As a consequence, "freedom of love" means in strict terms that love ends up setting forth a *voluntary decision* which one has to make on one's own and without coercion. Yet it is a decision and therefore however more freely it is made the more responsible it will be; how-ever more voluntary it is, the more conscious it will be; however more *decided* it is the least inconsequent, unstable and casual it will be.[28]

Such consent not only must be free from external compulsion but also must operate independently of the inward forces that so often make the will impotent. In this vital area of coexis-tence we must carefully distinguish form from substance.

The "I do" of the marital ceremony, if it is to constitute an authentic marriage, must be a choice that expresses both in capacity and intent a genuine commitment to the fullness of conjugal union. Under conditions of modern life, that authen-tic freedom may be, sadly, lacking. Many of us, having failed to undertake the commitment which the nature of love de-mands, have suffered terrible consequences. But we must not despair of our ability as human persons who wish to love, and be loved, to become masters of our own destinies.

III. *Marriage and the Family*

In giving themselves to each other in marriage, a man and a woman become a couple. They also constitute themselves as a community of conjugal life. Their sexual union includes the

28. Viladrich, *The Agony of Legal Marriage*, 132–33.

possibility that a new being will be conceived whose birth will profoundly affect their lives. Those who are spouses may also become parents. While such events are a matter of great joy, they can also place subtle strains upon the fundamental marital union.

The revival of interest in procreation among feminists vindicates the ancient linguistic roots of matrimony since the expression "marriage" was formed from the Latin word *mater* and the suffix *mon*, for the state of being a mother. And the renewal of the value of the family is of great social benefit, even if it may be misused for political purposes. But we should also be aware that throughout Western history there have always been tensions between marriage and family life. The union of person and sexuality inherent in the marital commitment of each spouse can be placed in jeopardy as their community of life assumes the character of a family.

Hegel argued that lovers should overcome their separate existence by giving themselves over completely to the new union they create out of their love. The independent personalities of the spouses, sustained by mutual personal love, are then collapsed into a higher synthesis of family and society. As a consequence of fertility, the partners are thought of as now belonging to a reality greater than themselves.[29] A similar disposition can be found in religious teaching that looks upon the family as an entity and casts a suspicious glance upon the love the spouses bear for each other. Such teaching upholds great truths, but the danger is that love and sexuality become bound up with the family rather than the person.[30]

The tension between marriage and family is also a matter of contemporary experience. For some women, the birth of a child is the occasion for an investment of love and affection that can take precedence over the bond which she has with her husband. Others contend that the virtues of the extended family are superior to the narrow and selfish character of the re-

29. See generally, Singer, *The Nature of Love*, vol. 2, chap. 12.
30. Nicholas Berdyaev, *The Fate of Man in the Modern World* (Ann Arbor: The University of Michigan Press, 1935).

lationship between the so-called "nuclear" couple. They resist any conception of the family that would emphasize marriage and the sexual relations of the spouses to the detriment of the larger reality of kinship. Family, in this enlarged sense, gives scope to the primacy of woman. In such "female collectivity" one may find women acting together "to dignify their lives, to lighten each other's labor, and growing in real love."[31]

The ideal of kinship, and the networks of relatives that it implies, suggests possibilities of a richer human life than what now obtains within the isolated, couple-centered family of suburban North America. Within a larger unit, however formed, a woman's opportunities to contribute to the continuities of life are greatly enhanced. As she directs her attention to the needs of both young and old, she is more agent than object. In these circumstances, a woman does not "briefly blaze as her husband's paramour and decline into the whining mother of one or two."[32] This celebration of an enlarged fertility puts to shame pleasure-seeking couples who look upon "frequent and prolonged copulation"[33] as the primary good of marriage. But the ideal of the extended family suggests a model of life that can distort the nature of reproductive love.

In the ancient world, procreation was a matter of blind necessity, dictated by forces indifferent to personal purpose. In the modern world, the tendency to equate human birth with technological images of reproduction reveals a deeper alien-

31. Germaine Greer, *Sex and Destiny: The Politics of Human Fertility* (New York: Harper & Row, 1984), 286. Compare the observation of Francine du Plessix Gray, in her study of women in the former Soviet Union: "Throughout my months in the U.S.S.R. I barely if ever heard one mention the word *Liubov* 'love' in its heterosexual, romantic sense. It confirmed my suspicion that love in the Soviet Union is a luxury, an accessory, but hardly a prerequisite for marriage or happiness as it is in Western Europe or the United States. For conversations with Soviet women make it clear that heterosexual love tends to recede in importance before the far deeper bonds of blood kinship, filial responsibility, matriarchal ties; and that they tend to look on marriage as a coolly pragmatic commodity resorted to for a variety of utilitarian reasons" (Francine du Plessix Gray, *Soviet Women* [New York: Doubleday, 1989], 54).

32. Greer, *Sex and Destiny*, 289.

33. Ibid., 271.

ation from the humanness of the experience.[34] No significant improvement in our understanding of procreation can be expected unless it is understood as an experience intimately linked to the profound love that spouses bear toward each other:

> The sexual instinct assures, perhaps, conservation of the species, but not its perfection. On the other hand, genuine sexual love, that is, ardor for another being, his body and soul in indissoluble union, is in itself primarily a gigantic force entrusted with improving the species. Instead of existing prior to its object, it is always born in response to a being who appears before us and who, by virtue of some eminent quality he possesses, stimulates the erotic process. . . .
>
> A mysterious longing! Whereas in every other situation in life nothing upsets us so much as to see the frontiers of our individual existence trespassed upon by another person, the rapture of love consists in feeling ourselves so metaphysically porous to another person that only in the fusion of both, only in an "individuality of two" can it find fulfillment. . . . However, the longing for fusion does not end with simple, uncreative union. Love is complete when it culminates in a more or less clear desire to leave, as testimony of the union, a child in whom the perfections of the beloved are perpetuated and affirmed.[35]

A husband and wife express their mutual affirmation through acts of sexual love. In addition to serving their own legitimate advantage, these acts also enable them to participate in the order of creation. The new human being they may bring into existence is not, ideally, the child of the mother or of the father. Rather, it is the personified union of the two. When conception occurs without reference to the bond between the couple, something of great importance in missing from the physical union. The deeper meaning of procreation in the common life of the lovers has failed to appear.

The spousal relation is inherently ordained toward, but not reducible to, procreation. Procreation is a sacred and profound experience, but it is not an end in itself. While the potentials

---

34. Virginia Held, "Birth and Death," in *Feminism and Political Theory*, ed. Cass R. Sunstein, (Chicago: University of Chicago Press, 1990), 87.
35. Ortega y Gasset, *On Love*, 36–37.

of the marital union cannot be limited to the interpersonal interests of the husband or wife, neither can the love between them be restricted to the horizon of fertility. If it were, sexual love would become sexual subservience. It is the love of the other *as a spouse* that makes possible any prospects of maternity or paternity. The spousal relation has priority; procreation is, or should be, a consequence of that love.[36]

The arrival of a child, by birth or adoption, signals the beginning of a family. In modern life, the proliferation of single-family dwellings creates an architectural illusion of familial self-sufficiency, which is cruelly dissolved by broader social realities. The home may provide for the elementary needs of nurture and survival, but any conception of higher purposes that the parents may entertain is subtly subverted by powers beyond their control.

The values of children are formed by influences that not only are external and perhaps inimical to parental authority and example (the mass media, for example) but also penetrate the intimate space of the home. The economic, social, medical, and educational services that were once provided by the household have now been assumed by the wider society or by the state. These changes may be lamented, but they are, in the main, inevitable aspects of social development. The problem is not what the family has lost, but what it has left.[37]

As a functional unit within a larger social complex, the present position of the family in human affairs is not a great im-

36. Pedro-Juan Viladrich, *The Agony of Legal Marriage*, chap. 5. This is also the position of the Holy Father, John Paul II. See Andrew N. Woznicki, *Karol Wojtyla's Existential Personalism* (New Britain: Mariel Press, 1980). The inversion which gives primacy to procreation over spousal love can be found in modern, as well as ancient, philosophy. For Schopenhauer, sexual love has the composition of the next generation as its objective. As a manifestation of the metaphysical desire of the will, this aim is expressed in the phenomenal world through the passion of the married partners. Consequently, "all love, however ethereally it may bear itself, is rooted in the sexual impulse alone" (Arthur Schopenhauer, "The Metaphysics of Love of the Sexes," in *The Philosophy of Schopenhauer*).

37. See the essays in *Kindred Matters* by Diana T. Meyers, Kenneth Kipnis, and Cornelius F. Murphy, Jr. (Ithaca: Cornell University Press, 1993).

provement over the insignificance of its existence in the ancient world. Serving the cycles of reproductive necessity, it allows little scope to higher human purposes. Moreover, as human procreation is increasingly viewed as a purely biological process, the subordination of family to economy and the state intensifies. If the family is to continue—to flourish, rather than stubbornly to persist—it will do so through a restoration of the value of parental, as well as of spousal, love.

Procreation reflects the mutual donation of the spouses to those qualities of paternity and maternity that are essential to the continuation of their mutual love. These commitments engage responsibilities which correspond to the dignity of a parent as either a masculine or feminine person. As a father and a mother, each has contributions to make and, while many tasks must be shared in common, their parental obligations can never be identical. Nor can the contribution that each should make be specified, in great detail, in advance of lived experience. What each gives as a parent to the life of the family is a gift, as well as the fulfillment of a duty; what one gives cannot be subject to a priori prescription. *As a person*, one gives all that one can give to the spiritual as well as the material well-being of a child, to the degree that such endowment can be bestowed within the home.

However much a woman may otherwise experience oppression in the home, as a mother she receives a great deal of respect and deference. The same is, unfortunately, not true of the father. In a modern home, he is often the least important person in residence. He is also under pressure to justify whatever authority he might wish to exercise for the good of the family. The abuse of the paternal role during the time of a patriarchal culture, along with the consequences of industrialization, have greatly diminished the significance of fatherhood. Any renewal of the paternal must take into account all the qualities of the masculine personality that are relevant to the best and optimal fulfillment of the role.

Some of the oldest conceptions of fatherhood explicitly identified him as a participant in royal authority. Aristotle makes this attribution not only by way of political analogy but also as a matter of anthropological insight. In relation to his child, the father is likened to a king because, like a king, the father stands in a superior relation to the one subject to him. And, like a king, he is of the same stock as those for whom he is responsible. In Aristotle's conception, there was also a chronological factor that accentuated the difference between parent and child. The relation between them was thought of as one aspect of the broader distinction between age and youth.[38]

In seeking to understand the relation between a father and his children, the significance of the age differential is often overlooked. Modern fathers are encouraged to be close to their children, to play with them more frequently, and to enter into the spirit of their youthful activities. These are valuable aspects of contemporary life; they increase the psychological security of the child and reduce the remoteness of the father from the life of the family. But intimacy can be overdone. Much of the general malaise of modern life is traceable to the leveling of the various ages of life and to the establishment of youthfulness as a standard of meaningful existence. The process can paralyze any attempt by a male parent to assert a legitimate authority over those children for whom he is responsible:

Youth as the period of highest vital efficiency and of erotic exaltation becomes the desired type of life in general. Where the human being is regarded only as a function, he must be young; and if youth is over, he will still strive to show its semblance. Add to that, for primary reasons, age no longer counts. The individual's life is experienced only momentarily . . . not remembered and cherished as the up-building or irrevocable decisions upon the foundation of biological phases. . . . The individual is no more than one instance among millions; why then should he think his doings of any importance? What happens, happens quickly and is soon forgotten. People therefore tend to behave as if they were all of the same age. . . . When the old

38. Aristotle, *Politics*, bk. 1, chap. 12, 1259b1–15. It is to be noted that we are talking about a relation between parent and child, not the relation between spouses. Royal images also surround the role of mother as queen. Aristotle also noted that a special friendship should exist between a father and his sons (*Magna Moralia* 9). For a general discussion, see Robert Bly, *Iron John*, chap. 4.

pretend to be young, of course the young have no reverence for their elders. These latter, instead of (as they should) keeping the young at a distance and setting them a standard, assume the airs of an invincible vitality, such as beseems youth but is unbecoming to age.[39]

Without some respect for the stages of life, we will not begin to understand the deeper meaning of parenting. Fathers who lack a sense of their own developing existence can not provide the wisdom and guidance their children hope to receive from them.

Children hope to receive from their fathers, as well as their mothers, some affirmation that will make them whole. The child has a spiritual destiny, and these deeper needs must be satisfied by both of his parents. Custom and ritual surround motherhood with immense religious importance but often neglect the comparable authority of the father. In a democratic age, not only has the father lost the intimations of royalty; he is no longer seen as one who mediates divine mysteries.[40]

We lack an elevated image of fatherhood. The impoverishment of the status and meaning of paternity contributes to a general sense of masculine insignificance. Some may fear that the enhancement of the position of father will only lead to new abuses and such concerns must be taken seriously. At the same time, it makes no sense to exalt motherhood while neglecting, or demeaning, the status of an equal parent. If marital love is to be fully reciprocal, there must be equal respect between the spouses for what it means to be either a masculine

39. Karl Jaspers, *Man in the Modern Age*, trans. Eden and Cedar Paul (London: Routledge & Kegan Paul, 1951), 50. For an argument by a family psychologist that children should pay more attention to adults than adults to children, after infancy, see John Rosemond, "Parenting," *Providence Sunday Journal*, E 10, 8/16/92.

40. On this, see Patrick M. Arnold, *Wildmen, Warriors and Kings*, (New York: Crossroads Press, 1991). In his book *What Men Want* (Cambridge: Harvard University Press, 1994), John Munder Ross points out that there are gender-specific tasks of fathering that should exist in a normal home. Excessive mothering can impede the progress of the child toward separation and independence. In addition to the effect which the father has on the gender identity of his child, the father also elicits, and restrains, instinctual impulses, including those connected with aggression (chap. 4).

or a feminine person throughout every dimension of their shared life.

Without the influence of both parents, a child will receive a distorted conception of the fundamental problems of existence. He or she will find it difficult to reconcile the fundamental polarities of beauty and goodness. Because of a schism between the paternal and maternal principles, such a child will not easily develop that harmony between the ethical and the aesthetic dimensions of being which is indispensable to a balanced life.[41]

Literature on parenting stresses the duties that the status entails, and there are good reasons for such an emphasis. But the primary realities cannot be fully expressed in the terminology of ethics. For what is involved is the generation of persons. At birth, an unrepeatable self has come into the world. The obligations that the event engages are obviously important, but of greater importance is the degree of welcome: how the new child is received, and whether it is made to feel at home. Acceptance cannot be compelled.

As the family seeks clear justification for itself in the modern world, it will no longer do simply to say that it serves to propagate the species. There must be reasons for the continuance of the family that touch the essential interests of the human person. As the primary natural habitat of human sociability, the family is the only form of human association where one's importance lies simply in being oneself. "Home is the place where, when you have to go there, they have to take you in."[42] It is where one can be born, grow up, and even die as a fully affirmed human person.

41. The distortions can be caused by an exaggerated emphasis upon either masculine or feminine formation. Kierkegaard's tragedy was that because of the disunion of his parents he overly intellectualized his life. See K. Stern, *The Flight from Woman,* chap. 10. That influence can be seen in Kierkegaard's conception of marriage, which tries to compensate for the instability of the ethical by an appeal to universal spiritual meaning (Soren Kierkegaard, *Works of Love,* trans. David L. Swenson and Lillian Marvin Swenson [Princeton: Princeton University Press, 1949], chap. 3).

42. Robert Frost, "The Death of the Hired Man," in *Complete Poems of Robert Frost* (New York: Holt, Rinehart and Winston 1964), 49, 53.

Parents can provide their children with an unconditional love which no social service agency can ever hope to duplicate. Yet these potentials of parental love will not be realized unless those who bring children into the world recapture the full significance of their calling in its greatest as well as its most elementary meaning. This is particularly true with respect to what is loosely called "education." Modern parents do not usually provide academic instruction; if they think of themselves as educators at all, they usually consider their role to be that of supporting the instruction that the child receives at school. Such support is valuable and, in some respects, indispensable. But parents can also unwillingly reinforce prevailing ideas concerning the purposes of education which are detrimental to the deepest needs of their children.

When parents uncritically submit to the convention that the purpose of education is to facilitate employment and practical success, they collaborate in a social process which places their child in a servile position within a materialistic culture. Children who are pressured by their parents to conform to prevailing norms of achievement cannot help but believe that love is, everywhere, conditional; that even at home they are not loved for their own sakes. To integrate their own family into the life of the broader community parents must inculcate in their children essential social and civic virtues. But if they take their calling seriously, they will avoid training their children to be subservient to the laws of the marketplace. It is part of the special dignity of parenting to make the family a school for love. Mothers and fathers teach by example, and they can show to their children the integrity and fulfillment that can be theirs through a developing respect for truth, goodness, and beauty in all their inexhaustible wonder and diversity. In transmitting these values to their children, parents have the power to surpass the often-pretentious standards of modern pedagogy.

The instabilities of modern marriage and the increase in divorce too often leads to a situation in which one parent, acting alone, must heroically bear all the parental responsibilities. These circumstances require utmost understanding, but they should not lead us to overlook the important links between procreation and mutual conjugal love. Nor should they lead us to ignore the significant benefits that come to any child who receives the positive and continuous influence of both of its parents.

As the conjugal union of a man and a woman, marriage has a natural orientation toward the procreation and education of children. But conjugal union is also a complementary encounter of espousal between a masculine and a feminine person. As we have already noted, fertility is not an end in itself. It should be a reflection of the love between husband and wife. With the arrival of children, the spouses are now a mother and a father; but their relationship as husband and wife is still the core of their union. It is important that even under such change of circumstances the spousal relationship retain its primary significance.

The ancients believed that the conjugal bond between a husband and wife aimed at something essentially different from what one observes in animal reproduction. With biological discernment, Aristotle saw that in lower animals sexual mating was limited to the purposes of reproduction, while animals that evidenced some degree of intelligence manifested a more enduring mutual regard. It was only in humans that there existed a complete collaboration. Aristotle reasoned that men and women aim "not just at existence, but at a happy existence."[43] Yet the mutual happiness Aristotle had in mind never transcended the experience of parenting. Emphasizing the different contributions that each makes to the household, he held out to the married couple the pleasurable assistance of offspring as the parents move toward their later years. In the Middle Ages, Aquinas was even more conservative in his assessment of spousal intimacy. Husbands and wives help each other in the work of procreation; but as for other needs a man may have, this great celibate thought they are more easily satisfied by help from other men.[44]

43. Aristotle, *Oeconomica* 3.
44. Aquinas, *Summa Theologiae* Ia. 92,1. (vol. 13, Blackfriars ed., 1964).

The idea that the range of mutual assistance a husband and wife owe to each other is limited by their roles as mothers and fathers is a traditional idea of continuing influence. But it lacks that deeper sense of companionship we now associate with married love. The shift can be seen in the novels of Jane Austen, who saw marriage as the essential friendship, as well as in the works of John Stuart Mill, who insisted that marriage should have no other motivation "except the happiness which two persons who love each other feel in associating their existence."[45]

The nature of the mutual happiness which spouses may legitimately anticipate remains subject to considerable ambiguity. The extended controversy within Roman Catholicism as to whether mutual aid was a primary, or secondary, objective of married life is an extreme expression of this confusion. More recent developments, which emphasize the fruitfulness and value of conjugal love in itself, independent of procreation, are a valuable corrective.[46] The desire to subordinate the interpersonal relation of the spouses to generative ends was also part of a tendency to reduce marriage to the family and, in so doing, to lessen the value of intimate love. This reduction led to a situation in which "sex, and love and marriage were bound up with the family, rather than with personality, and personality could not endure this state of affairs."[47] There was a failure to see that the love between spouses was a love between persons—persons who exist not only for their own sake, but also for intimate experiences of adult human friendship and mutual enhancement.

The difficulties involved in explicating a reciprocal love that is both personal and sexual can be seen in Kant's theory of marriage. He saw marriage as an agreement between two per-

45. "On Marriage," in vol. 21, *Collected Works of John Stuart Mill*, 41. On Jane Austen, see Allan Bloom, *Love and Friendship*, chap. 3.

46. See the discussion in Evelyn Eaton Whitehead and James D. Whitehead, *Marrying Well* (New York: Image Books, 1966), chap. 5.

But see *Veritatis Splendor* (The Splendor of Truth), encyclical letter of John Paul II, of October 5, 1993.

47. Nicholas Berdyaev, *The Fate of Man in the Modern World*, 124.

sons who grant each other equal, reciprocal rights. Each gains an exclusive sexual partner on condition that there is mutual respect for the other as a person. However, while the conditions of the exchange are meant to protect against abuse, the emphasis which Kant places upon rational principles leaves this conception at a chill distance from the dynamics of interpersonal love. And its emphasis upon duties leaves insufficient room for an active concern for the good of the other.[48]

Mutual love, rather than mutual aid, expresses more deeply the inner nature of interpersonal relation between married persons. Rather than being a possessory exchange, betrothed love is a donation of self by which two distinct persons live a shared existence. This perspective accentuates its pervasive character:

In its meaning as the dynamics of marital life "mutual aid" is not properly an end of marriage, but rather that dimension which is proper of marital life itself and which expresses itself in reciprocal service, mutual love, the entire set of interpersonal relations between the spouses, the existential realization of the conjugal life, and all that which is present in the generation and formation of children, the forming and developing of a home and family, and the ordained realization of the sexual inclination. . . . [I]n its total meaning, "mutual aid" is not so much an end as it is a constant and typical dimension of all marital life. . . . For this reason, if we understand mutual aid in the total sense of the dynamics of married life, that "mutual aid" is not properly an end but rather marriage itself insofar as it is lived within a community of life and love.[49]

Apart from but not in opposition to procreation, the mutuality of love between the spouses refers to the inexhaustible ways in which, as a couple, they complement each other as each other's good. But such intimacy seeks the other's good because the other, as a complete person, has his or her unique des-

48. Irving Singer, *The Nature of Love* (Chicago: University of Chicago Press, 1985), vol. 2, chap. 12; Howard Williams, *Kant's Political Philosophy* (New York: St. Martin's Press, 1983) chap. 5. See also Carole Patemen, *The Sexual Contract*, chap. 6.

49. Pedro-Juan Viladrich, *The Agony of Legal Marriage*, 203. John Paul II stresses an equality of mutual service in *Mulieris Dignitatem* (1988).

tiny. These interpersonal reciprocities are the qualities of a maturing married love: a "staying in love," in which both come to cherish the joint experience and the particular person with whom this life, with its joys and its sorrows, has been shared.[50]

Married love calls on qualities of affection and companionship that, once they become habitual, can sustain a durable long-term commitment. The romance and sexual attraction that highlight the beginning of the process remain an integral part of its continued vitality. So, surprisingly, does the persistence of self-love.

Neither a man nor a woman can commit themselves to an enduring union under conditions that would foreseeably jeopardize their own integrity, or their legitimate sense of self-esteem. The will to love cannot be completely severed from the need to be loved. In the love between the sexes, there is a perception, from the primary encounter onward, that the other has the capacity to satisfy, within reason, our deeper desires for happiness. Such expectation is at the core of all intimate relationships. We know, intuitively, that our deepest interests must be respected if we are to live in harmony with another in a conjugal union that will permeate all aspects of our personal existence.

In the dynamics of married love there is a continuous relationship between need and bestowal. In bestowal, the one who truly loves, loves beyond the capacity of the beloved to satisfy his or her needs. Love is also the affirmation of the other. The lover delights in the life and accomplishments of the other, because the good of the beloved has become an integral part of the lover's own happiness.[51] A deeper complexity lies in the fact that each spouse, in addition to his, or her, involvement in the marriage, also deserves to realize a personal fulfillment in the world beyond the home.

50. Singer, *The Nature of Love*, vol. 3, chap. 10.
51. "To be beloved is all I need, and whom I love, I love indeed" (Samuel Taylor Coleridge, "The Pains of Sleep").

IV. *Individual Autonomy and Marital Union*

When a man and a woman fall in love, romance is at the flood. Each is absorbed in the other, and, since they experience such emotional satisfaction, neither gives thought to the overall quality of the relationship or to its future. As lovers, the partners are not thinking or acting out of themselves. In ecstasy, one may be surrendering self to the other, but there is no decisive commitment by either to the other. It is for these reasons that romance and married love are often considered to be irreconcilable.[52]

The experience of falling in love brings much immediate happiness, but it is inherently unstable. The intensity of feeling being experienced by the lovers is, by its nature, variable. But there are other reasons why romance falls short of permanence. Each is so saturated with the other that neither gives sufficient attention to themselves. We have already observed the subtle connection between legitimate self-love and love for another. The love we have for another must be compatible with the love we have for ourselves. There must be a similarity, but not an identity, between the two loves.

In legitimate self-love we not only value our bare existence; we cherish our uniqueness. This is the core and continuity of our identities; it is also the ground of our love for another. For love between a man and a woman to be truly interpersonal, the attraction between them must be that of one uniqueness toward another. The self, while affirming itself, must be drawn toward the value which the other is in her or himself. However much it may be charged with emotion, love has its origin in the perception of something lovable in the beloved.[53]

If romantic love is to mature, it must chart a course between the shoals of instinct and idealization. Love experienced as the satisfaction of desire is passive. When sexual need is satisfied,

52. Denis de Rougemont, *Love in the Western World*.

53. Robert Johann, *The Meaning of Love* (Glen Rock, N.J.: Paulist Press, 1966).

passion dies. Don Juan had many conquests, but he never loved a woman. Rather, they loved him with a love that was not returned.[54] Real love is not a passion that consumes itself; it is a reaching out in the affirmation of its object. Such attachment must not be an idealization. When eros is awakened, it seeks to find its good in the incommunicable reality of the other. The lover sees and seeks a goodness and beauty embodied in the person of the opposite sex. The danger is that he or she may imaginatively transform the other into a symbol of perfection. The other is then loved insofar as he, or she, seems to be a reflection of an ideal. Lovers may be convinced that they are in love with another person, but they may, in fact, be in love with the ideal.[55]

In meaningful love, the other is seen as having a good proper to himself or herself. The value that is there causes the lover to reach out and seek some form of union with that abundance which is the intimate self of the other. In a love that is both personal and sexual, the lover hopes to come into vital contact with the one who is loved. The lover wants to be with the beloved in a union so close that the lover becomes part of the beloved's existence. But this union must be achieved without the lover renouncing his or her independent reality.

As the love that exists between a man and a woman develops, it tends toward marriage, which, as we have seen, is the closest possible union between persons. For married love to be true to its personal nature, it must in some respects be based upon equality. The reason is that love cannot be detached from personhood. The parties to a marriage must treat each other as equal, and unique, persons.

In the dynamics of love between the sexes, physical attraction plays an indispensable role. Yet every individual of the opposite sex possesses a value, in the first place, as a person. Their sexual value is, ultimately, of secondary importance. A man's encounter with femininity is an encounter with a con-

54. José Ortega y Gasset, *On Love,* chap. 2.
55. Irving Singer, *The Nature of Love,* vol. 1, chaps. 2 and 3. Id. chap. 7.

crete person, and the same is true of a woman's experience of masculinity.[56]

Although equality is an integral part of marriage, it cannot replace the unitive value of married love. In their desire to correct all the wrongs inflicted upon them by men, some feminists have called upon principles of equality to transform the relations between husbands and wives. They would change society from the root up, beginning with the family. If patterns of dominance and subservience within the home can be corrected, women as well as men would be able to pursue personal fulfillment, through education and employment, in the broader public world. To realize these objectives, it is thought that the relations between husbands and wives should conform, as far as possible, with standards of justice derived from ideals of equality.[57]

Since married men and women are equal as persons, their relations should be governed by reciprocal rules, which might be imagined as having been adopted under circumstances in which spouses prescind from all qualities that accentuate their differences. In chapter 2, "Reason and Gender," we noted some of the general consequences of egalitarian leveling upon the development of a unique masculine or feminine personality. With respect to marriage, an egalitarian conception presupposes that gender distinctions are primarily the result of social practices that work to the disadvantage of women. If the only differences between a husband and a wife are imagined as being those which are of an obvious and biological nature, their mutual marital obligations can be deduced from their status as equals. Allocation of rights and responsibilities within the family will then attain a new equilibrium, which will be to the advantage of all its members:

For if principles of justice are to be adopted unanimously by representative human beings ignorant of their particular characteristics

56. Karol Wojtyla (Pope John Paul II), *Love and Responsibility*, trans. H. T. Willetts (New York: Farrar, Straus, and Giroux, 1981).

57. E.g., Susan Moller Okin, *Justice, Gender, and the Family* (New York: Basic Books, 1989).

and positions in society, they must be persons whose psychological and moral development is in all essentials identical. This means that the social factors influencing the differences presently found between the sexes—from female parenting to all the manifestations of female subordination and dependence—would have to be replaced by genderless institutions and customs. Only children who are equally mothered and fathered can develop fully the psychological and moral capacities that currently seem to be unevenly distributed between the sexes. Only when men participate equally in what have been principally women's realms of meeting the daily material and psychological needs of those close to them, and when women participate equally in what have been principally men's realms of larger scale production, government, and intellectual and artistic life, will members of both sexes be able to develop a more complete *human* personality than has hitherto been possible.[58]

This family ethic extends to the domestic world principles of justice which moral philosophers such as John Rawls have conceived to be the foundation of equality which ought to exist between distinct individuals who must live together in a democratic society. The political conception is an attempt to assure that those who, in spite of their differences, must socially coexist, will do so according to principles they would assume if they were fairly represented as equal persons.[59] It remains to be seen how fully such principles can be applied to spousal relations.

The incorporation of these contractarian values into the world of marriage and family does much to enhance the personhood of women. It corrects the false impression that they are not capable of moral autonomy, and it also demonstrates that women are rationally able to comply with standards of fairness so long as others do the same. The application of equality to intimacy accommodates some of the divergences of moral sensitivity and perception which, as we saw in an earlier chapter, constitute a difference between men and women. The disinterestedness that the imagined deliberations require is

58. Ibid., 107.
59. Ibid. See also Susan Moller Okin, "Justice and Gender," *Philosophy & Public Affairs* 16 (Winter 1987), 42–72.

not a purely abstract procedure. As understood from a feminine viewpoint, the consent to equality calls for a certain empathy, requiring one to see a situation from different points of view. To reach agreement with others whose interests may be different from one's own demands that one think not only of oneself but also of all who are engaged in the common marital enterprise.

If the experienced relations between husbands and wives were actually governed by moral principles of reciprocal equality, it might be reasonable to expect that the hierarchical structures of dominance and dependence, which characterized a patriarchal culture, would finally be eliminated. The application of the principles could lead to an equal sharing of family responsibilities, especially household tasks, as well as the burdens of child care. A certain proportionality would be operative. As men took up a greater share of the burdens of nurture and intimacy, their wives would gain greater opportunities, previously denied them, to participate in the larger world of work and culture.[60]

It may be objected that it is inappropriate to apply principles of equality to the relations between married persons because an equality of friendship, rather than an equality of justice, should always exist between members of a family.[61] That argument could be countered by the observation that many mod-

60. Okin, *Justice, Gender, and the Family,* chap. 5. Compare this observation of John Paul II on equal parenting: "Although both of them together are parents of their child, *the woman's motherhood constitutes a special 'part' of this shared parenthood* and the most demanding part. Parenthood—even though it belongs to both—is realized much more fully in the woman, especially in the prenatal period. It is the woman who 'pays' directly for this shared generation, which literally absorbs the energies of her body and soul. It is therefore necessary that *the man* be fully aware that in their shared parenthood he owes *a special debt to the woman.* No program of 'equal rights' between women and men is valid unless it takes this fact fully into account" (*Mulieris Dignitatem,* chap. 6; italics in original).

61. Aristotle, *Nichomachean Ethics,* chap. 8.7. See also chap. 12. See also John M. Cooper, "Aristotle on Friendship," in *Essays on Aristotle's Ethics,* ed. A. Rorty (Berkeley: University of California Press, 1980), chap. 17. On the restoration of the idea of erotic friendship between a married couple, see Allan Bloom, *Love and Friendship,* chap. 3.

ern marriages cannot be described in terms of an affectionate reciprocity because a woman, by entering marriage, particularly if she becomes pregnant, may alter the whole course of her life and then be abandoned by her husband. Better to construct family life upon a basis of equal justice, so that if mutual generosity and affection fail, the injured party has a structure of principles to which she can appeal.[62]

The conceptualization of marriage in terms of equal justice is remedial in the sense that it is meant to relieve the deprivations and frustrations that women experience within the modern family. But this perception of oppression is not reciprocal. It ignores the extent to which men can and do experience a loss of personal identity and nonfulfillment in married life. As explained in the initial chapter, there is a mutual sense of personal deprivation at the heart of married life, and this situation with its deeper reciprocities must be corrected in a way that is compatible with the needs and legitimate desires of both men and women. To meet this challenge one must not abandon principles and depend upon the vagaries of affection. But one must also not undervalue the potentialities of eros.

The challenge is to determine the relation between love and justice. The insistence upon rights within a marriage may be a sign that the relationship is unraveling; yet no intimate union could endure without some sense of mutual entitlement. Eros promises more than what can be expected from a respect for rights; but, without such juridical respect, the promises of love can never be fulfilled. Nonetheless, the entitlements which arise out of a marital relationship are of a personal nature, and they must be grounded in the experience of espousal.

The justice of equality applies its principles of fairness to all, but it does so impersonally. Equality treats each marital partner as a moral person, but it imposes demands derived from qualities of being that are common to both.[63] By contrast, the marital relation arises from a love for a specific individual who is either a masculine or a feminine person. The sexual attrac-

62. Okin, *Justice, Gender, and the Family,* chap. 2.
63. Robert Johann, *The Meaning of Love.*

tion is, as we have said, that of one uniqueness for another. One *encounters* another atypical person. In the developing relationship, one seeks intimacy with that profound singularity; one does not desire an identical perfection. The lover does not hope for an ethical union with another moral person. He or she is drawn toward the embodied reality of the other. The attraction is to a particular reality of much greater depth than any similarities between them.

Marital justice cannot be derived from principles that descend upon the parties from some imagined antecedent position of pure understanding. Their mutual obligations must be based upon the reciprocal intentions that their marital vows are meant to verbalize. Where the ceremonial "I do" is freely expressed, each person, by an unrepeatable act of will, has made a gift of self to the other with respect to whatever is involved in their conjugal union. A decision of such magnitude must be uncoerced; once made, it creates the bonds that constitute the justice of marriage. Before that event, each was a completely independent man or woman. Now they are spouses. As such, they belong to each other as husband and wife.[64]

The idea of mutual belonging stirs images of possession— which, for feminists, recalls the script of patriarchy. These memories could be countered with tales of the sexual subservience of men, but then we are left with nothing but the sadness of mutual accusation. When the relations between the spouses are thought of in terms of mutual respect, the reciprocal obligations become more meaningful. But we are still left with a sense of dissatisfaction. For even if we are able to express the nature of the bond in a way that relieves the fears of

64. Pedro-Juan Viladrich, *The Agony of Legal Marriage*, chap. 4. Michael Sandel argues that an increase of justice within family relations will not necessarily lead to a moral improvement in such relationships, particularly where the purpose is to change the motives of the parties. He seems to have in mind the principles of equality which I have also criticized, but not the sense of the bonds of justice arising out of the marriage vows. See Michael Sandel, *Liberalism and the Limits of Justice* (Cambridge: Harvard University Press, 1982), chap. 1. See also Michael Walzer, *Spheres of Justice* (New York: Basic Books, 1983), chap. 9.

oppression, we still feel that some deeper, more personal interest has not been accommodated. For a more complete and happier understanding of what each is owed, we must again seek the aid of eros.

If the mutual obligations of a husband and a wife are to be fully intelligible, they must be seen in relation to the desires of love from which they originate. Men and women fall in and out of love, especially under the uncertain conditions of modern life. But if a man and woman truly love each other, they will want their love to endure. Love seeks union, a type of coalescence that will preserve their love and make it fruitful. The marital partners contribute, respectively, their masculinity and their femininity to the society they create out of their love. There is a possessory exchange, but it is an exchange of persons, not of sexual objects.[65] Through the debt of marriage, two become as one with respect to the requirements of their conjugal union. At the same time, each remains a person in his or her own right.

As men and women both become aware of the range and complexity of their own distinct personalities, the restrictions of marriage and family life become more difficult for both to bear. To be a person involves a continuous increase in separate identity and a need for an evolving self-direction.[66] Marital life embraces all the dimensions of mutual existence. Such encompassing can be perceived as an intrusion upon the individual quest for an autonomous existence. But intimacy can enrich as well as diminish the person. The self-reliant conceptions of personal growth that pervade our culture make it difficult for us to see how a close relation to another can advance our own autonomy. Yet dependence upon another can, paradoxically, promote one's independence. It all depends upon the quality and intensity of the mutual love.

65. Compare Viladrich, supra, note 60. This exchange is more adequately expressed as an entrusting to each other as persons. For a theological explanation, see *Mulieris Dignitatem*, chap. 5.

66. John Rawls, *A Theory of Justice* (Cambridge: Harvard University Press, 1971), chap. 7. See also Diana Meyers, *Self, Society, and Personal Choice* (New York: Columbia University Press, 1989).

As a husband and wife become more fully present to each other, interpersonal exchange and dialogue are maximized. The more the other is, the more lovable he or she becomes. Where affirmation is mutual, each becomes increasingly conscious of their own value. By giving themselves to the union of their love, the spouses enhance their own self-worth.

Where I love another directly, I break the little circle I form with myself. Where I would lodge the other simply as an idea, I discover a new existence; I am present to a new and transcendent revelation of that value I love in myself. And by that very fact, I cure myself of the exclusiveness, the poverty, the solitude that are my lot and my curse when, through egoism, I constitute myself the center of the universe and the absolute. The only way to fathom the depths of the value which I am in myself is to turn toward and be open to that same value where it exceeds the bounds of my proper subjectivity. I cannot really love myself without loving other selves. Only when drawn into communion with other selves is my own person confirmed in being and my own love equal to the perfection to which it secretly aspires.[67]

No person, of either sex, can commit themselves to a perpetual union under conditions which threaten their own integrity. But marriage is a commitment to a life in common. To balance independence with this conjugal community calls for a delicate reconciliation of values. Whether a balance is struck will depend upon qualities of character that each party brings to the marriage. It will also depend upon what they both understand by love.

Heterosexual love expresses the longing of a person to find a fulfillment, through intense communion with a person of the opposite sex. In terms of temporal life, this is the happiness promised by eros: "To be together always with someone who wishes to be together with you always."[68] It includes a desire for the companionship of the other and a will directed toward the good of that other. The union effected by marital love is not one of fusion; in reciprocal respect, the unique personality of each must be preserved. Otherness inheres in this intimate

67. Robert Johann, *The Meaning of Love*, 52.
68. Bloom, *Love and Friendship*, 541.

society, but it is not detached from union. For what is loved is the *self* of the other.

Throughout these reflections we have explored the giftedness, as well as the vulnerabilities, of modern men and women as they struggle to understand themselves as either feminine or masculine persons. The emancipation of women and the reconstruction of manliness are the two great humanistic tasks of this age. The emergence of these new images of personal existence have placed an extraordinary strain upon the relations between the sexes. Now is the time for reconciliation. Through a dialogue, a conversation among equals, we must come to understand how our distinctive sexuality influences every dimension of our personal and interpersonal lives.

Men and women now hope to realize new levels of personal fulfillment in economic, social, and political life, but to do so in a way that does not compromise their sexual identities. In the previous chapters we suggested some of the ways that such integrity is apparent in various aspects of our common public life. A sense of fulfillment must also be experienced in the domain of intimacy. Feminism has shown how much the public and private realm are interconnected, and it is clear that the reformation of our fragile cultural and political existence will depend upon improvements within the environment of the home. At this fundamental level, marriage and family life must be transformed in a way that is both fair and responsive to our deepest desires for love. A new humanism should find its origins in that most private context where adult persons affirm what is unique and different about each other.

Love in marriage requires attitudes of affection and companionship that will sustain life-long commitment. Actively concerned for each other's life and growth, spouses must encourage and support each other in their mutual aspirations for a full and satisfying life. There is a deep relation between being loved and being who we are. Such love is possible only between persons sufficiently mature to see their own good in the flourishing of their spouse. In the love between a husband and

a wife there is a reciprocal consciousness at work: each is interested in the life of the other, as he or she rejoices in the fact
of the other's existence. And, while each respects the right of
the other to personal fulfillment, such respect does not occur
in complete isolation from the life they hold in common.

In marriage, the need to reconcile liberty and community,
which is a common theme of public discourse, takes on a more
profound meaning. By espousal, one has made a disposition
of oneself for the good of another for which there is no parallel
in the political world. A man, by his word, owes himself to the
one to whom he has made his vows. In that exchange a woman
makes a reciprocal donation. Neither is subordinate, or superior, to the other; neither loses his or her separate selfhood.
But, as spouses, they are not absolutely independent individuals. There is not that autonomy that reigns when the other,
and his or her interests, are exclusive of my own.

In unitive love the lover is in contact with that profound center of being which the beloved is in his or her uniqueness. The
lover delights in the accomplishments of the beloved because
the well-being of the beloved is part of the lover's own happiness. This respect for the independence of the other must be
reciprocal, for to love is to will also to be loved.[69] The tension
between self-sufficiency and a shared life is relieved as mutual
love begins to create values that are interpersonally shared.
And, when bestowal is reciprocal, when each promotes the
good of the other, the barriers between individual identities
are lowered.

Within marriage, when will and desire become reconciled,
the dynamics of heterosexual love bring to each a new happiness of life, growth, and peace. Beyond this point, reason
must be silent; reflection has nothing further to say. Understanding lacks the power to decide, in a given situation, what

69. Irving Singer, *The Nature of Love*, vol. 3, chap. 10. To delight in the
achievements of the other is to recognize the other as a primary agent of his,
or her, attainment. There is a world of difference between this positive recognition of the other and Sartre's idea that the lover creates the being of the
other within the world. See Notebook 1 of Sartre's *Notebooks for an Ethics*.

should be the proper balance between the satisfaction of one's needs and the affirmation of the other. In the end, as at the beginning, we must return to experience. Within each particular marriage, a unique man and a unique woman have assumed the bonds of love. As a specific masculine or feminine person, each has hopes for self-fulfillment, and for fulfillment for their spouse. It is for them to decide how much they desire the happiness of love.

BIBLIOGRAPHY

Abbott, Walter, S.J. ed, *Documents of Vatican II*. America Press, 1966.
Aquinas, St. Thomas. *Summa Theologiae*. 13. Oxford: Blackfriars, 1964.
Arendt, Hannah. *The Human Condition*. Chicago: University of Chicago Press, 1958.
———. *The Life of the Mind*. New York: Harcourt Brace Jovanovich, 1978.
———. "What is Freedom?" In *Between Past and Future: Eight Exercises in Political Thought*. New York: Viking Press, 1968.
Aristotle. *Nicomachean Ethics*. New York: Garland Publishing, 1987.
———. *Oeconomica*. In *Aristotle*. Trans. G. C. Armstrong. Cambridge: Harvard University Press, 1964.
———. *Politics*. New York: Cambridge University Press, 1988.
Arnold, Patrick. *Wildmen, Warriors, and Kings: Masculine Spirituality and the Bible*. New York: Crossroad Press, 1992.
Augustine, St. *The City of God*. Ed. and trans. J. W. C. Wand. London: Oxford University Press, 1963.
Bacon, Francis. "Of Marriage and Single Life" (1625). Published in *Selected Writings*. Introduction and notes by Hugh Dick. New York: Random House, 1955.
Baier, Annette. *Moral Prejudices: Essays on Ethics*. Cambridge: Harvard University Press, 1994.
———."Trust and Antitrust." In *Feminism and Political Theory*. Ed. Cass R. Sunstein. Chicago: University of Chicago Press, 1990.
———. "Whom Can Women Trust?" In *Feminist Ethics*. Ed. Claudia Card. Lawrence, Kan.: University Press of Kansas, 1991.
Balsdon, J. P. V. D. *Roman Women: Their History and Habits*. New York: Barnes and Noble, 1983.
Bardacke, T. "Hemingway's Women." In *Ernest Hemingway, The Man and His Works*. Ed. John T. McCaffery. New York: Cooper Square Publishers, 1964.
Barth, Karl. "The Doctrine of Creation." Vol. 3, Book 4, *Church Dogmatics*. Ed. A. T. Mackay et al. Edinburgh: T. & T. Clark, 1961.
Bartlett, Katharine T. "Feminist Legal Methods." *Harvard Law Review* 103 (February 1990): 829–88.
Bardwick, Judith M. *In Transition: How Feminism, Sexual Liberation, and the Search for Self-Fulfillment Have Altered Our Lives*. New York: Holt, Rinehart and Winston, 1979.
Barzun, Jacques. *The Culture We Deserve*. Middletown, Conn.: Wesleyan University Press, 1989.

Beauvoir, Simone de. *The Second Sex.* Ed. and trans. H. M. Parshley. New York: Alfred A. Knopf, 1952.

Becker, Mary E. "Prince Charming: Abstract Equality." *Supreme Court Review 1987* (1987): 201–47.

Bednarik, Karl. *The Male in Crisis.* Trans. Helen Sebba. Westport: Greenwood Press, 1970.

Beiner, Ronald. *Political Judgment.* Chicago: University of Chicago Press, 1983.

Bender, Leslie. "Feminist (Re)Torts: Thoughts on the Liability Crisis, Mass Torts, Power, and Responsibilities." *Duke Law Journal* (September 1990): 848–912.

———. "A Lawyer's Primer on Feminist Theory and Tort." *Journal of Legal Education* 38 (March/June 1988): 3–37.

Benhabib, Seyla, and Drucilla Cornell, eds. *Feminism as Critique: On the Politics of Gender.* Minneapolis: University of Minnesota Press, 1987.

Berdyaev, Nikolai. *The Fate of Man in the Modern World.* Ann Arbor: University of Michigan Press, 1935.

Berman, Harold J. *Law and Revolution: The Formulation of the Western Legal Tradition.* Cambridge: Harvard University Press, 1993.

Bloom, Allan David. *Love and Friendship.* New York: Simon and Schuster, 1993.

———. *The Closing of the American Mind: How Higher Education Has Failed Democracy and Impoverished the Souls of Today's Students.* New York: Simon and Schuster, 1987.

Bloom, Harold. "States of Being." In *Blake: A Collection of Critical Essays.* Ed. Northrop Frye. Englewood Cliffs, N.J.: Prentice-Hall, 1966.

Bly, Robert. *Iron John: A Book about Men.* Reading, Mass.: Addison-Wesley, 1990.

Brown, Wendy. *Manhood and Politics: A Feminist Reading in Political Theory.* Totowa, N.J.: Rowman and Littlefield, 1988.

Buber, Martin. *Between Man and Man.* Trans. Ronald Gregor Smith. New York: Macmillan, 1965.

Buck, Pearl S. "America's Medieval Women." In *An American Retrospective: Writing from Harper's Magazine, 1850–1984.* Ed. Ann Marie Cunningham. New York: Harper's Magazine Foundation, 1985.

Campbell, Joseph. *The Hero with a Thousand Faces.* New York: Pantheon Books, 1949.

———, and Bill Moyers. *The Power of Myth.* New York: Doubleday, 1988.

Cantarella, Eva. *Pandora's Daughters: The Role and Status of Women in Greek and Roman Antiquity.* Trans. Maureen Bifant. Baltimore: Johns Hopkins University Press, 1987.

Card, Claudia, ed. *Feminist Ethics.* Lawrence, Kan.: University Press of Kansas, 1991.

Cassirer, Ernst. *The Question of Jean-Jacques Rousseau.* New York: Columbia University Press, 1954.

Cavitch, David. *D. H. Lawrence and the New World*. New York: Oxford University Press, 1969.

Chabod, Federico. *Machiavelli and the Renaissance*. Trans. David Moore. New York: Harper and Row, 1965.

Chodorow, Nancy. *The Reproduction of Mothering: Psychoanalysis and the Sociology of Gender*. Berkeley: University of California Press, 1978.

Clark, Gillian. *Women in the Ancient World*. New York: Oxford University Press, 1989.

Coleridge, Samuel Taylor. "The Pains of Sleep." In *The Norton Anthology of English Literature*. Ed. M. H. Abrams et al. New York: W. W. Norton and Company, 1974.

Cook, Blanche Wiesen. *Eleanor Roosevelt*. I: 1884–1933. New York: Viking Press, 1992.

Cooper, John M. "Aristotle on Friendship." In *Essays on Aristotle's Ethics*. Ed. Amélie Rorty. Berkeley: University of California Press, 1980.

Dalton, Clare. "Where We Stand: Observations on the Situation of Feminist Legal Thought." *Berkeley Women's Law Journal* 3 (1987/88): 1–13.

Daly, Mary. *Beyond God the Father: Toward a Philosophy of Women's Liberation*. Boston: Beacon Press, 1973.

D'Arcy, Martin. *The Mind and Heart of Love, Lion and Unicorn: A Study in Eros and Agape*. New York: Meridian Books, 1956.

Dinnerstein, Dorothy. *The Mermaid and the Minotaur: Sexual Arrangement and Human Malaise*. New York: Harper and Row, 1976.

DuBois, Ellen Carol. *Feminism and Suffrage: The Emergence of an Independent Women's Movement in America, 1848–1869*. Ithaca: Cornell University Press, 1978.

Ehrenreich, Barbara. *The Hearts of Men: American Dreams and the Flight from Commitment*. New York: Anchor Press, 1983.

Eisenstein, Hester. *Contemporary Feminist Thought*. Boston: G. K. Hall, 1983.

Eisenstein, Zillah R. *The Radical Future of Liberal Feminism*. New York: Longman, 1981.

———. "Elizabeth Cady Stanton: Radical-Feminist Analysis and Liberal-Feminist Strategy." In *Feminism and Equality*. Ed. Anne Phillips. New York: New York University Press, 1987.

Eisler, Riane. *The Chalice and the Blade: Our History, Our Future*. San Francisco: Harper and Row, 1987.

Eliot, George. *Middlemarch: A Study of Provincial Life*. 2 vols. New York: Harper and Bros., 1872–73.

Eliot, T. S. "The Victim and the Sacrificial Knife." In *D. H. Lawrence: The Critical Heritage*. Ed. Ronald P. Draper. New York: Barnes and Noble, 1970.

Elshtain, Jean Bethke. *Public Man, Private Woman: Women in Social and Political Thought*. Princeton: Princeton University Press, 1981.

———. "Against Androgyny." In *Feminism and Equality*. Ed. Anne Phillips. New York: New York University Press, 1987.

Finley, Lucinda. "Transcending Equality Theory: A Way out of the Maternity and the Workplace Debate." *Columbia Law Review* 86 (October 1986): 1118–1182.

Finnis, John. *Natural Law and Natural Rights*. New York: Oxford University Press, 1980.

Fleming, Thomas. *The Politics of Human Nature*. New Brunswick, N.J.: Transaction Books, 1988.

Fox-Genovese, Elizabeth. *Feminism without Illusion: A Critique of Individualism*. Chapel Hill: University of North Carolina Press, 1991.

Fraser, Nancy. "What's Critical about Critical Theory?" In *Feminism as Critique*. Ed. Seyla Benhabib and Drucilla Cornell. Minneapolis: University of Minnesota Press, 1987.

French, Marilyn. *Beyond Power: On Women, Men, and Morals*. New York: Summit Books, 1985.

———. *The Women's Room*. New York: Summit Books, 1977.

Freud, Sigmund. *Moses and Monotheism*. New York: Vintage Books, 1939.

Friedan, Betty. *The Second Stage*. 2d ed. New York: Summit Books, 1986.

———. *The Feminine Mystique*. New York: W. W. Norton, 1963.

Friedman, Marilyn. "Feminism and Modern Friendship: Dislocating the Community." In *Feminism and Political Theory*. Ed. Cass R. Sunstein. Chicago: University of Chicago Press, 1990.

Fromm, Erich. *The Art of Loving*. New York: Harper and Row, 1956.

———. *The Sane Society*. New York: Holt, Rinehart and Winston, 1955.

Frost, Robert. *The Complete Poems of Robert Frost*. New York: Holt, Rinehart and Winston, 1964.

Frye, Northrop. *The Educated Imagination*. Bloomington: Indiana University Press, 1964.

Gadamer, Hans Georg. *The Idea of the Good in Platonic-Aristotelian Philosophy*. Trans. P. C. Smith. New Haven: Yale University Press, 1986.

Gilder, George. *Men and Marriage*. Gretna: Pelican Publications, 1987.

Gill, Emily. "Models of Family and Polity." In *Perspectives on the Family*. Ed. Moffat, Gric., and Bayles.

Gilligan, Carol. *In a Different Voice: Psychological Theory and Women's Development*. Cambridge: Harvard University Press, 1982.

Gilmore, David. *Manhood in the Making: Cultural Concepts of Masculinity*. New Haven: Yale University Press, 1990.

Ginzberg, Ruth. "Philosophy Is Not a Luxury." In *Feminist Ethics*. Ed. Claudia Card. Lawrence, Kan.: University Press of Kansas, 1991.

Glendon, Mary Ann. *The Transformation of Family Law: State, Law, and Family in the United States and Western Europe*. Chicago: University of Chicago Press, 1989.

———. "Marriage and the State: The Withering Away of Marriage." *Virginia Law Review* 63 (1976): 663–720.

Goldberg, Naomi R. *Changing the Gods*. Boston: Beacon Press, 1979.

Gordon, Lyndall. *Eliot's New Life*. New York: Oxford University Press, 1988.

Graves, Robert. *Collected Poems*. Garden City: Doubleday, 1961.

Gray, Francine du Plessix. *Soviet Women: Walking the Tightrope.* New York: Doubleday, 1989.

Greenawalt, Kent. *Law and Objectivity.* New York: Oxford University Press, 1992.

Greer, Germaine. *Sex and Destiny: The Politics of Human Fertility.* New York: Harper and Row, 1984.

Guardini, Romano. *The Virtues: On Forms of Moral Life.* Trans. Stella Lange. Chicago: Henry Regnery, 1967.

Harding, Sandra, and M. B. Hintikka. *Discovering Reality: Feminist Perspectives on Epistemology, Metaphysics, Methodology, and Philosophy of Science.* Dordrecht, Holland: Reidel, 1983.

Hardwig, John. "Should Women Think in Terms of Rights?" In *Feminism and Political Theory.* Ed. Cass R. Sunstein. Chicago: University of Chicago Press, 1990.

Hawthorne, Nathaniel. "The Birthmark." In *Nathaniel Hawthorne: Young Goodman Brown and other Stories.* Ed. Stanley Appelbaum. New York: Dover, 1992.

Hayek, Friedrich A. von. "Legislation and Liberty." In *The Mirage of Social Justice.* Chicago: University of Chicago Press, 1976.

Hegel, Georg Wilhelm. *Hegel's Philosophy of Right.* Trans. T. M. Knox. New York: Oxford University Press, 1952.

Held, Virginia. "Birth and Death." In *Feminism and Political Theory.* Ed. Cass R. Sunstein. Chicago: University of Chicago Press, 1990.

———. *Feminist Morality: Transforming Culture, Society, and Politics.* Chicago: University of Chicago Press, 1994.

Henderson, Lynne H. "Whose Nature? Practical Reasoning and Patriarchy." *Cleveland State Law Review* 38 (1990): 169–92.

———. "Legality and Empathy." *Michigan Law Review* 85 (June 1987): 1574–1653.

Hill, Melvyn, ed. *Hannah Arendt and the Recovery of the Public World.* New York: St. Martin's Press, 1979.

Horgan, Paul. *Of America East and West: Selections from the Writings of Paul Horgan.* New York: Farrar, Straus and Giroux, 1984.

Horney, Karen. *Feminine Psychology.* New York: W. W. Norton, 1967.

Hsu, Francis L. K. *Americans and Chinese.* 3d ed. Honolulu: University Press of Hawaii, 1981.

Huizinga, Jonah. *In the Shadow of Tomorrow.* London: William Heinemann, 1936.

Iyengar, K. R. Srinivasa. *François Mauriac: A Novelist and Moralist.* London: Asia Publishing House, 1964.

Jaggar, Alison. "Feminist Ethics: Projects, Problems, Prospects." In *Feminist Ethics.* Ed. Claudia Card. Lawrence, Kan.: University Press of Kansas, 1991.

———. "Sexual Differences and Sexual Equality." In *Theoretical Perspectives on Sexual Difference.* Ed. Deborah L. Rhode. New Haven: Yale University Press, 1990.

James, Henry. *The Portrait of a Lady.* Cambridge, Mass.: Riverside Press, 1956.

James, William. *A Pluralistic Universe*. New York: Longmans, Green, 1912.

Jaspers, Karl. *Man in the Modern Age*. Trans. Eden and Cedar Paul. London: Routledge and Kegan Paul, 1951.

Jeansonne, Sharon Pace. *The Women of Genesis: From Sarah to Potiphar's Wife*. Minneapolis: Fortress Press, 1990.

Johann, Robert. *The Meaning of Love: An Essay Towards a Metaphysics of Intersubjectivity*. New York: Paulist Press, 1966.

John Paul II, Pope (Karol Wojtyla). *Love and Responsibility*. Trans. W. T. Willets. San Francisco: Ignatius Press, 1981.

———. *Veritatis Splendor (The Splendor of Truth)*. Encyclical Letter, August 6, 1993.

———. *Mulieris Dignitatem (On the Dignity and Vocation of Women)*. Apostolic Letter, August 15, 1988.

———. *Dives In Misericordia (Rich in Mercy)*. Encyclical Letter, November 30, 1980.

Jung, C. G. "Anima and Animus." In *Collected Works*, vol. 7. Princeton: Princeton University Press, 1977.

Kahn, Coppelia. *Man's Estate: Masculine Identity in Shakespeare*. Berkeley: University of California Press, 1981.

Kaminer, Wendy. "Feminism's Identity Crisis." *Atlantic* 272 (October 1993): 51–53.

Kant, Immanuel. *Anthropology from a Pragmatic Point of View*. Trans. Mary J. Gregory. The Hague: Martinus Nijhoff, 1974.

———. *Lectures on Ethics*. New York: Harper and Row, 1963.

———. *Observations on the Feeling of the Beautiful and the Sublime*. 1764. Trans. John T. Goldthwaith. Berkeley: University of California Press, 1960.

———. *Political Philosophy*. New York: St. Martin's Press, 1983.

Kass, Leon R., and Bill Moyers. "The Origin of Philosophy Is in Wonder." In *A World of Ideas*. Ed. Betty Sue Flowers. New York: Doubleday, 1989.

Kaufman, Andrew. " Judges and Scholars: To Whom Shall We Look for Our Constitutional Law?" *Journal of Legal Education* 37 (1987): 184–202.

Kay, Herma Hill. "Models of Equality." *University of Illinois Law Review* 1985 (1985): 39–88.

Keen, Sam. *Fire in the Belly: On Being a Man*. New York: Bantam Books, 1991.

Keller, Evelyn Fox. *Reflections on Gender and Science*. New Haven: Yale University Press, 1985.

Kierkegaard, Soren. *Works of Love*. Trans. David F. Swenson and Lillian Marvin Swenson. Princeton: Princeton University Press, 1946.

Kittay, Eva Feder, and Diana T. Meyers, eds. *Women and Moral Theory*. Totowa, N.J.: Rowman and Littlefield, 1987.

Kolb, David. *The Critique of Pure Modernity: Hegel, Heidegger, and After*. Chicago: University of Chicago Press, 1986.

Kolbenschlag, Madonna. *Kiss Sleeping Beauty Goodbye: Breaking the Spell of Feminine Myths and Models*. New York: Doubleday, 1979.

Kuehn, Thomas. *Law, Family And Women: Toward a Legal Anthropology of Renaissance Italy.* Chicago: University of Chicago Press, 1991.

Lacan, Jacques. *Feminine Sexuality: Jacques Lacan and the Ecole Freudiènne.* Trans. Jacqueline Rose. New York: W. W. Norton, 1983.

Laffey, Alice L. *An Introduction to the Old Testament: A Feminist Perspective.* Philadelphia: Fortress Press, 1988.

Larmore, Charles E. *Patterns of Moral Complexity.* New York: Cambridge University Press, 1987.

Lawrence, D. H. *Fantasia of the Unconscious.* New York: Viking Press, 1960.

———. *Studies in Classic American Literature.* New York: Thomas Seltzer, 1923.

Le Fort, Gertrude von. *The Eternal Woman.* Trans. Placid Jordon, O.S.B. Milwaukee: Bruce, 1962.

Lenin, V. I. "The Woman Question." In *Selections from the Writings of Karl Marx, Frederick Engels, V. I. Lenin, and J. Stalin.* New York: International Publishing, 1951.

Lerner, Gerda. *The Creation of Patriarchy.* New York: Oxford University Press, 1986.

Levinas, Emmanuel. *Time and the Other and Additional Essays.* Trans. R. A. Cohen. Pittsburgh: Duquesne University Press, 1987.

Lewis, C. S. *The Four Loves.* Glasgow: William Collins Sons, 1960.

Llano, Alejandro. *The New Sensibility.* Trans. Alban d'Entremont. Pamplona: University of Navarra, 1991.

Lloyd, Genevieve. *The Man of Reason: "Male" and "Female" in Western Philosophy.* London: Methuen, 1984.

———. "Augustine and Aquinas." In *Feminist Theology: A Reader.* Ed. Ann Loades. Louisville: John Knox Press, 1990.

Lombroso, Gina. *The Soul of Woman* (L'Anima Della Donna). New York: E. P. Dutton, 1923.

Lorris, Guillaume de, and Jean de Meun. *The Romance of the Rose.* Ed. and trans. Harry W. Robbins. New York: Harper and Row, 1977.

Lyotard, Jean-Francois. *The Post-Modern Condition: A Report on Knowledge.* Minneapolis: University of Minnesota Press, 1984.

MacKinnon, Catharine A. *Toward a Feminist Theory of the State.* Cambridge: Harvard University Press, 1989.

McMillan, Carol. *Women, Reason, and Nature: Some Philosophical Problems with Feminism.* Princeton: Princeton University Press, 1982.

Maloney, Michael Francis. *François Mauriac, A Critical Study.* Denver: Alan Swallow, 1958.

Marcel, Gabriel. *Being and Having.* London: William Collins, 1965.

Maritain, Jacques. *Challenges and Renewals: Selected Readings.* Ed. Joseph W. Evans and Leo R. Ward. Cleveland: World Publishing, 1968.

———. *Distinguish to Unite; or, The Degrees of Knowledge.* New York: Scribner, 1959.

———. *Education at the Crossroads.* New Haven: Yale University Press, 1943.

———. *Man and the State.* Chicago: University of Chicago Press, 1951.

————. *Moral Philosophy; An Historical and Critical Survey of the Great Systems.* New York: Scribners, 1964.

Massaro, Toni. "Empathy, Legal Storytelling, and the Rule of Law." *Michigan Law Review* 87 (August 1989): 2099–2127.

May, Rollo. *Love and Will.* New York: W. W. Norton, 1969.

Mead, Margaret. *Male and Female: A Study of the Sexes in a Changing World.* New York: William Morrow, 1949.

Mencken, H. L. *A Mencken Chrestomathy.* New York: Alfred A. Knopf, 1949.

————. *In Defense of Woman.* New York: Alfred A. Knopf, 1917.

Meyers, Diana T. *Self, Society, and Personal Choice.* New York: Columbia University Press, 1989.

————. "The Socialized Individual and Individual Autonomy." In *Women and Moral Theory.* Ed. Eva Feder Kittay and Diana T. Meyers. Totowa, N.J.: Rowman and Littlefield, 1987.

————, Kenneth Kipnis, and Cornelius F. Murphy, eds. *Kindred Matters.* Ithaca: Cornell University Press, 1993.

Mill, John Stuart. "The Subjugation of Women" (1869). In volume 21 of *Collected Works of John Stuart Mill.* Ed. John M. Robson. Toronto: University of Toronto Press, 1984.

————. *Essays on Equality, Law, and Education.* Volume 21 of *Collected Works of John Stuart Mill.* Ed. John M. Robson. Toronto: University of Toronto Press, 1984.

Millet, Kate. *Sexual Politics.* New York: Avon Books, 1971.

Minow, Martha. *Making All the Difference: Inclusion, Exclusion, and American Law.* Ithaca: Cornell University Press, 1990.

————. "Feminist Reasoning: Getting It and Losing It." *Journal of Legal Education* 38 (March/June 1988): 47–60.

————. "Justice Engendered." *Harvard Law Review* 101 (1987): 10.

Mitchell, Juliet, and Ann Oakley, eds. "Reflections on Twenty Years of Feminism." In *What Is Feminism?* New York: Pantheon Books, 1986.

Moffat, R., et al., eds. "Studies in Social and Political Theory." In *Perspectives on the Family* 8. Lewiston, N.Y.: Edwin Mellen Press, 1990.

Moore, Michael S. "The Interpretive Turn in Modern Theory: A Turn for the Worse?" *Stanford Law Review* 41 (April 1989): 871–957.

Moore, Robert, and Douglas Gillette. *King, Warrior, Magician, Lover: Rediscovering the Archetypes of the Mature Masculine.* San Francisco: Harper and Row, 1990.

Moore, Thomas. *Care of the Soul: A Guide for Cultivating Depth and Sacredness in Everyday Life.* New York: Harper Collins, 1992.

Moyers, Bill. *A World of Ideas: Conversations with Thoughtful Men and Women about American Life Today and the Ideas Shaping Our Future.* Ed. Betty Sue Flowers. New York: Doubleday, 1989.

Murdoch, Iris. *The Sovereignty of Good.* New York: Schocken Books, 1971.

Murphy, Cornelius F. *Descent into Subjectivity: Studies of Rawls, Dworkin, and Unger in the Context of Modern Thought.* Wakefield, N.H.: Longwood Academic, 1990.

―――. "Dialectical Reasoning and Personal Judgment." *University of California at Davis Law Review* 26 (Spring 1993): 673–90.

Murphy, Cullen. "Women and the Bible." *Atlantic* 272 (August 1993): 39–45 +.

Murry, John Middleton. *Son of Woman: The Story of D. H. Lawrence.* New York: Jonathan Cape and Harrison Smith, 1931.

Noonan, Peggy. *What I Saw at the Revolution: A Political Life in the Reagan Era.* New York: Random House, 1990.

Nozick, Robert. *Anarchy, State, and Utopia.* New York: Basic Books, 1974.

Nussbaum, Martha C. *The Fragility of Goodness: Luck and Ethics in Greek Tragedy and Philosophy.* New York: Cambridge University Press, 1986.

―――. *Love's Knowledge: Essays on Philosophy and Literature.* New York: Oxford University Press, 1990.

Nye, Andrea. *Feminist Theory and the Philosophies of Man.* London: Routledge, 1988.

O'Brien, Connor Cruise. "Toward European Disunion." *Harper's* 285 (July 1992): 18–22.

O'Brien, Mary. *Reproducing the World: Essays in Feminist Theory.* Boulder: Westview Press, 1989.

Okin, Susan Moller. *Women in Western Political Thought.* Princeton: Princeton University Press, 1979.

―――. *Justice, Gender, and the Family.* New York: Basic Books, 1989.

―――. "Reason and Feeling in Thinking about Justice." *Ethics* 99 (January 1989): 229–49.

Olsen, Frances. "Unraveling Compromise." *Harvard Law Review* 103 (November 1989): 105–35.

Ong, Walter J. *Fighting For Life: Contest, Sexuality, and Consciousness.* Ithaca: Cornell University Press, 1981.

Ortega y Gasset, José. *On Love.* Trans. Tony Talbot. New York: Meridian Books, 1957.

Parekh, Bhikhu. *Hannah Arendt and the Search for a New Political Philosophy.* Atlantic Highlands, N.J.: Humanities Press, 1981.

Parsons, Alice Beal. *Woman's Dilemma.* New York: Thomas Y. Crowell, 1926.

Pateman, Carole. *The Sexual Contract.* Stanford: Stanford University Press, 1988.

Percy, Walker. *Signposts in a Strange Land.* Ed. Patrick Samway. New York: Farrar, Straus and Giroux, 1991.

Perry, John Weir. *Lord of the Four Quarters: Myths of the Royal Father.* New York: G. Braziller, 1991.

Pieper, Josef. *About Love.* Trans. Richard and Clara Winston. Chicago: Franciscan Herald Press, 1974.

―――. *Leisure: The Basis of Culture.* Trans. Alexander Dru. New York: Pantheon Books, 1952.

Pincoffs, Edmund. *Quandaries and Virtues: Against Reductivism in Ethics.* Lawrence, Kan.: University Press of Kansas, 1986.

Pinder, John. *The European Community: The Building of a Union.* New York: Oxford University Press, 1991.

Pisan, Christine de. *The Book of the City of Ladies*. Trans. Earl Jeffrey Richards. New York: Persea Books, 1982.

Pitkin, Hanna Fenichel. *Fortune Is a Woman: Gender and Politics in the Thought of Niccolo Machiavelli*. Berkeley: University of California Press, 1984.

Pomeroy, Sarah B. *Goddesses, Whores, Wives, and Slaves: Women in Classical Antiquity*. New York: Schocken Books, 1975.

———. *Women in Ancient Egypt*. New York: Schocken Books, 1984.

Posner, Richard. *The Economics of Justice*. Cambridge: Harvard University Press, 1981.

Pound, Roscoe. *Law Finding through Experience and Reason, Three Lectures*. Athens: University of Georgia Press, 1960.

Power, Eileen. *Medieval Women*. New York: Cambridge University Press, 1975.

Radding, Charles M. *The Origins of Medieval Jurisprudence: Pavia and Bologna, 850–1150*. New Haven: Yale University Press, 1988.

Rawls, John. *A Theory of Justice*. Cambridge: Harvard University Press, 1971.

Rescher, Nicholas. *Ethical Idealism: An Inquiry into the Nature and Function of Ideals*. Berkeley: University of California Press, 1987.

Rhode, Deborah L. *Justice and Gender*. Cambridge: Harvard University Press, 1989.

———. "The 'Woman's Point of View.'" *Journal of Legal Education* 38 (March/June 1988): 39–46.

Rich, Adrienne. *Of Woman Born: Motherhood as Experience and Institution*. New York: W. W. Norton, 1976.

Rist, John M. *Human Value: A Study in Ancient Philosophical Ethics*. Leiden: E. J. Brill, 1982.

———. *Stoic Philosophy*. London: Cambridge University Press, 1969.

Rorty, Amélie. *Mind in Action: Essays in the Philosophy of Mind*. Boston: Beacon Press, 1988.

Rorty, Richard. *Consequences of Pragmatism: Essays, 1972–1980*. Minneapolis: University of Minnesota Press, 1982.

Rosemond, John. "Parenting." *The Providence Sunday Journal*, E10 (August 16, 1992).

Ross, John Munder. *What Men Want: Mothers, Fathers, and Manhood*. Cambridge: Harvard University Press, 1994.

Rossi, Alice S., ed. *The Feminist Papers: From Adams to de Beauvoir*. New York: Bantam Books, 1973.

Rougemont, Denis de. *Love in the Western World*. Trans. M. Belgion. New York: Pantheon Books, 1956.

———. *Love Declared: Essays on the Myths of Love*. Trans. Richard Howard. New York: Pantheon Books, 1963.

Ruddick, Sara. *Maternal Thinking: Toward a Politics of Peace*. Boston: Beacon Press, 1989.

Ruether, Rosemary Radford. *Religion and Sexism: Images of Woman in the Jewish and Christian Traditions*. New York: Simon and Schuster, 1974.

Russell, Letty. *Growth in Partnership*. Philadelphia: Westminster Press, 1981.

Sandel, Michael. *Liberalism and the Limits of Justice*. Cambridge: Harvard University Press, 1982.

Sartre, Jean-Paul. *Notebook for an Ethics 1*. Trans. David Pellawer. Chicago: University of Chicago Press, 1992.

———. *Search for a Method*. Trans. Hazel Barnes. New York: Viking Books, 1963.

Schauer, Frederick. *Playing by the Rules*. New York: Oxford University Press, 1991.

———. "The Jurisprudence of Reasons." *Michigan Law Review* 85 (1987): 847–70.

———. "Rules and the Rule of Law." *Harvard Journal of Law and Public Policy* 14 (Summer 1991): 645–94.

Scheler, Max. *Formalism in Ethics*. Trans. Manfred S. Springs and Robert L. Funk. Pittsburgh: Duquesne University Press, 1973.

Schmitt, Carl. *The Concept of the Political*. Trans. G. Schwab. New Brunswick, N.J.: Rutgers University Press, 1976.

Schneiders, Sandra M. *Beyond Patching: Faith and Feminism in the Catholic Church*. New York: Paulist Press, 1992.

———. *Women and the Word*. New York: Paulist Press, 1986.

Schochet, Gordon J. *Patriarchalism in Political Thought: The Authoritarian Family and Political Speculation and Attitudes Especially in Seventeenth-Century England*. New York: Basic Books, 1975.

Schopenhauer, Arthur. *The Art of Controversy and Other Posthumous Papers*. Trans. T. Baily Sanders. New York: Macmillan, 1896.

———. "The Metaphysics of Love of the Sexes." In *The Philosophy of Schopenhauer*. Ed. Erwin Edman. New York: Random House, 1928.

———. *The Pessimist's Handbook*. Ed. and trans. T. Bailey Sanders. Lincoln: University of Nebraska Press, 1964.

Schreiner, Olive. *The Story of an African Farm*. New York: Garland, 1875.

Schumaker, E. F. *A Guide for the Perplexed*. New York: Harper and Row, 1977.

Seltman, Charles. *Women in the Ancient World*. New York: St. Martin's Press (n.d.).

Sennett, Richard. *The Fall of the Public Man*. New York: Knopf, 1977.

Shahar, Shulamith. *The Fourth Estate: A History of Women in the Middle Ages*. Trans. Chaya Galai. London: Methuen, 1983.

Shaw, Bernard. *Nine Plays*. New York: Dodd, Mead and Company, 1946.

Sher, George. "Other Voices, Other Rooms?: Women's Psychology and Moral Theory." In *Women and Moral Theory*. Ed. Eva Feder Kittay and Diana T. Meyers. Totowa, N.J.: Rowman and Littlefield, 1987.

Simmel, Georg. *On Women, Sexuality, and Love*. Trans. Guy Oaks. New Haven: Yale University Press, 1984.

Singer, Irving. *The Nature of Love*. 3 vols. Chicago: University of Chicago Press, 1985.

Singer, Isaac Bashevis, and Richard Burgin. *Conversations with Issac Bashevis Singer*. Garden City, N.Y.: Doubleday, 1985.

Skinner, B. F. *Beyond Freedom and Dignity.* New York: Knopf, 1971.

Smith, J. C. *The Neurotic Foundations of Social Order: Psychoanalytic Roots of Patriarchy.* New York: New York University Press, 1990.

Smith, Patricia. *Feminist Jurisprudence.* New York: Oxford University Press, 1993.

Smith, Steven G. *Gender Thinking.* Philadelphia: Temple University Press, 1992.

Soble, Alan. *The Structure of Love.* New Haven: Yale University Press, 1990.

Stacey, Judith. "Are Feminists Afraid to Leave Home?" In *What Is Feminism?* Ed. Juliet Mitchell and Ann Oakley. New York: Pantheon Books, 1984.

Starobinski, Jean. *Jean Jacques Rousseau: Transparency and Obstruction.* Chicago: University of Chicago Press, 1988.

Stein, Edith. *On the Problem of Empathy.* 2d ed. Trans. Waltrant Stein. The Hague: Martinus Nijhoff, 1970.

Steiner, George. "Bad Friday." Review of *Simone Weil: Portrait of a Self-Exiled Jew,* by Thomas Nevins. *New Yorker* 68 (March 2, 1992): 86–91.

Steinem, Gloria. *Revolution from Within.* Boston: Little, Brown, 1992.

Stern, Karl. *The Flight from Woman.* New York: Farrar, Straus and Giroux, 1965.

Strauss, Leo. *Thoughts on Machiavelli.* Glencoe: Free Press, 1958.

Sullivan, Roger J. *Immanuel Kant's Moral Theory.* New York: Cambridge University Press, 1989.

Summers, Christine Hoff. "Feminism and Resentment." In *Symposium, Feminist Theory Reconsidered, Reason Papers* 18. Fall 1993.

Summers, Robert S. "Theory, Formality, and Practical Legal Criticism." *Law Quarterly Review* 106 (July 1990): 407–30.

Taylor, Charles. *Sources of the Self: The Making of the Modern Identity.* New York: Cambridge University Press, 1980.

———. "Alternative Futures: Legitimacy, Identity, and Alienation in Late Twentieth Century Canada." In *Constitutionalism, Citizenship, and Society.* Toronto: University of Toronto Press, 1985.

Taylor, Jerome. *In Search of Self; Life, Death and Walker Percy.* Cambridge, Mass.: Cowley, 1986.

Tillich, Paul. *Love, Power, and Justice.* New York: Oxford University Press, 1954.

Tribe, Laurence. *Abortion: The Clash of Absolutes.* New York: W. W. Norton, 1990.

Vecchio, Silvana. "The Good Wife." In *A History of Women,* 2.

Vickery, John B. *Robert Graves and the White Goddess.* Lincoln: University of Nebraska Press, 1972.

Viladrich, Pedro-Juan. *The Agony of Legal Marriage: An Introduction to the Basic Conceptual Elements of Matrimony.* Trans. Alban d'Entremont. Pamplona: University of Navarra, 1990.

Virgil. *The Aeneid.* Trans. C. Day Lewis. New York: Doubleday, 1953.

Visser't Hooft, Willem Adolph. *The Fatherhood of God in an Age of Emancipation.* Geneva: World Council of Churches, 1982.

Vivas, Eliseo. *D. H. Lawrence—The Failure and the Triumph of Art*. Evanston: Northwestern University Press, 1960.

Walzer, Michael. *Spheres of Justice*. New York: Basic Books, 1983.

Weber, Max. *Politics as a Vocation*. Trans. H. H. Gerth and C. Wright Mills. Philadelphia: Fortress Press, 1962.

Wechsler, H. "Toward Neutral Principles of Constitutional Law." *Harvard Law Review* 73 (1959): 1–35. Reprinted in Herbert Weschler, *Principles, Politics, and Fundamental Law*. Cambridge: Harvard University Press, 1961.

Weigle, Marta. *Creation and Procreation: Feminist Reflections on Mythologies of Cosmogony and Parturition*. Philadelphia: University of Pennsylvania Press, 1989.

Weil, Simone. *Waiting for God*. New York: Harper and Row, 1951.

Weinrib, Ernest J. "Legal Formalism: On the Immanent Rationality of Law." *Yale Law Journal* 97 (May 1988): 949–1016.

———. "Enduring Passion." Review of *An Essay on Personality* by Roberto Mangabeira Unger. *Yale Law Journal* 94 (June 1985): 1825–1841.

Werhane, Patricia H. *Adam Smith and His Legacy for Modern Capitalism*. New York: Oxford University Press, 1991.

West, Robin. "Jurisprudence and Gender." *University of Chicago Law Review* 55 (Winter 1988): 1–72.

———. "Taking Freedom Seriously." *Harvard Law Review* 104 (November 1990): 43–106.

Whitehead, Alfred North. *The Function of Reason*. Boston: Beacon Press, 1929.

Whitehead, Evelyn Eaton, and James D. Whitehead. *Marrying Well: Stages on the Journey of Christian Marriage*. New York: Image Books, 1981.

Williams, Bernard. *Ethics and the Limits of Philosophy*. Cambridge: Harvard University Press, 1985.

Williams, Joan C. "Abortion, Incommensurability, and Jurisprudence." *Tulane Law Review* 63 (June 1989): 1651–1672.

———. "Deconstructing Gender." *Michigan Law Review* 87 (February 1989): 797–845.

Wishik, Heather Ruth. "To Question Everything: The Inquiries of Feminist Jurisprudence." *Berkeley Women's Law Journal* (1985): 64–77.

Wojtyla, Karol (Pope John Paul II). *Love and Responsibility*. Trans. W. T. Willets. San Francsico: Ignatius Press, 1981.

Wolgast, Elizabeth H. *The Grammar of Justice*. Ithaca: Cornell University Press, 1987.

Wollstonecraft, Mary. *A Vindication of the Rights of Women*. Ed. Charles Hagleman, Jr. New York: W. W. Norton, 1967.

Woolf, Virginia. *A Room of One's Own*. New York: Harcourt, Brace, 1929.

———. *Three Guineas*. New York: Harcourt, Brace, 1938.

Woznicki, Andrew N. *A Christian Humanism: Karol Wojtyla's Existential Personality*. New Britain: Mariel Press, 1980.

Young, Marion. *Justice and the Politics of Difference*. Princeton: Princeton University Press, 1990.

————. "Impartiality and the Civic Public." In *Feminism as Critique.* Ed. Seyla Benhabib and Drucilla Cornell. Minneapolis: University of Minnesota Press, 1987.

Zulueta, Francis de. *The Institutes of Gaius.* Book 1. Oxford: Clarendon Press, 1940.

INDEX

abortion, 82, 109–11. *See also* feminist jurisprudence

abstract normativity, 87, 112. *See also* equality

Adams, Abigail: on the power of husbands, 13

administration of justice: effect of ideological convictions upon, 116; use of neutral principles in, 117–19. *See also* feminist jurisprudence; law

Adonis, 22

Aeneas: prayer of, 128

aesthetic disposition: hedonism compared with, 86

affectivity: and living well, 134; and public life, 122

age: insignificance of in modern life, 157

amity: in public life, 132

ancient world: procreation in, 153; status of women in, 1–6

androgyny: and gender distinctiveness, 37; and intellectual life, 46, 52–53. *See also* gender

Aquinas, Thomas (Saint): on the distinction between masculine and feminine natures, 8; on spousal intimacy, 161

Arafat, Yasir: Nobel Peace Prize awardee, 103

archetypes: of paternal authority, 98; of struggle, 100; of the unconscious, 46

Arendt, Hannah: on the nature of thinking, 47, 77

Aristotle: on differences between age and youth, 156–57; denigration of domestic life, 89, 124; on equality of friendship in family life, 169; on friendship between fathers and sons, 157; on heterogeneity of values, 79; on kingship, 98; on mutual happiness of parents, 161; practical reasoning in the works of, 108–9; on paternity, 156–57; on the nature of the public world, 89; on the soul, 67

Aristotelians: resistance to socioeconomic understanding of public world, 125; failure of, to grasp public value of domestic life, 123. *See also* Aristotle

athletics: and ideals of manhood, 100; and warfare, 103

Austen, Jane: on the friendship of married love, 162

autonomy: and the goods of life that lie beyond the self, 87; and relations between married persons, 150, 175; as aspiration of both men and women, 58; and personal identity, 42, 172.

Bacon, Francis: on domestic responsibilities, 22

Baier, Annette: on the virtue of trustworthiness, 54, 122

Balkans: current war in, 127

Barth, Karl: on relations between men and women, 34, 43

Barwick, Judith: on relationships, 29, 40

Barzun, Jacques: on the development of culture, 85

Beauvoir, Simone de: on contingency, 76; on the drudgery of domestic life, 19; on relations between the sexes, 19–20; on women's attitudes toward logic and morality, 74

Berdyaev, Nicholas: on marriage and personality, 162

birth: as coming into the world of an unrepeatable self, 159

ness of men and women, 167. *See also* equality

egoism: as antithetical to love, 173

Eisenhower, Dwight: as model of a soldier-statesman, 103

Eliot, George: on outlets for female talents, 8; intellectual range of, 70

Eliot, T. S.: unhappy marital experience of, 23, 27

Elizabeth I (Queen of England), 9, 91

emancipation of women: beginnings of, 14–16; and freedom of thought and action, 44–45; and reform of the legal order, 106–22; and violence of men, 92–93; as opportunity for self-determination, 87, 115, 174. *See also* feminism; feminist jurisprudence; sexual oppression; women

empathy: and disinterested deliberation, 169; as sympathetic understanding of the plight of another, 120. *See also* reason; intuition

Enlightenment: and relations between husbands and wives, 10–13; and individualism, 54; and legal theory, 73; and modern thought, 50–55

entrepenurial spirit, 101

equality: and differences between men and women, 31–43, 58, 118; and the disadvantaged, 126; and the equal dignity of the sexes, 42; and household tasks, 169; and intimacy, 168; impersonal nature of, 170; and opportunities for advancement, 85; and personal attributes, 170; as sameness, 58. *See also* sexual equality

eros: as arbitrary desire, 136; as awakening of desire, 141; and death instinct, 142; and genital satisfaction, 137–38; and happiness of love, 138; and marital obligations, 170–72; dependence of, upon morality, 150; as natural urge for a complete life, 136–37; as related to but distinct from sexuality, 137

European Community. *See* community

experience: as means of understanding the nature of love, 135, 176

family: and arrival of a child, 155; as kinship, 153; and marriage, 151–53; as natural habitat, 159; and principles of equal justice, 167–68; as societal function, 155–56. *See also* home; marriage; spousal relationship

father: decline in authority of, 22, 156, 158; relation to child, 157; images of, 158; importance of masculinity to, 156–58; as participant in royal authority, 156–57

Faust: legend of, 84

feeling intelligence, 87. *See also* women

female sexuality: Church Fathers view of, 6

feminine mystique, 18. *See also* Friedan, Betty

feminine personality: formation of, 32

feminism: contemporary expression of, 16, 40; and domestic oppression, 19, 89–113; and empathetic responsibilities, 79; experiential attitude of, 73–74; and masculine ways of knowing, 45, 73, 88; nineteenth-century form of, 14–16, 92–93; attraction to pragmatism, 85. *See also* feminists; feminist jurisprudence; feminist morality

feminists: and equality, 167; opposition to hierarchies, 104; and imposed identities, 105; on law, 106–22; on love and public life, 133, 174; attitudes toward political action and power, 123, 104; interest in procreation, 152. *See also* feminism; feminist jurisprudence; feminist morality; radical feminism; women

feminist jurisprudence: and abortion, 109; critique of the legal order, 106–22; factual preferences of, 115–16; and hierarchical legal norms, 118; legal reasoning in, 107–8; legal myths, deconstruction of, 106; neutral principles,

kings: establishment of order by, 99;
dignity of, 98; and conceptions of
manhood, 99
kinship: as network of relatives,
153; and reproductive love, 153.
See also family; marriage; spouses

law: and contingencies, 118–19; decisions of, as both principled and
contextual, 117; and discrimination against women, 106–7; justifications for, 117; as impersonal
mechanism, 118–19; as intelligible
in itself, 116; role of the will in,
111. *See also* feminist jurisprudence; legal method; legal process
Lawrence, D. H.: on antagonism between men and women, 24–26
legal method: as hierarchical and
authoritarian, 111–12
legal process: conflict between abstract and concrete values in, 111
Lenin: on middle-class domestic life,
19
liberal theory: and impersonal procedures, 76
liberty: absolute expression of, as
dehumanizing, 146. *See also*
freedom
libido dominandi, 91
Lombroso, Gina: on relation between suffering and injustice,
120–21; on womanhood, 73
love: and adult responsibility, 29,
81; as affirmation of another, 163;
commitments of, 144; craving for,
as sign of immaturity, 139; deepening of, 114; as delight in the accomplishments of the beloved,
164; as a donation of the self, 163;
experiential understanding of, 135,
176; "falling in love," 142, 165;
freedom of choice in, 141, 151 ;
and the goods of the soul, 48;
happiness of, 135–38, 175; and
human finitude, 139; between
husbands and wives, 37–39, 144,
150; of an ideal, 166; and the
imagination, 144, 166; and impersonal public action, 133–38; and
the independent personalities of
lovers, 166, 172; in intellectual
life, 48, 84; and justice, 170; mag-

netic quality of, 140; as need, 138,
143; objective and subjective qualities of, 141; philosophical understanding of, 135, 175; procreation
as a completion of, 153; as a
reaching out to a unique person
of the opposite sex, 144, 165–66,
175; reconciliation of need and bestowal in, 139–40, 164; and romantic involvement, 142, 165; as
self-consuming passion, 166; and
self-fulfillment, 138; transitive nature of, 144; undeserved, 138; unselfish, 138; unitive quality of,
139, 141; will to, 164. *See also*
marriage; married love
Lukas, John, 82

Maastricht Treaty, 126
Machiavelli: theory of politics, 90–
91; 93–94
male: combative contests of, 100;
delight in danger, 102; desire for
autonomy, 34; destructive energies of, 53, 81, 102; kinship of
force and order within, 90; love of
abstract and objectified procedures, 47, 112; passivity of, 143;
sexual identity of, 30–31; violence
of, 32, 92, 102; vocation to change
of, 102. *See also* maleness; manhood; manly; men
maleness: abandonment of, 96; as
character formation, 36; fulfillment in private rather than public
life, 95. *See also* male; manhood;
manly; men
Mandela, Nelson: as peacemaker,
103
manhood: and broader universe of
meaning, 53; lack of positive images of, 41, 96; stereotypes of, 96;
as uncertain and precarious, 30,
90
manliness: anthropological foundations of, 102 ; reconstruction of,
174
manly, 88
Maritain, Jacques: on intellect and
intuition, 66, 68
marital justice, 71
marital obligations: deduced from
principles of equality, 167; and

radical feminism: experiential attitude toward law, 71–75; and dominance of men within the family, 17–21, 167–69; and the obsolescence of the masculine, 93; and subjectivism, 111. *See also* feminism; feminists

rationalism: and abstract thought, 52–54; defined, 48; as disembodied, 51, 76, 87; and eros, 136; and ethical theory, 76–77; male-centered quality of, 76; and disparagement of natural existence, 67, 87; as practical intelligence, 82–83; and science, 49, 76, 112. *See also* masculinization of thought; pragmatism; reason

Rawls, John: theory of justice, 168; on the nature of the human person, 172

Reagan, Ronald: description of, 112

reason: and action, 88; as an autonomous power, 54; deontological form of, 52; and emotion, 68, 76, 136; and eros, 84; and experience, 60, 118; and the feminine dimension of existence, 71–85; and gender, 44–48, 67–69; and imagination, 68; instrumental aspect of, 82; connection to intuition, 68–69, 89; and jural phenomena, 115–16; and liberty, 66–67; and the meaning of love and marriage, 135, 146, 175; and moral progress, 48; and mothering, 59–60 ; and non-contextual values, 82–84; and objective being, 66–67; and control of passion, 47, 68; as passionate faculty, 84; and practices, 60, 62; and pragmatism, 82–83; as purposive, 80–85; situated thinking as a form of, 79

reconciliation: between men and women, 37, 40–43; 86, 106, 174

Renaissance: position of women in, 9

reproduction: differences in male and female understanding of, 62; and married love, 39–40; and reconstruction of the public world, 104, 123; and responsibilities of relatedness, 59–60. *See also* mothering

righteousness: and the aesthetic disposition, 50–51, 86 ; and the beautiful, 88; and feminine desires for felicity, 50, 97

Roman Catholicism: conflict within, over the primary and secondary purposes of marriage, 162. *See also* Catholic Church

Roman society: status of women in, 5

Romance of the Rose: medieval classic, 22

romantic love: dangers of, 142; maturity of, 165. *See also* love

Roosevelt, Eleanor: on the attitudes of men toward public life, 130

Rorty, Richard: on reason and practices, 61

Ross, John Munder: on gender-specific tasks of fathers, 158

Rougemont, Denis de: on tensions between romance and married love, 143, 165

Rousseau: on the illusory quality of love, 146; on marriage, 146–47; moral theory of, 50; and the sexual exploitation of women, 92

rule of law: and Hobbesian state of nature, 118–19; relation to sexual oppression, 117. *See also* feminist jurisprudence

rules: in the legal process, 116; and the value of social union, 122

Rwanda: civil strife in, 127

Sand, George: relationship with Chopin, 28

Sandel, Michael: on justice in family relations, 171

Sartre, Jean Paul: on love, 141, 175

Schmitt, Carl: on the distinction between friends and enemies, 91

Schopenhauer, Arthur: aphorism on marriage, 23; on reasoning powers of women, 7; on sexual love, 155

Schreiner, Olive, 19

science: application of methods to ethics, 75–76; objectives of, as different from those of philosophy, 65; and technological development, 145

Second Vatican Council. *See* Catholic Church

self: as cause rather than object of love, 138

self-esteem: in contemporary life, 29; gender as aspect of, 140; and love from others, 28, 138–39; in marriage, 164; and self-approval, 140; of women, 30

self-identity: and gender distinctiveness, 58; importance of inclusive relationships to, 131; and personhood, 171

self-love: compatible with love for another, 165, 173

self-realization, 56

self-reliance, 72

self-sufficiency: exaggeration of, as a sign of an unfulfilled life, 139; and enhancement derived from a shared life, 175

selfless love: and human pride, 138–39

sexual activity: instinctive and compulsive aspects of, 144

sexual asymmetry, 35

sexual attraction: complexities of, 140

sexual difference: constructive use of, 37; and gender, 72–75; as mystery, 43; and the person, 42; and reproduction, 39–44, 62. *See also* sexual polarity

sexual discrimination, 5, 7, 14–20, 44, 57, 71–72, 107, 124. *See also* sexual oppression; subordination of women

sexual equality: and collaboration of men and women, 106; and personal happiness, 41, 167–68; and retention of unique differences, 88. *See also* egalitarianism; equality

sexual experimentation, 146

sexual hierarchy, 21. *See also* patriarchy

sexual identity: ambiguities of, 32; movement toward, 37; and personal life, 75

sexual love: as ardor for a person of the opposite sex, 153; compulsive aspects of, 144; as the giving of oneself to another, 141; and the

order of creation, 154–55; as sexual subservience, 155. *See also* marital love

sexual oppression: female experience of, 1–20, 96; masculine experience of, 21–26; and the masculinization of thought, 44; and politics, 90–95; and the rule of law, 117. *See also* sexual discrimination; subordination of women

sexual polarity: and human vitality, 37–38, 44, 56–58; and espoused love, 37

sexual reconciliation, 42

sexual subservience, 1–20, 171

sexual union, and the possibilities of procreation, 151–52

sexuality: crisis of, 136, 146; related to eros, 137; and personal existence, 174

Shaw, George Bernard: on the reversal of sexual initiatives, 23

Singer, Irving: on intimate heterosexual relations, 40; on distinction between romantic and marital passion, 143; on married love, 164

Singer, Isaac Bashevis: on the plight of modern men, 31–32

Skinner, B. F.: on science and personal autonomy, 77

social security: as general protection against human vulnerabilities, 125

society: distinctiveness of, 125; economic values in, 125; foundational issues of, 127

Socrates: on women, 3

soldiers: anonymity of, 101; and ideals of manhood, 100

South Africa: transformation of, 127

Soviet Union: breakup of, 127; and women's attitudes toward love and marriage, 153

spiritual authority: and prohibitory injunctions, 97

spousal love: as love between persons, 162

spousal relationship: meaning of, 149; and personal independence, 150; principles of justice applied to, 168; and procreation, 154–55

spouses: and bonds of marriage, 171; independent personalities of,

love, 145, 146; as power to affirm
the well-being of another, 145;
Rousseau's conception of, 146
wisdom: absence of in masculine
behavior, 97; as the objective of
philosophy, 60
Wittgenstein, Ludwig: philosophy
of, 60
Wollstonecraft, Mary: on the sexual
bondage of women, 14
woman: defined, 39; and harmonious existence, 51; and individualism, 56; intellectual capacities of,
69, 76; moral dispositions of, 75–
78; as mother, 26, 33, 49, 156; as a
person, 6; power of, 1–2, 24, 33;
subjection to man, 8–9; symbolized as fortune, 91. *See also* feminism; women
womanliness: masculine dependence upon, 33–35; men's fear of,
31
women: and abstraction, 54; in the
ancient world, 1–5; and individual
autonomy, 55; and contractarian
values, 168; creativity of, 33, 47;
emancipatory struggle of, 14–21,
44–46, 104–8; status in the Enlightenment, 10–14; exclusion
from intellectual life, 47–52; exclusion from public life, 90–91; and

feeling intelligence, 87; and the
integration of subjective and objective existence, 113; and modern
freedom, 17–18, 40, 44–45, 123,
174; and the masculinization of
thought, 44–52; and practical reason, 59–62, 80; and patriarchy, 1–
18; relations with men, 28–31, 34,
40–43, 103; in the Renaissance, 9;
scientific achievements of, 70;
skepticism of, 85–86; subordination of, 1–16, 36, 44–45, 72, 93;
and family, 152–53; supreme authority of, 94; values of, 52, 96,
111, 119–20. *See also* feminism;
feminists; feminist jurisprudence;
values
wonder: as basis of philosophy, 64,
87
Woolf, Virginia: on the creative
power of women, 47; on masculine dependence upon women,
28, 36; on the violent quality of
male professions, 130

Xenophon: on sexual equality, 3

Yahweh: male father-god, 1, 34
Young, Iris Marion: on the opposition of reason to desire, 127
youthfulness: as desired mode of
life in the modern world, 157

Harvey's chinese fud
285-5550

♪ *Beyond Feminism: Toward a Dialogue on Difference* was composed in Palatino by Brevis Press, Bethany, Connecticut; printed on 60-pound Glatfelter Supple Opaque Recycled and bound by Thomson-Shore, Inc., Dexter, Michigan; and designed and produced by Kachergis Book Design, Pittsboro, North Carolina.